Some Highligh

..., named JOHN, formerly a Hair-in Kingston:—He has been absent two years, ce then has been seen about Kingston, Montego-ad Martha-Brae, also with Fishermen at Port—Whoever gives information where said Negro oured, so as he may be found, shall be handsome-arded, by application on the above Estate.

Kingston, Dec. 2, 1779.

RUN AWAY from the Subscriber, the beginning of last month, a Negro Fellow named

TILLY,

but has for some time passed by the Name of BILLY.—He is a Creole, and a very knowing marked on one of his shoulders, M.S.——As he en in Spanish-Town a few days ago, it is ima-se is gone to Leeward, as he has lived in most parishes there.

y person taking him up and lodging him in any Gaols in this Island, or bringing him to the Sub-shall receive Two Pounds Fifteen Shillings; y person harbouring him after this Public Notice, epend upon being prosecuted to the utmost rigour law.

THOMAS LEIGH.

Kingston, December 3, 1779.

RUN AWAY from the Subscriber, the following Slaves, viz.

MARY, a Mulatto Woman, a Sempstress, with her two Children, NED and WILLIAM.

SAM, (the above's brother), a to Fellow, a Carpenter by Trade.——The above tos pass as Free people, but the contrary will be to any person by the Subscriber.

TALINA, a young Woman, with her Child y.——All the above Slaves were formerly the rty of Moses Lamera, deceased.——Whoever ap-n s and brings them to me in Kingston, shall be omely rewarded; and it proof can be had of their harboured by any person or persons, they may de-upon being prosecuted with the utmost rigour of w:—if they will deliver up themselves to me in urse of this week, they shall be kindly received.

ISAAC FEURTADO.

St. Ana's, July 20, 1779.

RUN AWAY

from the Subscriber, About five weeks ago,

A NEGRO BOY, named

JACK,

Of the Congo Country,
t 15 or 16 years of age, and has no Brand Mark.
speaks tolerable good English, and it is supposed
e has taken the Clarendon road, being well ac-

MADEIRA WIN
Of a former importation.

31— Kingston, 27th November, 1779

FOR LIVERPOOL
THE
SHIP BENSON
JAMES BALL, MASTER.

Will be ready to take in freight in the course of a w nd sail a SINGLE SHIP the 12th of January n Shippers will please to apply to said master, or to

BENSON and CARTER

---

31 Spanish Town, Nov. 27, 1779

STOLEN or STRAYED

ON Sunday night the 14th Insta out of a Guiney grass piece near the Barrack

A GREY HORSE

about 14 hands high, has a kind of Spanish mark on near buttock, was shod all round, on account of a bruise, and had on his near hind-foot a barred Whoever can give information of the said horse, so the owner may have him again, shall receive T PISTOLES reward, and all reasonable charges pa

JOHN ROCHAT
Lieut. 60th Regiment.

31—3m November 27, 177

Run away, the following Negroes

AUGUST, of the Mundingo coun about five feet nine, and a yellowish complex pitted with the small pox, marked on the left shor I.M. has been about five years in the country, is posed to be at leeward, having got out of gaol at vanna-la-Mar, about two years ago; he was lear to be a cook.

DUMFRIES, who formerly belonged to cap Crockatt, Mr. Jefferson, and Archibald Campbell, all of St. Ann's where he now conceals himself was lately taken up at Rio Bueno estate and b out of stocks there.

FORTUNE, formerly belonged to Mr. Will Bonny of Mount Pleasant in St. John's, is said to escaped out of Montego-Bay gaol.

YAW, he waited on Mr. Pope, late Deputy-M shal for St. James, and has been a long time in about the gaol of Montego-Bay; a short, thin, b legged fellow, a creole of St. George's parish, belo ing to Fort Stewart Estate, in said Parish.

KATE, a wench, formerly the property of B Harris, late of St. John's, is supposed to be harbo by one Jereu, about Saint Elizabeth's, who has c dren by her.

STREPHON, belonged to Jennings late of S Ann's, is said to be harboured by a mulatto girl e Raymond.

PLUM-PUDDING, who lately lived about S

Slave Women
in Caribbean Society

1650–1838

Abolitionist roundel. Whilst stressing the common humanity of women, this depicts the European woman selflessly helping the supplicant black woman, suggesting slaves were dependent on benevolent Europeans for their freedom. In fact slaves, women and men, fiercely resisted slavery and were not the helpless victims portrayed by the abolitionists.

Slave Women in Caribbean Society

1650–1838

BARBARA BUSH

Senior Lecturer in Social & Political Studies
Parson Cross College, Sheffield

Indiana University Press
BLOOMINGTON AND INDIANAPOLIS
James Currey
LONDON

Published by
James Currey Ltd
54b Thornhill Square, Islington
London N1 1BE

Indiana University Press
10th and Morton Streets,
Bloomington, Indiana 47405

First published 1990

4 5 98 97 96 95 94

British Library Cataloguing in Publication Data
Bush Barbara
Slave women in Caribbean society 1650–1838.
1. Caribbean region colonies. Black women slaves.
Social conditions, 1650–1838
I. Title
305.5′67′088042

ISBN 0-85255-058-8
ISBN 0-85255-057-X Pbk

Library of Congress Cataloging-in-Publication Data
Bush, Barbara
Slave women in Caribbean society, 1650–1838/Barbara Bush.
p.   cm.
Includes bibliographical references.
ISBN 0-253-31284-1.—ISBN 0-253-21251-0 (pbk.)
1. Women slaves—Caribbean Area—Social conditions.
2. Women—Black—Caribbean Area—Social conditions.
3. Social classes—Caribbean Area—History.
I. Title.
HT1071.B87   1990
305.5′67′082—dc20

Maps by Almac
Typeset in 11/12pt Baskerville by Colset Pte Ltd, Singapore
Printed by Villiers Publications, 26a Shepherds Hill, London N6

Contents

Contents

Illustrations

Maps

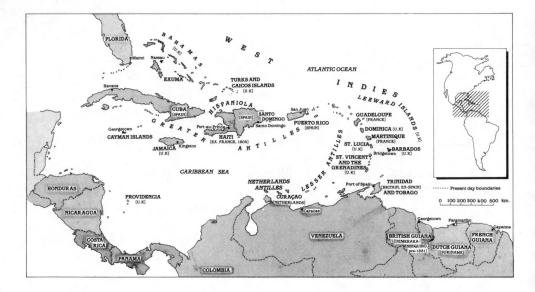

1 *The Caribbean, Surinam and the Guianas, c. 1832*

Preface

The idea for this work on slave women first came to me when I was living in Trinidad. My interest in women's history merged with my fascination for the West Indies with its rich diversity of peoples and cultures. With the exception of Lucille Mathurin Mair's pioneering study very little of any substantial nature had actually been written on slave women and I felt a need existed for a comprehensive study of their role in slave society. When I returned to England I completed a postgraduate thesis on slave women which, with suitable amendments to reflect the important new developments in both women's history and the history of slave societies, has ultimately been transformed into this book.

My original aim was to draw together all the fragmented evidence, challenge existing and, arguably, inaccurate appraisals of the life of women slaves, and present a fresh analysis of their social and economic role in plantation society. As my research progressed so did my commitment to my chosen area but a number of problems soon emerged. The 'historical invisibility' of women, the scarcity of hard evidence, was the most obvious. History for the most part has been written by men, for men, and thus records largely what men want to see. In the case of black women this 'invisibility' was complicated by the ethnocentric nature of contemporary writings by both planter and critic of slavery alike. If the former's rare comments on slave women were bluntly racialist, the latter's were tinged with paternalist sentimentality. Both were inaccurate. I found I was working in difficult and controversial territory and I am indebted to scholars such as Eugene Genovese, Michael Craton, Sidney Mintz, Orlando Patterson, Edward Kamau Brathwaite, Richard Dunn, Barry Higman, Herbert Gutman, Elsa Goveia and others whose pioneering works in the general field of New World slave and post-slave societies provided me with a more positive theoretical frame of reference.

I also found inspiration in the writings of black women. From the early 1970s activist writers such as Angela Davies began to challenge existing stereotypes of black womanhood. In strong polemical articles they forcefully demolished negative stereotypes and stressed the need for black women to assert their equality with white women, pointing to the iniquities in the slave system which ascribed to them inferior economic and sexual roles which have persisted up to the present day. This has resulted in a number of serious historical studies of women under slavery.

Much of the literature in this genre is Afro-American but in the Caribbean too there has been a growing movement to redress the burden of history and stress the essential integrity of black womanhood long submerged in a society with clear-cut race, class and gender divisions. With the growth of black consciousness in the Caribbean, black women began to find a new voice which may have disturbed some but was an inevitable development. Any open-minded observer of Caribbean society could see that the social divisions created by slavery were still deeply entrenched. According to Lucille Mathurin, in plantation slave society, 'the black woman produced, the brown woman served and the white woman consumed'. When I lived in the West Indies this heritage was still strongly felt, with the result that many black women felt a good deal of resentment about their continuing inferiority in this hierarchy based on colour and class.

Because of the obvious historical dimensions to the problem, an analysis of the role of slave women is fundamental to any understanding of the present status of Caribbean women. Many women are still affected by poverty and underdevelopment, a legacy of slavery and colonialism, while men's fear of the strong black woman, derived from slavery, in the view of some black writers, continues to influence relationships between the sexes. Indeed, one can still detect antagonisms on the part of West Indian men towards their women in the lyrics of popular calypso. But such observations also pose important questions about reading history backwards and the pitfalls of over-use of the present to explain the past.

A further consideration in explaining the origins of this book is the complex relationship between race, class and gender. As a woman, the female slave shared a common subordination with all women but, where gender united black and white women, race and class divided them. These divisions still have relevance today in the debates between women of different class backgrounds and between black and white feminists. As workers, women slaves were rendered equal to men and regarded as barely human. On the surface, at least, slave status denied women not only their humanity but also their essential femininity. The slave woman's plea 'Am I not a woman and a sister?' is the silent voice behind this book.

Whilst the major focus is on the woman slave, the reconstruction of her life was only possible in the wider context of slavery and the development of the slave community. This book should thus be of interest to the more general reader as well as to those with a specific interest in woman's history. I have tried to reach an acceptable balance between academic rigour and accessibility to the reader new to the subject. Hence I have not overloaded the text with footnotes; major quotes are given detailed references but, otherwise, references to sources made in the text may be checked in the full bibliography at the end of the book. For the more general reader, or students who wish to read more around the subject, I have provided a selected number of further readings, in addition to more detailed footnotes, at the end of each chapter, which may be checked in the bibliography.

In writing this book, I have received invaluable support from my family and friends and I would like to acknowledge warmly their collective contribution to its successful completion. I am particularly indebted to Michael Craton, who supervised my original research, and my mother and Akli Slimani, who helped with revision of the manuscript.

1

The 'Invisible' Black Woman in Caribbean History

An Introduction

Until recently, academic literature on the West Indies made little or no reference to the slave woman *per se* or singled her out for special attention, as an individual whose experience and reactions to slavery were somehow intrinsically different from those of the male slave. Because of the cultural misconceptions and growing ethnocentric beliefs, black women were seen by contemporary observers in a different light from European women. Physical labour for white women was proscribed in the West Indies, but Africans of both sexes were put to work in the fields. Black women were further differentiated from white women in a sexual sense. From the tales of early travellers to Africa, West Indian whites gleaned a superficial and inaccurate impression of West African sexual mores, polygyny in particular. They were appalled by the idea of a man having more than one wife in some West African societies, whilst refusing to admit to the hypocritical double standard (chastity for women, sexual licence for men) which existed in their own society. Polygyny gave them an excuse to perpetuate this double standard on the plantation in a particularly invidious way. In the eyes of white men, the sexual function of black women placed them in a separate category to black men.. Out of this basic division grew the belief that slave women had different aspirations, needs and functions. As the anthropologist Peter Wilson has observed:

> From early on black women were treated differently from black men and were more readily and firmly attached to the alien society of the whites . . . To black women concubinage offered the opportunity to improve their social standing, but according to white values.[1]

The crux of Wilson's interpretation of women in slave society is that they were 'more readily and firmly' attached to white society. Conventional histories of slavery took a similar viewpoint and it was commonly assumed that black women accommodated more readily to slavery. In consequence, their involvement in, for instance, slave resistance was ignored or, more

Europe supported by Africa & America.

1.1 *'Europe supported by Africa and America'. The exact sense the artist wished to convey is not clear, but the female form is used symbolically to depict the interdependence between the three continents through colonisation and the slave trade. As in the abolitionist roundel (p. ii) the European woman is placed in a central and implicitly superior position.*

damagingly, misconstrued. It has been argued that the woman's physical proximity to white men placed her in a position encompassing 'the contradictory human possibilities of betrayal and devotion', which generated 'suspicion, guilt and degradation' around the individual woman (King, 1973). Apart from denying the woman a valid role in slave resistance, such analyses have perpetuated various highly misleading myths about the slave woman, several of which centre around erroneous and inaccurate interpretations of her role in the slave family.

With the recent growth of interest in the lives the slaves created for themselves, the slave woman, despite the paucity of relevant literature, has begun to emerge from historical obscurity. Historians are increasingly coming to challenge the traditional one-dimensional view of the slave woman. More emphasis is being placed on her contribution to slave resistance. In the words of Lucille Mathurin Mair, slavery and the slave trade, providing as they did a 'crude levelling of sexual distinctions', ensured that the woman shared 'every inch of the man's physical and spiritual odyssey' (Mathurin Mair, 1975).

The last decade has seen a blossoming interest in the history of women slaves in the American South represented by studies by Elizabeth Fox-Genovese (1986), Darlene Clark Hine and Kate Wittenstein (1981), Deborah Gray White (1985) and Jaqueline Jones (1985). Arlette Gautier (1983) has produced a comprehensive study of women slaves in the French Caribbean, but, with the exception of Mathurin Mair's pioneering work on Jamaican women, no similar study of women slaves in the British Caribbean has yet been published. Issues relating to female slaves have gained new prominence in medical and demographic histories of slavery. Demographic differences between American and Caribbean slave populations have directed attention to confronting fundamental questions of life, death and physical well-being and a more holistic comparative study of hemispheric slavery. But, despite these recent developments, the woman slave is still given short shrift. The reasons for this lie in the way historians have approached the study of slavery over the past several decades, particularly their interpretation of original source material.

Early modern works on slavery perpetuated and consolidated contemporary images of the slave. The master/slave relationship was based on inherent racism. As Orlando Patterson has explained, to sustain their dominance, Europeans in slave-owning colonies had to ensure the 'social death' of slaves. This involved attempting to isolate them from their social and cultural heritage and resulted in a relationship of domination rooted in the social, psychological and cultural power of the master class. Naked force was a key element in this relationship, but so were the institutional structures of slavery and intellectual justification (Patterson, 1982). Legal, philosophical, religious, biological and scientific reasons were used to instil the notion of inferiority into black people. The long saga of slave resistance can be interpreted in part as a struggle against this process of reification (dehumanisation and powerlessness).

The extent of resistance to the system was frequently underplayed by early modern historians of Caribbean slavery. They portrayed the slave as a passive or ingratiating figure and emphasised ascribed inferior racial traits. 'The West Indian negro [slave]', wrote Lowell Ragatz in 1928, 'had all the characteristics of his race. He stole, he lied, he was simple, suspicious, inefficient, irresponsible, lazy, superstitious and loose in his sexual relations.'[2] Such historians took a distinctly Eurocentric view of slavery, in which women slaves scarcely merited a mention.

The first challenge to these ideas came from two seminal studies – Melville Herskovits's *The Myth of the Negro Past* (1941), which established the continuity of African cultural forms in the New World and the vitality of Afro-American culture, and Herbert Aptheker's *American Negro Slave Revolts* (1943), which demolished the view of the passive, submissive slave. This was followed by Kenneth Stampp's *The Peculiar Institution: Slavery in the Ante-Bellum South* (1956), which drew attention to day-to-day resistance and, as recent appraisals of his work stress, contributed significantly to eradicating the racism in earlier historical works and promoting a new assessment of slaves as 'ordinary human beings' (Abzug and Maizlish, 1986). The slave had come into *his* own at last. What had formerly been accepted as negative traits of the black personality – lies, deceit, treachery, idleness – were now regarded as facets of everyday insubordination. 'The record of slave resistance', wrote Stampp, 'forms a chapter in the endless struggle to give dignity to human life.' Stampp's work spearheaded a rapid growth in the study of slave resistance in the United States, which synchronised with the development of black consciousness.

Yet Stampp still tended to reiterate conventional views about slave family life and the role of women and arguably underestimated the vitality of slave culture. The later cultural histories of slavery in the American South by Genovese (1974), Blassinghame (1972), Rawick (1972–3) and Gutman (1976) partially rectified this imbalance. Emphasising the positive aspects of slave family life, they presented the woman slave in a more sensitive way. In *Roll, Jordan, Roll,* Eugene Genovese widened the parameters of slave resistance. He asserted that the way in which the slaves built their own community and struggled for improvements within the system was arguably a more important form of resistance, in terms of overall achievement, than outright rebellion. 'Accommodation itself', he suggested, 'breathed a critical spirit and disguised subversive actions and often embraced its opposite, resistance.' Thus the slaves who appeared to be well assimilated into the world of the masters – domestics and skilled artisans – were in effect the most adept at this resistance within accommodation. Perhaps Genovese stretched the concept of resistance to an unacceptable limit, but his work was of immense value in drawing attention to the complexities of the slave community and the importance of black cultural institutions to the survival of the individual slave.

Work on slavery in the United States has stimulated a parallel development in the study of Caribbean history, which until the 1960s was dominated by economic debates. Studies by Patterson (1969) and Goveia (1965) tended to reproduce a somewhat negative image of slave society but stimulated new research into the more positive aspects of the slave community and the development of Afro-Caribbean culture represented by Edward Kamau Brathwaite's *The Development of Creole Society in Jamaica* (1971). Because of the significant contribution women made to slave cultural life, such works focused more directly on women and highlighted the existence of negative stereotypes and images. More recent works have focused increasingly on examining the slave experience from the black perspective (Craton, 1978) and charting the depth of resistance to the system (Beckles 1982; Craton, 1982; Gaspar, 1985). There have also been exciting new developments in demographic and quantitative studies of slavery – Barry Higman's *Slave Populations in the British Caribbean, 1807–1834* (1984) is of particular note here. Together with studies by Kiple (1984) and Sheridan (1985), they have initiated a redefinition of women's work and childbearing role, albeit from a somewhat clinical perspective.

These important developments have done much to retrieve the 'invisible' male from his anonymity but the woman slave's essential humanity remains submerged, despite the fact that historians like Michael Craton have acknowledged their central role under slavery. To understand why, it is necessary to examine some of the more enduring stereotypes and misconceptions of the personal lives of slaves. Stereotypes can be defined as:

> figures who conform to more or less identical patterns of behaviour, resemble each other physically, and . . . react in predictable ways to similar stimuli; and who may exist independently of – and often in the very teeth of – historical change.[3]

The common image of the woman slave, culled from planter and abolitionist sources alike, is a compound of the scarlet woman, the domineering matriarch and the passive workhorse.

The woman's role in the domestic life of the slaves has spawned the most enduring myths. This is largely the result of the way in which contemporary observers interpreted the slaves' private lives according to the values of middle-class European society. Whites, both anti- and pro-slavery, denied the slaves a viable family life; just as the urban poor and peasants of eighteenth- and nineteenth-century Europe were accused of promiscuity as a subordinate class, so were blacks, but racial complexities enhanced the distortions in the case of slaves. This ethnocentric class bias resulted in a denigrating attitude to slave mores which has persisted up to the present day, especially in relation to discussions on the slave family. As Herbert Gutman has pointed out, modern theories of the slave family grew out of the racialist notions of slave owners. The twin evils of familial instability and sexual immorality arising from this are still used to describe black family life both in slavery and freedom. Thus, in any study of the domestic life of slaves, we must be continually aware of what Sidney Mintz has defined as 'the gaps between actual behaviour, the informants' description of such behaviour and the historical records themselves'.[4] This is of particular relevance to the woman slave. The historical evidence must be looked at in new contexts and from additional and considerably widened perspectives, if the realities of her life in slave society are to be retrieved from historical obscurity.

To reach any fresh appraisal of the black woman's contribution to slave society, it is necessary, primarily, to expand the narrow perspectives from which her life has been viewed. First, a clear distinction must be made between her work life and her private domestic life. Although some overlap naturally existed between these two areas of everyday existence, the distinction is crucial to any analysis of the slave woman's response to slavery. In her work life, the woman related primarily to the formal external plantation system and the world of the white masters. Here, she was essentially a valuable economic asset, subject to a harsh and repressive legal code and, constantly reminded of the ugly realities of a sugar monoculture based on chattel slavery. In contrast, the private domestic life of the woman slave was part of the 'inner', more hidden slave community. It involved her relationships with fellow slaves, in which her actions were guided largely by the 'unofficial' social and moral codes of the slaves as opposed to the 'official' codes of behaviour imposed upon her by the plantocracy.

In the external work sphere, the woman's role differed only marginally from that of the male slave. The female slave laboured as hard and as long, and was subjected to the same harsh punishments. Thus, a knowledge of the slave laws, their origins and functions and the socio-economic and power structures of the West Indian colonies is highly relevant to understanding the woman slave, not only as worker but also as rebel. Because the woman was subjected to the same conditions as the male slave, she reacted to enslavement, punishment and coercion in similar ways, from everyday resistance to outright rebellion.

If the woman slave, as a worker, was regarded by the planter as an asexual unit of production, in her domestic life her role became strongly differentiated from that of the male slave. This was especially true with respect to childbearing and childrearing. Moreover, her life within her own black community as mother and wife was clearly influenced by African cultural traditions. She often had to struggle to retain her cultural identity. Thus, it was outside her formal role as a working slave that she exhibited some of her greatest strengths, despite her unique vulnerability as a woman. The slave woman, in the contribution she made to the family and community lives of the slaves as well as in her work life, frequently had to reject the laws and rules of the whites. She was forced to resist the system in order to preserve her integrity as a woman and protect her family and friends. Hence, her role in slave society can only be effectively determined in the perspective of slave resistance in general, the second major perspective.

In a multitude of forms, resistance was an important aspect of slave life in all New World societies. In the West Indies, the primary focus of this study, 'standing up to the man' frequently culminated in organised revolts. Planters in the Caribbean lived in a state of perpetual insecurity, under constant threat of slave insurrections. In the West Indies, in particular, additional preconditions for revolt existed in the high black-to-white ratio and the extremely harsh conditions on sugar plantations. Herbert Aptheker

(1943) defined a slave revolt as an act involving more than ten people whose ultimate aim was freedom. By this definition, numerous slave revolts occurred in the West Indies from the earliest days of slavery, especially in the larger and richer islands such as Jamaica. The role of the slave woman in this scenario of organised revolt can no longer be ignored.

Resistance is a continual and primary theme running through this study. Changes in the character of slave revolts over time reflected changes and developments in the institution of slavery itself, which affected all aspects of the life of the individual slave. Hence the pattern of slave revolt forms a useful contextual framework in addition to providing a challenging theoretical background to any in-depth study of women slaves in the Caribbean.

A third perspective is culture. As the transposed African cultural patterns of the slaves heavily influenced their response to enslavement, any study of the woman slave would be inadequate if it ignored her cultural heritage. The Guyanese historian Walter Rodney (1969) has argued that the traditional culture of the Africans was 'the shield which frustrated the efforts of the Europeans to dehumanise Africans through servitude'. Indeed the preservation of cultural identity has been seen by radical black writers like Frantz Fanon (1968) as a vital indicator of the will and ability of a subordinate people to survive and resist the cultural impositions of their white masters and thus maintain their unique identity. Slavery may be seen as a process of 'zombification' of the individual but it also unleashed a black quest for a revitalising spirit capable of reaffirming an individual's sense of cultural identity and personal worth which is still in evidence today where black people are oppressed (Depestre, 1969).

It could be argued that the dislocation of the middle passage, the diverse origins of the slaves and the structure of the slave plantation left the slaves bereft of their traditional cultures. Yet a greater cultural unity existed among slaves than has previously been assumed. Sidney Mintz and Richard Price, for instance, suggest that there were 'deep-level cultural principles, assumptions and understandings' which were shared by Africans in any New World colony and which probably served as 'a limited but crucial resource' in the early adaptation of African slaves, as well as a vital catalyst in the development of unique Afro-American institutions.[5]

Many cultural similarities did exist between the different societies in West Africa, the area of origin of the majority of slaves in the Caribbean. This is particularly true in the case of religion, marriage and kinship patterns. As Walter Rodney (1969) has observed, the similarity of African survivals in the New World points not to tribal peculiarities but to the 'essential oneness' of African culture. In this context, any examination of the cultural matrix of slave society can be rendered meaningless without due reference to West African cultural patterns.

If slaves failed to resist the process of alienation which was inherent in the slave system, they faced 'psychic annihilation'. The preservation of cultural identity was paramount to survival. An indispensable aspect of that identity was the existence of strong kinship bonds between slaves, for these were an emotional anchor for otherwise dispossessed human beings. Was the black woman, as the pivot of the slave family, instrumental in preventing this 'psychic annihilation'? Women slaves faced a hard struggle against demoralisation in their work life, but the full force of the attack on their culture was in their domestic environment.

Culture can be defined as an individual's existential relationship to the material environment, an integral part of everyday life from birth to death. Thus, cultural resistance is essential if the culture of any given community is severely threatened. In the Caribbean, the subtle dialectic between the opposed cultures of Africa and Europe ensured that creole society was formed in an atmosphere of conflict and resistance, but also adaptation and reciprocal assimilation between all strata of the population, black and white. Slave society was not a static entity but a 'complex interactional process, full of tension and contradiction' (Patterson, 1982). A duality of behaviour characterised the individual's response to enslavement, which has carried over into modern Afro-Caribbean society. The anthropologist Peter Wilson has outlined a marked dichotomy between what he terms, 'reputation' and 'respectability'; reputation (Afro-Caribbean value-orientated) undermines respectability (European value-orientated) and is a form of non-cooperation which can involve strong resistance. 'Reputation', similar to Orlando Patterson's concept of the slaves' retrieval of honour, may be the key to understanding the hidden and complex mechanisms of not only slave resistance, but the very nature of slave society itself. Thus it is essential to interpret the behaviour of the slave woman within this context of duality in addition to the broader perspective of her African cultural heritage.

A final but no less important perspective is that of gender. In common with women in virtually all cultures, the slave woman was subordinate to *all* men and hence suffered sexual as well as economic oppression. In this sense, her white European counterpart fared little better than she did herself. However, the slave woman, subjected to both black and white partriarchy, in addition to experiencing class exploitation was also a victim of racism. It is in this framework of triple oppression that her achievements should be measured. Primarily, then, the object of this study is to illuminate more fully the 'invisible' woman and reveal the vital and significant contribution she made to West Indian slave society. It will show how, in both her work life and her domestic life, she exhibited a strength and independence with which she has not previously been accredited. Above all, it will record how she struggled, alongside her menfolk, to live, to maintain her dignity, to survive and to retain her essential integrity and her culture, despite the enormous odds against her. Her positive role in slave resistance will be stressed but the greater emphasis will be placed on her private domestic life, her efforts to reconstitute and cohere the slave family, the corner-stone of slave solidarity and community stability.

In time-scale the book spans the whole period of slavery but the emphasis is placed on the later period of slavery, for which a greater variety of source material is available. I have included relevant cross references to African and modern Caribbean societies and, although the major part of the discussion deals with the British Caribbean, I have referred to other slave-owning colonies for comparative purposes. The main focus is the ordinary black woman slave rather than the coloured domestics and this effectively excluded free women of colour. Mention will be made of maroon* women, however, because of their important role in black resistance in the slave colonies.

Whilst acknowledging the diversity of slave experience – differences between rural and urban occupations, small and large estates and regional differences – much of the discussion relates to the experience of women on the large sugar plantation as this played a dominant role in determining the character of slavery, particularly, as Higman notes, after 1810. By 1807 there were 775,000 slaves in the British Caribbean (declining to 665,000 in 1834). This represented two-thirds of all slaves in the Caribbean and one-quarter of all slaves in the Western Hemisphere (Higman, 1984). As Jamaica had more slaves than any of the other British islands, a good deal of the evidence I have used is from there. Although I have tried to cover most aspects of the women's experience, this study is by no means definitive and at times I have had to generalise from specific examples due to paucity of evidence and absence of slave testimony. But if the purpose of history is to open up new lines of enquiry and establish continuity between past and present this study will hopefully meet those criteria.

Chapter 2 provides a critical examination of the origin and nature of the myths, images and stereotypes of black women. The following two chapters are concerned with the black woman in the context of institutionalised slavery, her legal status and economic function. Resistance, from everyday acts of non-cooperation to insurrection, is the central theme of Chapter 5. The subsequent three chapters explore the slave woman's role in the slave family and community life and her attitudes to childbearing. The concluding section provides a general overview of the woman's specific contribution to the cultural life of the slaves. The scope of the study demands an interdisciplinary approach, although this is by no means innovatory where Caribbean historiography is concerned (Green, 1977).

In approaching this analysis I have tried to view the life of the woman slave from the inside looking out and not vice versa, in the same way as the full richness of working-class history is only revealed when observed from the standpoint of the ordinary man and woman, not from the imposed definitions of the ruling classes. Although, as Kenneth Stampp (1956) has pointed out, we risk appearing presumptuous in pretending to know how slaves felt, this risk must be taken if we are to redress the historical imbalance resulting from the crude bias of contemporary literature. In the course of the written history of slavery, black men and women have consistently been denied their culture and dignity and conceived of *en masse* rather than as

---

*This term is derived from the Spanish *cimarrones* meaning 'mountaineers', that is blacks who fled to the mountains from the plantations and established free communities.

individuals. The woman slave in particular has been consistently objectified by historians in their search for 'hard fact'. This work, in contrast, will stress the individuality of the woman slave, and interpret her reactions to enslavement from her own viewpoint, and not through the eyes of the white observer. In exploring her role in slave society thus, this study will also show not only how the black woman survived enslavement, but also how her determination and spirit of resistance were crucial to the survival of her family, her community, her culture and her own personal integrity and human dignity. In the broader perspective, it is hoped it will contribute to a wider understanding of slave society in general, for the slave woman cannot be seen as an isolated entity. To focus on her specific identity in the slave context is to come to a closer understanding of the unique nature of Afro-Caribbean society both past and present, for the very *identity* of West Indians is rooted in the historical experience. This study is a contribution to a deeper understanding and appreciation of that experience.

Further reading

Chioma Steady (1981)
Coombes (1974)
Davies (1981)
Fanon (1968)
Green (1977)
Mathurin Mair (1975)
Rodney (1969)

2

'The Eye
of the Beholder'

Contemporary European Images
of Black Women

O Sable Queen! thy mild domain
I seek, and court thy gentle reign,
So soothing, soft and sweet
Where meeting love, sincere delight,
Fond pleasure, ready joys invite,
And unbrought raptures meet.

Do thou in gentle Phibia smile,
In artful Benneba beguile
In wanton Mimba pout
In sprightly Cuba's eyes look gay
Or grave in sober Quasheba
I still shall find thee out.[1]

The 'Sable Queen' was one of the more pleasant contemporary images of
the black woman. Part of white male mythology, it reflected a common and
often near-obsessional interest in the 'exotic charms' of African womanhood. Not all European impressions of the black woman were so favourable.
The plantocracy ascribed to her two distinct and, in many senses, contradictory functions. Whereas the male slave was valued solely for the economic contribution he made to the plantation, the woman was expected to
perform both sexual as well as economic duties. Childbearing fell into the
former area, but also sexual duties performed for white masters. In the West
Indies, sexual relationships between black and coloured women and white
men were widespread, commonplace and generally accepted by the plantocracy to be an integral part of the social structure of the islands. The
European assessment of black female sexuality has been seminal in the
development of many unfavourable misconceptions about black womanhood in general. It has coloured and influenced both contemporary and

11

modern attitudes to the black woman, not only in her sexual sphere, but also as a worker, mother and wife.

The history of the black woman in slave society in the West Indies is submerged beneath a layer of damaging stereotypes and common misconceptions about slave society in general. Europeans observed her life from a narrow and biased perceptive, frequently in almost complete ignorance of what transpired in the slave village; they utilised their scanty and inaccurate knowledge in order to pronounce with confidence upon all aspects of the life of the woman slave, including her private domestic life. An ignorance of the African cultural background of the slaves and the inability of contemporary observers to see any aspect of the life of an individual slave, other than in the context of their own culture, further distorted the popular image of the slave woman. This ethnocentric bias was reinforced by contemporary belief in the ascribed inferiority of blacks.

Africans of both sexes were regarded as 'slaves by nature' – childlike, primitive, idle and of a lower intelligence level than Europeans. This notion had religious sanction in the eighteenth century. The frontispiece of a collection of pro-slavery essays, *Tracts upon the Slave Trade* (London, 1788), stated that 'Scriptural Researches on the Slave Trade' had indicated that Africans were designated to be slaves in 'Conformity with the principles of Natural and Revealed Religion, delineated in the Sacred writings of the Word of God'. Hence, stereotypes of black womanhood can be seen to fall into two broad categories – those which are generally applicable to all slaves and those which have originated from the unique sexual functions of the individual woman. In contemporary accounts of slavery the woman was often labelled 'promiscuous', cruel and negligent as a mother and fickle as a wife. As a worker, she has been portrayed as passive, downtrodden and subservient, a resigned slave who contributed little to the cause of slave resistance. So strong were these images that they have come to be regarded as *sui generis* of black women even in the modern era. The alleged 'immorality' and 'licentiousness' of the slave woman became the basis of numerous misconceptions about the nature of slave marriages and slave family life. Moreover, the emphasis on the earthiness, sexuality and physical strength of the black women initiated unfavourable comparisons between black and white women, especially on a moral plane.

Although white women were also subject to patriarchal domination and contemporary records indicate that, in the early days of slavery, there was a marked lack of respect for poorer white women, such class differences became less marked with the maturation of slave society, as all white women were elevated above black and coloured women (Beckles, 1986). With the ending of white indentured labour after 1700 even white women of humble origins could aspire to the leisured, pampered position of higher-status women. The preservation of racial distinctions between black and white women now became crucial in establishing the social position of these upwardly mobile *arrivistes*. European women in the West Indies represented a tiny minority. The adverse juxtaposition of black against white womanhood was not perhaps as central a factor in the development of institutionalised racist dogma as it was in the Southern United States. Nevertheless, it had a significant influence on the stereotyping of black women.

A stereotype is a composite picture of an individual which, while reflecting an element of reality, distorts it. It is inflexible and can exhibit a massive durability, even in the face of historical change. Although, as in the case of the Jews, stereotypes can reflect a fear of the potential superiority of a group which inspires hatred, the majority of stereotypes applicable to slaves, 'good' or bad, were used to consolidate the latter's inferior position. If historical evidence is closely examined, certain stereotypes can be seen to be at variance with contemporary facts. Where considerable stereotyping occurs, however, the situation is increasingly complicated by the fact that stereotypes draw upon actual cultural traits and can contain a 'kernel of truth', no matter how distorted this may be. This is especially relevant where contemporary discussions of slave morality are involved. The image of the black woman held by abolitionists differed from that of the planter, yet is was equally a distortion of reality based on racist images of African culture.

Such contemporary impressions were often derived from dubious travellers' tales of Africa. Though often wildly inaccurate, these facilitated the development of enduring stereotypes which became consolidated during the eighteenth century and were incorporated into the arguments for and against the retention of chattel slavery. An image of the slave was constructed to fit both the planter rationale of slavery and the humanitarian's reasons for its abolition. As David Dabydeen (1985) has shown, such images were reflected in the art of eighteenth-century England.

The stereotyping which was particularly damaging to black women characteristically fell into the realm of sexual morality. As the pressure from abolitionists grew towards the end of the eighteenth century, arguments for and against slavery increasingly focused upon the code of morality of the slaves. Both pro and anti factions, however, were agreed on the general immorality of slaves, but attributed it to different causal factors, the planters to the 'primitive' nature of blacks, the abolitionists to the evils inherent in the system of slavery. Despite differences both factions were agreed upon the 'moral degeneracy' of women slaves. The overall result was the crystallisation of a number of myths.

The impact of contemporary stereotyping upon the projected image of the black woman in the historical context was twofold; as a worker she was portrayed as a defeminised neuter unit, as a woman she came to represent the delights of forbidden sex and in consequence her sexual attributes were highly and often sensationally exaggerated. Similarly, her 'matriarchal' position in the slave family was greatly overemphasised. The composite image of the slave woman created by the eighteenth-century white observer has proved extremely durable, despite the existence of contradictory evidence in contemporary writings which shows it to be inaccurate. Thus an understanding of how popular myths and stereotypes about black women originated, how they developed and became consolidated, and the fallacious assumptions upon which they were based is a crucial prerequisite to a more realistic interpretation of the role of black women in slave society.

Europeans were aware of African peoples from the time of the Greek writer Herodotus. With the growth of contact with West Africa, during the fifteenth and sixteenth centuries, as the transatlantic slave trade developed, European sailors and merchants returned from the African coast with tales of the exotic tropics. The difference in physical characteristics between Europeans and Africans had an immediate and profound impact. The blackness and nakedness of the native inhabitants was remarked upon by virtually every traveller. This 'impudent nakedness' of the Africans soon came to be associated with the uninhibited sexuality of a 'lewd, lascivious and wanton people'. Europeans were particularly 'surprised and offended' by the nakedness of African women, which stood out in strong contrast against the physical modesty of respectable European women.[2] Yet, as James Walvin notes, despite their shocked senses, Europeans characteristically displayed 'a curiosity bordering on the obsessional' about the sexual habits of Africans. The equation between lack of modesty of black women and lack of sexual morality was easily made. These early impressions of black sexuality were reinforced by European society's repressed attitude towards sex. With the rise of Christianity, sexuality came to be associated with the devil and the colour black to symbolise all the evil and sinful elements in life. As women in Europe were traditionally regarded as the instigators of evil-doing, blackness was also associated with feminity; hence the link between black women and the delights of a forbidden sexuality would have easily (and possibly almost unconsciously) been made by European men during their initial contacts with African societies.

By the late eighteenth century, early observations relating to black women had gradually become commonly accepted. Since the earliest days, bawdy tales about the sexual aggressiveness of negro women by Europeans involved in the slave trade were loosely bandied about. People in frequent contact with Africans or African slaves were expected to give descriptions of 'hot constitution'd Ladies' who were so 'lascivious' by nature that they 'made no scruple to prostitute themselves to the Europeans for a very slender profit, so great was their inclination to white men'.[3]

The sexual attractions of black women apart, the majority of descriptions pertaining to their general physical appearance were not very flattering. In accordance with the ideal of womanhood in Europe, the female physical build was expected to be markedly different from that of men. This was apparently not the case where African women were concerned. As one early African traveller, William Towerson, observed:

> the men and women go so alike that one cannot know a man from a woman but by their breasts which in the most part be very foule and long, hanging downe low like the udder of a goate.[4]

The supposedly strong physical and muscular build of African women provided a perfect rationale for their economic exploitation on slave plantations. The 'corporeal equality of the sexes' amongst black people became a firmly entrenched notion amongst European observers, enduring well into the nineteenth century. Writing of Dahomey in the 1860s, for instance, the British explorer Sir Richard Burton concluded that 'the masculine physique of the women' enabled them to compete with men in 'enduring toil, hardships and privations'.

The 'feminine harshness of feature' and 'robustness of form' of black women was unfavourably compared to white women. Likewise the connection between physical strength and animality was quickly made. Comparisons between African women and female animals were not infrequent. Both Towerson and Sir Hans Sloane compared the breasts of African women who had borne children to the udders of goats. On a related, but more practical, level, there was a distinct aversion in the West Indies, commented on by Sloane, and at a much later date Edward Long, to the use of black women as wet nurses. Planters eschewed black nurses 'for fear of infecting their children with some of their ill-customs'. The blood of black women was 'corrupted' and their milk 'tainted', differing distinctly from that of European mothers.

During the great debate on slavery, plantocratic writers, in support of their racialist arguments, stressed particularly this link between the black woman and the animal world. Edward Long, for instance, suggested that African females had a close, natural affinity with the orang-utan. 'An orang-outang husband', he declared, 'would not be any dishonour to a Hottentot female.' In keeping with these denigrating notions, black women were naturally believed to have no difficulty in childbirth and had their babies as easily as 'a female orang-outang'.[5] Such extreme analogies were easily arrived at. The pure African woman did not fit the Graeco-Roman ideal of beauty which prevailed in Western Europe. European concepts of feminine beauty were bound up with notions of purity, delicacy, modesty and physical frailty. The black woman was viewed as physically strong, exuding a warm animal sensuality, an inferior subspecies of the female sex. This image easily allowed for the economic and sexual exploitation of black women.

Not all images of the black women were so unfavourable. Richard Ligon greatly admired 'the lovely smiles and faces and graceful, softly-muscled bodies' of black girls he met in the Cape Verde Islands (off the north-west coast of Africa) and Barbados. Mulatto women were generally viewed by contemporary observers in a more favourable light than pure African women and the individual slave women whose beauty impressed European men were usually of mixed blood. 'Mary Wiggins and an Old Cotton-tree', wrote 'Monk' Lewis, 'are the most picturesque objects that I have seen for these twenty years.' But Mary Wiggins was a beautiful mulatto slave on Lewis's Jamaican estate whose 'air and countenance' were compared to that of the Virgin Mary as portrayed in Renaissance art. Likewise, John Stedman's mulatto mistress, Joanna, was no ordinary Surinamese slave woman. 'Her face', he wrote:

Joanna.

2.1 *'Joanna'. Joanna was John Stedman's reputedly beautiful slave mistress. Note how the facial features and dress emphasise the European ideal of beauty and femininity. The naked breast and pose, however, hint at the alleged sensuality of African women which led to sexual, as well as economic, exploitation of black women. Evidence indicates, however, that Stedman respected Joanna and purchased her freedom.*

16

was full of native modesty . . . with cheeks through which glowed, in spite of the darkness of her complexion, a beautiful tinge of vermillion, when gazed upon. Her nose was perfectly well-formed, rather small; her lips a little prominent.[6]

In effect, Joanna fits perfectly, in physical features and behaviour, the contemporary European ideal of a refined, modest woman. Both Lewis and Stedman were unusually sensitive contemporary observers. The love, respect and admiration they felt for individual slave women is not reflected in the general writings from the later period of slavery. Although abolitionists, in highly sentimental appeals to the British public, expounded in romanticised and idealised terms upon the virtues of 'Sable Beauties' and 'Ebony Queens', allusions to the physical unattractiveness of black women predominated.

Despite the unflattering picture painted by white men, in practice the physical appearance of black women failed to repel them sexually. Few men, however, openly admitted to their attractions for and relationships with slave women. The majority were hypocrites. They utilised the alleged physical and moral inferiority of black women, in contrast to European women, to establish them firmly in the role of the 'other woman'; one set of moral standards was applicable to white women, another less honourable set to black; the superiority of white women was stressed. The nineteenth-century English historian, Macaulay, astutely observed that it was in the interests of the defenders of slavery for the English public to believe white men were physically repelled by black women. Strongly against this calculated moral whitewashing, he stressed how in reality white men 'in torrid zones' frequently preferred black women to white women. 'White men', he wryly concluded, 'have never found black women too ugly to be concubines, *only* wives.' Supporting Macaulay's observations, John Stedman intimated that white men actually *preferred* black women. '[White] creole women', he wrote, 'do not have a very alluring appearance . . . the colonists in their amours prefer the Indian, Negro and Mulatto girls.' Far from feeling an aversion to black women, white men in Surinam valued them highly for their remarkable 'cleanliness, health and vivacity'.

By the late eighteenth century, the black and, even more so, the coloured woman was well established, in the eyes of the white man, in her role as concubine. According to plantocratic commentators like Bryan Edwards slave women were free of any restrictive moral codes, 'refused to confine themselves to a single connexion with the other sex' and boldly disposed of themselves sexually 'according to their own will and pleasure'. Thomas Atwood declared that marriage among slaves was unstable, the more so because it was 'common for women to leave their husbands for others'; slave women were prostitutes who submitted to white men for money or clothes and likewise sold their own daughters for 'a moderate sum'.

The belief was prevalent that the slave woman was always amenable to the sexual advances of white men; by this means she could gain favours and acquire prestige. Frequently, in contemporary literature, she was portrayed as a sexual temptress or procuress. Edward Long fulminated about the

17

conniving and licentious ways of the black woman while Emma Carmichael, writing in the penultimate years of slavery, blamed the moral ruin of white men in the West Indies upon the seductive capabilities of the black woman. Although the latter writer, as a white woman, was undoubtedly personally hostile, a marked tendency did exist, on the part of white men, to transfer the blame for their sexual improprieties on to the 'forwardness' of black women and thus exonerate themselves.

In contrast, the opponents of slavery, especially the religious faction, saw the black woman not as a scheming black Jezebel, but as an innocent victim of the unholy lust of callous and brutal white men. The abolitionists thus became chivalrous defenders of the 'violated chastity' of 'sable females'. For propaganda purposes, descriptions of the 'defilement' of black women were often couched in emotive tones. 'When the women are taken on board a ship, naked, trembling, terrified,' wrote the fanatical slave trader turned abolitionist John Newton, describing the horrors of the middle passage, 'they are often exposed to the wanton rudeness of white savages.' Religious abolitionists saw black women as 'the instruments of licentious gratification' of white men who were responsible for the general immorality in the sugar colonies; slaves were but innocent and malleable 'children'. These righteous Englishmen aspired to raise black women up to the strict moral standards to which their own womenfolk were expected to adhere. They even went so far as to appeal to British women, 'distinguished for their virtues and delicacies', to help save their naive and maltreated black sisters. This intense concern over the sexual exploitation of black women, however, was closely connected with the campaign to discredit the plantocracy and promote the cause of abolition. Abolitionists did not deny that black women were promiscuous, or that slaves in general lacked a moral code, they merely represented the latter as corrupted innocents. Their appeals in defence of slave women were founded upon the basic premise that *all* of them were morally ruined and stripped of their womanly dignity. In this sense, the abolitionist image of the black woman did not qualitatively differ from that of the plantocracy.

Contemporary statements on the general 'immorality' of slave women cannot be separated from late eighteenth-century beliefs about the slave family. The promiscuous behaviour of female slaves and the high incidence of miscegenous unions in the West Indies were regarded as important contributory factors to the general instability of slave family life. Often, contemporary judgements on the role of the slave woman as mistress, mother and wife were steeped in ignorance and myth. Most observers exhibited a degree of cultural arrogance which denied Africans any valid system of morals. Planters, for instance, accused the slaves of lacking 'civilised' marriage patterns, but this did not worry them overmuch. Marriage amongst the slaves, they argued, was unnecessary and 'promiscuity' was a natural state of affairs.

In contrast, abolitionists, especially those of a religious orientation, approached the problem of the moral turpitude of the slaves with missionary zeal. As they believed unflinchingly in holy Christian wedlock, they desired to convert the slaves to Christianity, and thus extend to them the benefits of true Christian marriage. Not unnaturally, they believed that the attitudes of the planters and the general conditions of slavery in the West Indies militated against their objectives. As John Riland observed, the true significance of 'the sacred institution' could hardly be grasped by slaves when none of the basic preconditions existed. For this reason, Riland, like many fellow abolitionists, criticised hypocritical planters, who allowed slaves Christian marriage (on the insistence of unscrupulous and mercenary clergymen) without providing an adequate moral environment.

The abolitionist image of the black woman as a potentially 'good' Christian wife was no less unrealistic than portrayals of her as a fallen woman. The wifely model was the middle-class European woman, subject to strict patriarchal authority. 'Every man', wrote John Riland, 'expects to be master of his own house, and to have the authority over his children.' In Riland's view the male slave could not realise these expectations because his wife could not 'obey his wishes'. She was 'forced from his roof' to labour in 'a promiscuous gang' of men and women: thus 'domestic enjoyment' for slaves was totally impossible.[7]

Until recently modern authors have proved no less vulnerable in the tendency to view slave marriages and the role of the slave women as mother and wife from the perspective of European moral and cultural values. In *The Peculiar Institution*, for instance, Kenneth Stampp (1956) challenged many traditional concepts about slave behaviour but his views of slave marriage maintained a strong cultural class and gender bias. He believed that the slave family 'had nothing like the social significance' that it had in white society, largely because the slave woman was primarily a full-time worker for her owner and 'only incidentally' a wife, mother and 'homemaker'. Stampp thus concluded that the slave family was not a true family, as the husband was not the head of the household, the holder of property, or the provider and protector.

Before they were challenged by black writers themselves and innovatory historians like Gutman and Higman, it was *de rigueur* for writers to stress how the peculiar situation of the woman slave on the plantation contributed significantly to the development of the unstable matrifocal black family and, indeed, the general lack of morals among slaves. In so doing, they too readily accepted the contemporary images of the black woman; late eighteenth-century myths about black morals and marriages have proved more resilient than the truth. Fernando Henriques (1962–8), for instance, alluded to widespread promiscuity on slave plantations which was often encouraged by slave masters in an environment where all slave women were the property, sexual or otherwise, of the master. Similarly, the image of the woman slave engaged in 'sporadic relations not far removed from prostitution', subscribed to by Orlando Patterson (1969), differs but little from impressions of slave women conveyed by contemporary writers.

Although the tendentious question of the nature of the slave family and the woman's role within it will be explored more fully at a later stage, in terms of contemporary images of the slave woman *per se*, it is important here to examine in detail the development of such myths about her intimate life. The most deeply entrenched and durable myths, as has already been stressed, are those which focus upon the ironically contrasted views of the 'promiscuous harlot' and the 'domineering matriarch'. Historians, such as Elsa Goveia (1965), have traced the emergence of marital and sexual instability to the breakdown of West African cultural institutions. Such cultural institutions, 'polygamy'* in particular, have been consistently misinterpreted. To contemporary observers 'polygamy' was an especial *bête noire*. Bryan Edwards, for instance, believed that its practice by West Indian slaves had resulted in 'a shocking licentiousness and profligacy of manners' in most slave women. Planters saw 'polygamy' as the root cause of much of the promiscuous behaviour of women but, paradoxically, also believed that within polygynous unions women were no more than domestic slaves, liable at all times to cruelty and torture. In the words of Lucille Mathurin, who strongly contests this view of black womanhood, polygyny was judged by Europeans as a 'repulsive institution, symptomatic of black masculine oppression and its offshoot, black female debasement' (Mathurin, 1975).

Contemporary observers misinterpreted the role of slave women largely because of their distorted opinions on the status of women in contemporary African societies. Eighteenth-century Europeans were comparatively ignorant of the workings of such societies. As already noted, much of their scanty knowledge came from travellers, whose journeys were generally restricted to the coastal areas of Africa and whose comments were often highly subjective. Captain John Adams, for example, declared that the women of the Fanti tribe (Gold Coast) did most of the heavy agricultural work as well as performing 'all the drudgery attendant on the housekeeping'; their husbands, however, passed their days 'gossiping, drinking and sleeping'; whilst conveniently ignoring the fact that such 'drudgery' was the habitual lot of the mass of European women at the time. Most West Indian whites accepted the prevailing view of the African woman as a 'beast of burden'. 'Ebo women', observed Edward Long, 'labour well, but the men are sullen and refuse to submit to drudgery.'[8] Long believed that male slaves were 'adverse to any laborious employment' because in Africa women performed all the hard labour. This image of abject African womanhood was conjured up repeatedly and was supported by contemporary observations on the free Jamaican maroon societies, which retained strong Africanisms. Brian Edwards, for instance, asserted that maroon women were but 'slaves and drudges' to their menfolk and yet, ironically, it was the selfsame author who accused his fellow planters of being 'utterly ignorant' of the 'manners, propensities and superstitions' of the Africans.

Because most contemporary writers were indeed so 'utterly ignorant' their comments on such cultural institutions as polygyny should not be taken

---

*This term, which simply means marriage to more than one person at the same time, is loosely used. Polygyny – mating or marriage with more than one *woman* at a time – is more concise in the context of slavery.

up too readily. Apart from isolated observers like Robert Dallas, who argued against Edwards's notion that maroon men treated their wives brutally, most writers emphasised the abject condition of polygynous wives. To some extent, in so doing, they justified the economic exploitation of black women by illustrating that they were accustomed to hard, physical labour.

Such contemporary views of African womanhood were indeed a far cry from reality. Many contradictions are inherent in the works of individual authors. Contemporary writers presented two conflicting images of the black woman, the abject creatures subjected to harsh patriarchal rule and the wanton women who flouted all codes of accepted morality, neither of which was accurate. Modern writings on polygyny in traditional West African society show that, in many respects, the African woman in a polygynous marriage is in a more favourable position than her European counterpart. African women have a separate role from men, but not necessarily unequal status. Men and women alike make an indispensable contribution to the family economy. Contrary to popular opinion, women in Africa do not do all the heavy labour: the primary economic functions of women are light cultivation and local marketing, which gives them a degree of independence from men. For instance, amongst the Ibo (whose women were such drudges according to Long and Edwards), men do all the heavy work such as house-building and yam-growing, whilst women keep the vegetable gardens. Dallas had an inkling of this role division in African households; maroon women, he noted, cultivated provision grounds but did not regard this as 'an imposition upon them by the men'.

In many respects, the role of women in traditional African society corresponds much more closely to that of women in pre-industrial Europe than to the position of women in the modern western nuclear family. Unfortunately, eighteenth-century commentators assessed the sexual division of labour in the African family from a middle-class perspective, enhanced by their racialist notions. It is as a result of this that the misconceptions about the role of the black woman as mother, wife and worker arise. The deeper implications of analysing diverse social institutions in the framework of one specific set of cultural norms have been thus summarised by the French historian Philippe Ariès:

> The concept of family, the concept of class . . . and perhaps elsewhere, the concept of race, appear as manifestations of the same intolerance towards variety, the same insistence on uniformity.[9]

The men who passed judgement on the morals of the slave woman and castigated her behaviour as a mother and wife exhibited this insistence on 'uniformity' condemned by Ariès. The role of the woman, in both traditional African society and slave society, diverged considerably from the role of middle-class women in eighteenth-century Europe. Hence, the behaviour of black women was deemed aberrant and uncivilised; women were ascribed a role which corresponded to the images of them constructed by white observers. The composite picture of black womanhood which emerged during the period of slavery influenced plantocratic attitudes towards the woman slave as worker *and* woman. An ignorance of the ways and customs of West African tribal society, combined with a marked ethnic and class bias, moulded the opinions of planter and abolitionist alike. The contemporary belief in the heightened sexuality and immoral behaviour of the black woman, which 'justified' her sexual exploitation by white men, has been particularly damaging with respect to modern conceptions of the woman's role in slavery. Not only has it given rise to the notion that women accommodated more easily to slavery because of their close proximity to white men (and hence did not resist their enslavement), but it has also aided the development of popular theories on the pathological nature of the black family in the Caribbean.

If the black woman is to be conceded a more positive and meaningful role in slave society, it is necessary to probe above and beyond the limits of the standard historical images of the black woman; the cultural values which were important to the slaves, *not* those of their masters, must provide the contextual framework. Finally, the actual historical experience of black womanhood should be accorded the respect it warrants. As is shown in subsequent chapters, in strongly resisting slavery in a multitude of ways, in refusing to succumb to the pressures inherent in slave society, the individual slave woman *herself* was refusing to conform to the image white society had created for her.

Further reading

Bush (1981)
Cutrufelli (1983)
Dabydeen (1985)
John Newton, *The Journal of a Slave Trader . . . 1750–1754*
Mathurin Mair (1975)

3

Slave Society, Power and Law

The Institutional Context of Slave Women's Lives

Slave society was not a simple structure based on a rigid division between black and white, slave and freeman. The British West Indian colonies during the era of slavery were complex and dynamic social organisms. All classes, free and enslaved, on the plantations and in the urban settlements, were 'symbiotically interrelated' by interdependence and emulation and by a 'perverse admixture of fear, hatred, sex, grudging respect and occasional affection'.[1] Despite this 'symbiotic' link, however, tension and alienation between the different social classes also existed and had as important a role in the shaping of slave society, as did the assimilative trends. According to Edward Brathwaite (1977), conflict was an essential part of the process of creolisation (the movement from first-generation African-born to second-generation West Indian-born slaves). As the acculturation of African slaves took place, the interaction of European, slave and African elements of creolisation resulted in tension. These subtle dynamics of cultural conflict had a strong influence on slave resistance.

The historiography of the West Indies reflects the difficulties of arriving at a suitable definition of slave society. The earlier modern historians often portrayed social organisation in the colonies as 'a degraded state', disorganised and uncreative, defining slave society only in terms of juxtaposition to, and relationship with, the external metropolitan sphere. Until challenged by writers like Edward Brathwaite, historians involved in research into West Indian history continued to adopt this negative and static approach to slave society, accentuating the insular nature of plantation society and the high degree of social fragmentation and lack of cohesion.

In 1969, Orlando Patterson defined a society as a 'territorially based, self-sufficient collectivity possessing a coherent system of values' and concluded that slave society did not conform to this definition. At the peak of its

development in the late eighteenth century, it was 'near to the Hobbesian*
state of nature', functioning in a pessimistic atmosphere of 'acute anomie'.
More recently, Patterson has refined his ideas on the meaning and definition
of slavery, arguing that it was a 'permanent, violent domination of natally
alienated and generally dishonoured persons'. This is more than a simple
legal definition and allows for active participation of slaves in the creation of
slave society. Slaves, he argues, had an 'irrepressible yearning for dignity
and recognition' which led to resistance. Such resistance produced different
responses from masters, which determined the character of slave societies.
In the Caribbean, for instance, planters relied more on brute force than in
the Southern USA and when they became absentee masters in England,
leaving the running of the plantations to overseers and managers, society
became more degenerate and cruel.

Generally Patterson's impressions of slave society remain pessimistic. His
concept of 'natal alienation' – the loss of ties of birth in ascending and
descending generations – is particularly relevant. He also argues that the
'social death' of slaves was achieved through such alienating strategies as
stripping slaves of their own religion, giving them new and often ridiculous
names, and denying them formally recognised social relationships such as
marriage. In this essentially violent relationship no genuine love or trust
could exist between freemen and slaves as any intimacy was usually 'calcula-
ting and sado-masochistic'. Here Patterson draws heavily on the ideas of the
German philosopher G. W. F. Hegel (1770–1831), particularly his concept
of the 'ultimate slave'. For Hegel slavery was 'human parasitism' with
owners 'feeding' on their slaves to affirm their own liberty and power at the
expense of the enslaved. From this perspective slavery degraded both master
and slave (Patterson, 1982).

While Patterson has some thought-provoking and valid ideas on the
nature of slavery which, given the legal definition of slaves as chattels (goods
or property), are difficult to refute, he does not discuss in any depth the
cultural resilience of slaves and the degree to which they were able to create a
viable life for themselves (this is dealt with in more depth in Chapters 6 and
8). He also arguably underestimates the degree of positive interaction
between white, coloured and black although he does acknowledge the
diversity of experience of individual slaves. This varied according to the
reason why slaves were acquired, the proximity or distance from the master
and the personal characteristics of slaves – skill and gender, for instance.
The size of the slave population in proportion to the free and the level of
absenteeism of slave owners were also significant. However, Patterson does
not believe that differences in the mode of production and type of crop
affected the way slaves were treated. In contrast, Barry Higman stresses the
differences between urban and rural slaves and production on coffee estates
and cattle pens, as opposed to sugar plantations (Higman, 1984).

Complex social mechanisms integrated individuals – black and white –

---

*After the seventeenth-century English philosopher, Thomas Hobbes, who argued that, without strong
social controls, societies would degenerate into chaos.

into Caribbean society. Social cleavages did exist based on race, class and gender and oppression of slaves resulted in the development of a parallel slave subculture. But such cleavages did not necessarily represent a society plunged into chaos and anarchy. Slave society was, in effect, a dynamic and complex entity which had a positive and creative identity. As Edward Brathwaite (1971) has stressed, creole culture developed in the West Indies largely through a 'reciprocal interchange of cultural traits between black and white'. The adaptive culture of the slaves did have its roots firmly in Africa, but it did not develop in isolation and thus, even in conflict, related positively to West Indian society as a whole.

Slave women contributed significantly to the social fluidity of West Indian society. Domestic slaves, in particular, played an important role in the integration and diffusion of black and white culture, throughout the long process of creolisation. According to Edward Long, white women suffered from 'constant intercourse with negroe domestics' whose 'drawling, dissonant gibberish', modes of dress and manners they 'insensibly adopted'. Given the social isolation of European women in Jamaica and the constant contact which they had with black domestics, Long's observations are probably relatively accurate. Women on remote plantations were more vulnerable than those in towns. To quote Long:

> We may see in some of these places, a very fine young woman awkwardly dangling her arms, with the air of a negroe servant lolling almost the whole day upon beds or settees, her head muffled up with two or three handkerchiefs, her dress loose, and without stays. At noon, we find her employed in gobbling pepper-pot, seated on the floor, with her sable hand-maids around her.[2]

Poor urban female slave-owners were also spatially close to slaves and little better educated. Maria Nugent, a less caustic observer, also believed white creole women to be 'not untainted' by contact with black people whilst John Stedman noted that female slaves in habitual contact with whites, especially the light-skinned 'orderly and obedient' housekeepers and long-term mistresses of white men, emulated the white women.

As creolisation accelerated after the ending of the slave trade in 1807, in many outward aspects slaves did assimilate into and accommodate to the wider, white-dominated society. Yet, as will be argued in the final chapter, the influence of African-derived values remained strong. As Barry Higman (1984) has shown, even after 1807, there were still a significant number of Africans in Caribbean populations although two-thirds of these now came from the Bight of Biafra and Central Africa whereas before 1750 the main origin of slaves was the Gold Coast, the Bight of Benin and the Windward Coast (in between the Gold Coast and Sierra Leone).

Slaves had a dual existence. The manner in which individual slaves related to the external white-orientated society differed intrinsically according to their relationship to the black community. If mutual acculturation and interdependence existed between black and white, it frequently developed within an atmosphere of fear, hatred and mistrust. Much of this resulted from the fact that the social, economic and legal basis of Caribbean society was established by whites. White men of British origin were the main owners of slaves in the British West Indies – sex, colour and nationality correlated with wealth. Barry Higman's data reveal that only 6.5 per cent of freedmen were slave owners and whilst there was some ownership by white women this was concentrated in towns, in units of 1–10 slaves. The premier male planters were often distant in space and education, and authority and power was mediated through other white men – attorneys, managers, overseers – who had closer daily contact with blacks (Higman, 1984).

White domination was based on power which operated at an institutional level in the context of the legal and economic structures of slavery but also at the most basic level over the body of slaves. For the French historian Michel Foucault, the body is the ultimate contact point of power relations; in the Caribbean, white men and women alike could exercise such intimate power over their slaves through punishment, torture and the control of their physical needs and environment. In Foucault's words, the productive body (producing labour, that is) also had to be a subjected body (Foucault, 1977). At an even deeper level, sexuality itself became a fundamental component of the power white men exercised over both black and white women. Power is thus diffuse and manifests itself in manifold forms comprising a 'dense network' of power relationships which could occasionally become inverted in, for instance, the power otherwise subordinate white women had over black men or the ways in which certain black and coloured women could manipulate white men (discussed more fully in Chapter 6). Within these webs of power there are also diverse points of resistance (Foucault, 1978–9). Personal power can thus be contradictory for, as Hegel pointed out, it resulted often in dependence on the object of power. Without the slave the master had no identity and no power to exert.

The essence of power in slave society was thus complex and diffuse and worked through social, psychological and cultural channels as well as the more overt mechanisms of punishment and physical deprivation. As Patterson notes, the honour and esteem of the slave master came primarily through his power over the slave, but it was also sanctioned by the institutional framework of slave laws. These laws were derived from the authority of the master, which originated in the socio-psychological dehumanisation of the slave (Patterson, 1982). The hegemonic nature of the law contributed significantly to the development of conflict and was a singularly divisive element of slave society. A slave's life was dominated from birth to death by a legal code based on ancient precepts but drawn up by planter assemblies. The prime concern of these self-interested bodies was the protection of property and the social control of an unwilling work-force. Thus, in their rejection of, and open resistance to, the slave laws, the slaves exposed the contradictions and weaknesses inherent within a social system based upon coercion and punishment. The survival of this system depended upon the enforcement of a repressive legal code.

'In countries where slavery is established', wrote Bryan Edwards, 'the leading principle on which the government is supported is fear; or a sense of that absolute coercive necessity which, leaving no choice of action, super-cedes all questions of right.'[3] The law constitutes the fundamental basis of all societies dependent upon slavery. Thus, a familiarity with the function and operation of West Indian slave law is crucial to an objective analysis of the life of the individual slave woman.

Both protective and coercive or 'policing' clauses were incorporated into West Indian slave law. The former were devised to protect the slave from harsh treatment and to lay down minimum standards for his or her well-being. These laws were frequently abused, for, until the very last years of slavery, masters had almost absolute control over their human property. As the law was essential to the efficient running of a plantation economy, punitive and coercive clauses comprised the major part of island slave codes. Power and law were inextricably interrelated in slave society, especially in the Caribbean, where blacks heavily outnumbered whites. Because of the constant threat of insurrection, laws to repress slaves were manifold, whereas laws to protect them were very loosely adhered to.

Slaves guilty of running away, theft or other crimes were tried by slave courts consisting of two or more justices acting without a jury. Concealment of runaways was also punished and Elsa Goveia notes that Leeward Island legislation made provision for regular searches of negro houses (Goveia, 1965). Evidence of slaves was not admitted for or against other slaves and owners were given wide discretion in enforcing social control under English law.

The slave laws of the British West Indies differed in structure and content from those which governed the French and Spanish slave colonies. The *Code Noir* and *Siete Partidas*, based on Roman law, were both drawn up by metropolitan governments and hence, in theory at least, were more humane than the legal codes of the British colonies, where planter assemblies had virtually complete autonomy in the formulation of slave laws. In the *Siete Partidas*, for instance, the slave was envisaged as a person and not merely a chattel. Under their respective legal codes, masters in the French and Spanish possessions had duties towards as well as rights over their slaves. However, in the British West Indies, once acquired by their masters, slaves became their owner's private property, as was his horse or cow. As chattel slaves, they could be sold for debts if other moveable assets were exhausted, and disposed of in accordance with the laws of inheritance of real estate. In effect, the legal definition of the slave under British West Indian law denied him much of the protection afforded, in theory at least, by the French and Spanish codes, as well as patently ignoring the existence of family ties amongst the slaves. As Michael Craton has observed of slaves in the British West Indies:

> Denied the protection of the anti-slavery bias of the English Common Law because they were not English, they were also cut off from much of the protection provided for slaves under Roman law . . . because they were decreed as property, the peaceful enjoyment of which was even more sacred to the Englishman than personal liberty.[4]

In the British colonies, the slave was viewed as an object of barter from the earliest days of slavery. One early commentator, who visited Barbados in 1655, noted that planters sold slaves 'from one to the other as we do sheep'.[5] Summing up the difference between the French, Spanish and English slave codes, as they affected the individual, Elsa Goveia has written

> Early English slave law almost totally neglected the slave as a subject of religious instruction, as a member of the family, or as a member of society, possessing some rights, however inferior. In so far as the slave was allowed personality before the law, he was regarded chiefly, as a potential criminal.[6]

Until the first tentative ameliorative legislation in the 1780s, the status of the woman slave under the slave laws was almost identical to that of the male slave. She was subjected to the same punishments as men and the law offered her little or no protection from, for example, sexual abuse or overwork and maltreatment during pregnancy. In contrast to British West Indian slave law, the French and Spanish codes recognised, in theory at least, the necessity to protect women slaves in certain important areas. Père Labat, whilst travelling in the West Indies in 1695, noted that, in the French islands, the King had imposed a fine of 2,000 pounds of sugar if a man was convicted of being the father of a mulatto. When a master so 'debauched his slave', both mother and child were confiscated and 'given to the hospital'.[7] The *Code Noir* also incorporated clauses stipulating that families were not to be broken up when slaves were sold, as well as penalising the concubinage of free men with slaves, except in cases where the union was converted into legal marriage. Similarly, under the *Siete Partidas*, female slaves could be compulsorily manumitted in compensation for abuse, violation or prostitution of a woman by her owner.

It may be argued that the French and Spanish laws relating to miscegenation, for example, existed primarily not to protect the woman slave but to prevent the growth of a large mulatto population. Although the laws against concubinage were notoriously inefficient in terms of protection of the family and the promotion of marriage among slaves, the continental slave codes were more comprehensive and humane. Under French law, for instance, it was illegal to split families, and marriage was actively encouraged. Gwendoline Hall (1971) asserts that, in this respect, it was 'unequivocally protective' of the slave family and evidence indicates that these provisions were enforced.

In contrast, with respect to the protection of slave women from sexual abuse, the limitation of miscegenation and the acknowledgment of the rights of the slave family (which were all closely interrelated), earlier British slave law is patchy and inadequate. For example, Antigua was the only British colony to legislate against miscegenation during the seventeenth and eighteenth centuries. Isolated clauses did exist on some island statute books to protect the slave family; an act passed in Jamaica in 1733 stipulated that 'slaves should be sold singly, unless in the case of families, when a man and his wife, his, her or their children, are not to be sold singly'.[8] But, as Bryan

Edwards cynically observed, legislation of this genre was difficult, if not impossible, to enforce, and hence habitually disregarded by planters. In practice, until the ameliorative legislation of the late period of slavery, the slave women and slave families were afforded little or no special protection.

Because of the marked indifference of planter assemblies to the need to protect the slave woman and the slave family, any theoretical analysis of the status of the slave woman under the law rests upon an examination of the morphology, rather than the content, of slave laws. In the British colonies, slave law changed in response to fluctuations in the economy and socio-political pressures, both external and internal. During the seventeenth and eighteenth centuries, there was little change in the content of the slave laws. Early slave law is hard to piece together but what does emerge is that scant attention was paid to the welfare of slaves of either sex. One of the first comprehensive slave codes, the Barbados Slave Code, passed by the assembly in 1661, saw negroes as 'heathenish' and 'brutish', an 'uncertain, dangerous kind of people', unfit to be governed by English law (Dunn, 1977). It was deemed necessary to govern them by means of a harsh, punitive code.

The philosophical rationale upon which the Barbados Code depended became the basis of British West Indian slave law in general. Women were granted no special rights, for extraction of labour from slaves was heavily dependent on a harsh legal code. Both sexes were subjected to the same punitive laws, with perhaps the rare exception of pregnant women. Long quotes one such early law, which stipulated that female slaves, when pregnant, were 'to be respited from execution until after their pregnancy'.[9]

Towards the end of the eighteenth century the threat of the abolition of the slave trade, compounded by uncertain economic conditions and a rise in the price of slaves, induced the plantocracy to introduce the first ameliorative laws (so named because they were directed at bettering conditions). From the 1780s onwards, individual colonies amended existing legislation, purportedly to improve the material existence of slaves, reduce the mortality rate and promote a healthy natural increase amongst the slaves. Because of a growing interest among planters in the childbearing potential of the female slave, many of the new laws were designed, in theory, to protect the pregnant woman and encourage mothers to have large numbers of children. Under the Leeward Islands Act of 1798, for instance, female slaves 'five months gone' were to be employed only on light work and were to be punished by confinement only 'under penalty of five pounds'. A 'roomy negro house' of two rooms was to be built for every negro woman pregnant with her first child and the proprietor was to compel her 'under penalty of twenty pounds' to lie in at a hospital for lying-in women. Ameliorative legislation passed in the Leewards in 1798 and Jamaica in 1809 included provisions that female slaves 'having six children living' should be 'exempt from hard labour' and the owner 'exempt from taxes' for such female slaves. These laws are random but typical examples of the amelioration laws as they related to the specific childbearing role of women slaves.

Similarly, in their efforts to increase the fertility rate of women slaves, island assemblies passed laws intended to encourage stable matrimony and offered bonuses to slave parents. Where, previously, women had been accorded little protection under the law against sexual abuse, new laws in this delicate area appeared on the statute books, motivated not by chivalry but by practical considerations. The plantocracy associated the poor child-bearing record of women slaves with promiscuity and lack of stable marriage. It was widely held that the sexual exploitation of black women by white men contributed in no small degree to the general 'immorality' of slave society and thus should be legislated against. The Leeward Islands Act of 1798, for instance, subjected whites to a fine of £100 on legal conviction of 'having criminal commerce' with any female slave who was married. The Law of Jamaica of 1826 stated that 'any person committing a rape on a female slave shall suffer death, without benefit of the clergy'. The same penalty was meted out to men convicted of abusing slave girls under ten years old.[10] However, legislation of this nature was rare and there is insufficient evidence to determine whether it was enforced in practice or reduced the sexual abuse of women slaves.

The abolition of the slave trade in 1807 resulted in the increasing intervention of the metropolitan government in internal island affairs. In 1815 the Slave Registration Act* was passed and further ameliorative legislation was incorporated into the slave codes of the British West Indian colonies. Despite the new emphasis on the welfare of the slaves, however, the majority of laws on the statute books remained punitive. One opponent of slavery, in discussing ameliorative legislation, felt that most of these concessions to the improved welfare of slaves were made under pressure, 'grudgingly and of necessity'. He described the new laws as 'specious in words but inoperative in practice – mere rags to cover the blotches and ulcers of the system'.[11] Allowance must be made for a certain degree of bias in the above author's judgement, for it was the 'pious object' of abolitionists to 'mitigate' the evils of slavery and work towards its ultimate abolition. An objective appraisal of the effectiveness of the new laws in a historical context, however, indicates that his criticism was valid. This is especially true of the laws applicable to the slave woman in her role as mother and wife. Penalties placed upon slave owners for contravention of the law were unrealistic and it was virtually impossible to convict a master of crimes against his own slaves. As Elsa Goveia has observed, the amelioration laws lacked any efficient executive principle and their enforcement was difficult because of the non-admissibility of slave evidence against free persons (Goveia, 1965). Thus changes in the texts of the slave laws themselves cannot be taken as accurate indices of actual slave conditions – a point which is highly relevant to this present study of slave women.

The essential function of the slave laws, from the beginning of slavery to full emancipation, was to control the slaves, not to promote their material welfare. The existence of so many 'policing' laws is an indication of the

---

*This legislated against the unlawful importation of slaves into the British slave-owning colonies.

unwillingness on the part of the slaves themselves to co-operate with the system. On the contrary, they frequently broke laws in the course of a general resistance to the institution which made them so indispensable. Where slaves overtly confronted the law, they faced the plantocracy with a moral dilemma for, in showing their capacity to resist, they proved that, despite their definition under law, they were human beings possessed of free will. Thus slave crimes were, in reality, a form of slave resistance; slaves did not repudiate law and morality, but formulated legal and moral codes administered by their own headmen. Such 'laws' frequently conflicted with the official laws of the European master-class. A dual moral code existed in the slave community which John Stewart aptly described thus:

> to pilfer from their masters they consider as no great crime, though to rob a fellow slave is accounted heinous; when a slave makes free with his master's property, he thus ingenuously argues 'what I take from my master, being for my own use, who am his slave, or property, he loses nothing by its transfer'.[12]

In consequence of the high number of 'policing' laws in British West Indian slave codes, many areas of slave resistance involved *breaking* these laws. In this sense, the repressive nature of slave laws was counter-productive; the harsher the system and the more rigid the controls, the greater was the insubordination of the slaves. Unfortunately, where profits were at stake, the productivity of slaves was of paramount concern, even if labour could only be extracted by harsh controls and punishment. Until the penultimate years of slavery, women, as valuable workers, were subjected to the same punishment as men and held an identical chattel status under British West Indian slave law. The legal status of women slaves differed from that of men only in that the status of slave children was derived solely from their mother. Only after the Slave Registration Act was greater legal recognition of the slave father given as individual slaves had to register under the surname which the slave and his 'lawful issue' or her 'natural issue' would henceforth be called.

Only in one sensitive area of slave law, the laws on manumission, were women, as a result of their sexual unions with white men, arguably in a more favourable position than slave men. According to Edward Long – and his observations are supported by modern research – domestic slaves (a high proportion of whom were women) had a greater chance of being granted their freedom than other slaves. Moreover, slave women who had lived in long-standing unions with white men would possibly have had the opportunity of benefiting under their 'husband's' wills, a not uncommon event, which Long would have restricted by law. In reality, the number of women who gained their freedom as a result of inter-racial unions was probably small and restricted to privileged and/or light-skinned mulattos. The mulatto offspring of relations between white men and black or coloured women represented a high proportion of all freed slaves. However, having a white father did not automatically guarantee freedom. The chance of manumission was closely related to the status of individual mothers. As Long observed:

The lower rank of offsprings of miscegenous unions remain in the same slavish conditions as their mother; they are fellow labourers with the Blacks, and are not regarded in the least as their superiors.[13]

The manumission laws in the British West Indies were more stringent than those in the French and Spanish possessions and slave owners were reluctant to manumit slaves. In addition to draining labour from the estate, manumission was a great expense to the slave owner, as a large sum had to be lodged at the local vestry upon the freeing of a slave. Despite their closer proximity to white men, ordinary women slaves possibly had only a marginally better chance of achieving manumission for themselves and their children than the male slave. The economic value of women was high, as will be subsequently shown, and planters were loath to relinquish valuable assets. Unlike skilled male slaves, women could rarely accumulate money to buy freedom and were dependent on men – mainly European men – to provide the required sum of money. This had serious implications for their future status. Hence, although females were manumitted at a higher rate than men, 'so-called free women' arguably remained far more dependent than free black or coloured men (Patterson, 1982).

The laws on manumission apart, in general, the slave laws of the British West Indies adversely affected many major areas of the slave woman's life. In her role as childbearer and mother, she was afforded little protection. The clauses in the ameliorative acts specifically relating to the welfare of female slaves, like the protective clauses applicable to all slaves, were often dead letters. Consistently, there was a marked discrepancy between the law in theory and the law in practice. This was especially noticeable where the working conditions and punishment of female slaves were involved.

Further reading

Archer, ed. (1988)
Brathwaite (1971)
Dunn (1973)
Hall (1971)
Higman (1984)
Patterson (1982)

4

Plantation Labour Regimes

The Economic Role of Slave Women

Women in the formal plantation economy

The sole reason for the existence of black women in the Caribbean was their labour value. Although in the early days of slavery planters had made some attempt to promote marriage and healthy patterns of reproduction, with the increasing dominance of sugar monoculture, it was more economically viable to buy fresh slaves from Africa until abolitionist pressure at the end of the eighteenth century threatened the continued supply through the iniquitous middle passage. From the earliest days of the slave trade women were regarded by Europeans as eminently suited to field work because of their perceived 'drudge' status in polygynous marriages. A large part of the labour on sugar estates consisted of digging holes for canes, hoeing and weeding – tasks generally accepted in slaving circles as 'women's work' in Africa. Planters professed a preference for males and demographic evidence indicates that more males than females were brought to the Caribbean during the eighteenth century (Sheridan, 1985). However, in the complex and hierarchical division of labour that existed on large plantations, men were valued for craftsman skills or work in the semi-industrial processes of the sugar mill and at least half or more of ordinary field gangs were comprised of women, a pattern which was also evident in the French Caribbean (Gautier, 1983).

There was no common experience of female slaves as conditions varied from island to island and changed with the development of the large-scale plantation system. Barry Higman has provided a detailed breakdown of the diversity of work regimes in the British Caribbean, highlighting the main points of contrast between rural and urban slave, sugar and other types of production on, for instance, coffee and pimento estates or cattle pens.

However, when slaves were emancipated in 1834, 68.5 per cent of all employed slaves classified for compensation paid to slave owners were field labourers and inferior field labourers. Slaves employed in agricultural extraction of produce from the land (predial slaves) comprised 85 per cent of the total slave labour force. According to Higman, between 1810 and 1834 the sugar estate played a dominant part in defining the character of slavery and thus discussion of women's role will be restricted primarily to this area of slave economic activity. During the later period of slavery large-scale sugar production occupied 80 per cent of all economically active slaves with the exception of Jamaica where the figure was 53 per cent. The 1834 slave registration returns for 82,807 slaves show that 49 per cent were 'labourers in sugar cultivation' and 78 per cent of slaves lived on sugar estates. Cotton or other agricultural production occupied 5.3 per cent of slaves, 11.6 per cent were labourers *not* in agriculture, 13 per cent were domestics and 20.1 per cent had no occupation, being either too young, too old or sick (Higman, 1984).

From the earliest days, West Indian sugar plantations incorporated certain features of the woodland and savanna economies of West Africa, where hoe cultivation predominated. The newly arrived slaves continued the West African traditions of tilling their own kitchen gardens and cultivating provision grounds, in addition to labouring on their master's plantation (Dunn, 1973). In the first stage of colonisation of the West Indies, the economy of the islands was mixed; tobacco was grown, smallholdings predominated and owners relied upon white indentured labour to work their holdings. As the planters gradually turned from tobacco to the far more profitable sugar cane, small farms were consolidated into large plantations and owners came to rely more and more upon imported African slaves to meet their labour needs. Plantation management became increasingly more complex as the near monoculture stage of production was approached.

Viable plantation units required a large number of slaves, who came to be differentiated into different classes, with the skilled artisans and drivers forming the elite. After this elite, in descending order, came the domestic servants, the slaves involved in more menial 'ancillary' tasks such as washerwomen, the field labourers, the children's gangs and the 'unemployable', sick or superannuated. This social hierarchy was further complicated by divisions between black and coloured, African and creole.

Within this complex occupational stratification of slaves, the position of the woman slave was generally less favourable than that of her male counterpart. The Jamaican planter, William Beckford, gave a brief outline of occupations ascribed to the different sexes in plantation society:

A negro man is purchased either for a trade, or the cultivation and different process of the cane – the occupations of the women are only two, the house, with its several departments and supposed indulgences, or the field with its exaggerated labours. The first situation is the more honourable, the last the most independent.[1]

Apart from the midwife, doctoress or chief housekeeper, the slave elite

Plantation Le Resouvenir.
comprising a view of Mr Hamiltons residence, Coffee Lodge, & the chapel & dwelling house of the late Rev. J. Smith.
LONDON.
Printed for Thos Kelly, 17. Paternoster Row, Jany 21 1826.

4.1 *'Plantation Le Resouvenir'. There is no clue as to where this plantation was located, but the French names suggest Dominica or St Lucia, islands which had changed from French to English possession. The 'Coffee Lodge' suggests it is a coffee rather than a sugar plantation. The architecture is typical of Caribbean 'colonial' style.*

consisted almost solely of men: women in general were restricted to the lower ranks. Richard Sheridan analysed the occupational pattern of Roaring River Estate, Jamaica, in 1756 and found that, of the 92 women on the estate, 70 were field workers, whereas, of the 84 men, only 28 were working in the cane fields. The women not engaged in field work had a variety of occupations; Creole Phibba and Mulatto Mary were 'house wenches', Mulatto Dolly and Juran were cooks and Sue was a washer. Two women were doctoresses (traditional folk healers) and two others carried water to quench the thirst of field negroes; Old Bones took care of the 'Piquinio gang' as a driver, supervising the labour of small children (Sheridan, 1974). A similar occupational pattern existed on the Worthy Park Plantation in 1789, where, out of 162 women, 70 worked in the fields, compared with 29 men out of a total of 177 (Craton and Walvin, 1970). The pre-eminence of field work as the slave woman's major occupation is also shown in Richard Dunn's analysis of the occupational pattern of Mesopotamia, Jamaica, in 1809 (Dunn, 1977). Yet, despite the preponderance of women in field work, planters allegedly preferred men. Bryan Edwards wrote:

> I have to observe, that though it is impossible to conduct the business, either of a house or of a plantation without a number of females . . . the nature of the slave-service in the West Indies (being chiefly field labour) requires, for the immediate interest of the planter, a greater number of males.[2]

In consequence, according to contemporary accounts, only a third of slaves imported were women. The occupational patterns of individual plantations referred to above do not, however, support plantocratic statements on female labour. Plantation lists analysed by Craton and Dunn reflect neither a marked preference for male field hands nor a high ratio of male to female slaves. On the contrary, such modern research into the occupational distribution of sugar plantations indicates that planters may have exaggerated the adverse sex ratio to play down the exploitation of women slaves as field hands.

Although conditions of labour varied slightly from island to island, it is unlikely that the occupational distribution on plantations changed very much from the development of sugar monoculture, apart from an increase in skilled occupations as plantations became larger and more complex. According to Richard Dunn, a typical labour pattern found in plantation accounts of 1706 indicates that 64 per cent of slaves were field hands, 14 per cent domestics and 12 per cent overseers and craftsmen (Dunn, 1973). By the end of the eighteenth century, in Thomas Atwood's estimation, the proportion of 'working field negroes' per plantation was about two-fifths of the total number of slaves, the remainder being 'tradesmen, watchmen, stock-keepers, invalids, house servants, nurses and young children'.

As the higher occupations were largely restricted to men, women slaves would have comprised a significant percentage of common field hands from the earliest days of slavery. It can be argued that most of the more arduous tasks on the plantation, such as cane-cutting, holing and sugar-boiling, were performed by men, while women undertook the less demanding, though no less essential, tasks. Evidence from the French Caribbean collated by Arlette Gautier indicates that the way tasks were subdivided suggests a clear division of labour. Women cut canes, weeded and manured whilst men cut trees, extracted stones and carried heavy weights. In a symbolic gesture of feeding – traditionally women's responsibility in all cultures – women fed the mill, which could be dangerous work as, for instance, fingers could be trapped in rollers. Only women looked after children and chickens. A similar sexual division of labour existed among domestics. Men were valets and coach drivers, women cleaned and did the laundry. The head overseer, who had considerable power through control of work regimes and many aspects of the lives of slaves, was always a man (Gautier, 1983). The complex sexual division of labour on slave plantations – in the French Caribbean at least – would thus appear to be a combination of traditional African roles, imposed European values about the relative worth of male and female labour, and pragmatic economic calculations which designated all slaves as work units rather than human beings.

In view of the high numbers of women involved in field work, it is unlikely that women were spared the heaviest forms of labour, especially during busy periods, such as crop time. Dallas, who divided slaves into three basic classes, wrote that the first and most important class was comprised of 'the most robust of both sexes' whose chief employment consisted of 'preparing and planting the soil, cutting the canes, feeding the mill and aiding the manufacture of sugar and rum'. This observation, made around 1800, implies little differentiation between men and women, regardless of the nature of tasks undertaken. The only concessions made were for children, who picked grass and weeded, and convalescents and pregnant women, who were given 'light labour'.

Although conditions of labour and the treatment of female slaves changed in response to the social and economic development of the West Indian sugar colonies, from early sources it would appear that the taxing nature of the work performed by women slaves was an ever-present feature of plantation life. Richard Ligon, who owned a plantation in Barbados, wrote:

> The work which women do, is most of it weeding, a stooping and painful work; at noon they are called home by the ring of a bell, where they have two hours repast, at night they rest from six, till six o'clock.[3]

On an average seventeenth-century plantation there was nearly one labourer per acre of cane. Men and women did the work of animals. A negro field labourer had three tools, an axe, a hoe and a bill. Slaves were kept at work all year round, even though sugar-growing was only seasonal (Dunn, 1973). When sugar monoculture was fully established in the eighteenth century, the arduous nature of the field labour intensified. None the less, Beckford's account of the daily routine of a field labourer in the 1780s in Jamaica corresponds relatively closely to Ligon's earlier account of Barbadian plantation life. The slaves, observed Beckford:

37

generally turn out at six o'clock in the morning and (after breaks for breakfast and dinner) seldom continue in the field out of crop time after sunset, which is never later than seven; so from this hour, till six the ensuing morning, they may call time their own, part of which they consume in broken sleep, the rest in supper, and in preparation for breakfast.[4]

Women slaves, then, excluded in the large part from the elite occupations, suffered far more than male slaves from inevitable restriction to their ascribed occupations. Confined to the lower ranks, their opportunities of social mobility were severely limited; the favours and privileges accorded the elite slaves were available only to the majority of female slaves through concubinage or the 'selling' of sexual favours; a favoured slave or the natural daughter of the owner or overseer was often taken into service in the house. The majority of women, however, remained working in the fields, in harsh conditions and maintained by their owners at a bare subsistence level. Demographic analysis by Higman confirms the dominance of women in field gangs after 1800. On sugar plantations only 10 per cent were domestics compared with 20 per cent on coffee and cotton plantations. There were now a larger number of creoles and more females of colour were likely to find themselves in the field gang than coloured men, although Africans were still regarded by whites as stronger, if less intelligent, than creoles.

Although planters maintained the general treatment of sugar slaves was mild and 'indulgent', Higman's data confirm that slave morbidity and mortality were highest and the birth rate the lowest on sugar plantations of the notional optimum size of 250 slaves. Next highest in mortality were the coffee plantations, followed by cocoa, cotton, pimento plantations, cattle ranches or pens, the towns and finally marginal subsistence units (Higman, 1984). Sugar plantations were generally regarded as health hazards by whites and were characterised by unhygienic conditions, accidents, suicides, punishments, poor diets (even famine at times when food imports were disrupted) and endemic diseases such as yaws. The labour regime ensured that women shared the same back-breaking work, miseries and puishments as men. In crop time (four to six months between October and March) slaves were turned out of their quarters at sun-up and worked till sunset with little time to call their own. There was also extended night-work during this period. Higman has estimated that between 1807 and 1832 a typical day worked by field workers was 12 hours in Jamaica and 10 hours in the eastern Caribbean but that was averaged out over the whole year (Higman, 1984). Field workers were treated as the capital stock of the plantation, on a par with animal stock and maintained at bare subsistence level. Though they performed the hardest labour and worked the longest hours, their conditions were far inferior to those of domestics or skilled craftsmen and they suffered from greater ill-health and higher mortality rates. In addition they had to produce food in their free time on slave provision grounds to supplement the often inadequate diets provided by masters.

Despite the fact that slave owners neglected the material welfare of their ordinary field hands, a good profit was extracted from them. The profitability of slaves appears to have been a constant from the beginning of sugar cultivation. Richard Ligon wrote of planters in Barbados:

> they have bought this year no less than 1000 negroes, and the more they be, the better able are they to buy, for in a year and a half they will earn as much as they cost.

Whether the economic value of slaves induced planters to treat them well is, however, debatable. Ligon, for instance, believed that slaves were 'preserved with greater care than the [white] servants', as the latter were only indentured for five years, while the slaves were 'subject to their masters forever' and thus constituted a lifelong investment.[5] Conversely, one contemporary critic of slavery, William Edmundson, a Quaker, writing of seventeenth-century Barbados, accused planters of keeping their slaves 'in Ignorance and under Opression' and of starving them 'for want of Meat and Cloaths Convenient'.[6] Sir Hans Sloane also regarded the West Indian slave regime as essentially harsh and dehumanising.

By the 1780s the average cost per annum of maintaining a field slave was about £12 sterling inclusive of food, clothing, medicine, poll tax and insurance. At a slightly later date, Bryan Edwards estimated that the annual profit from one able field hand was £25. It would appear that West Indian planters received a good return on their investments, regardless of the high mortality rates of new African slaves in particular. From an analysis of statistical data for the years 1765 to 1775, Richard Sheridan has estimated that, if a prime field hand in Jamaica laboured for twelve years, he (or perhaps, more appropriately, she), would return 6 per cent per annum; fifteen years' labour produced a return of 9 per cent, while, if the slave survived twenty years' labour, he would bring a return of 11 per cent per annum for his owner (Sheridan, 1974).

Whether many ordinary field hands ever survived long enough to verify Sheridan's neat computation is debatable, but there is no doubt that, as the backbone of the plantation economy, they were highly valued assets. In the case of the prime female slave, her utility value is reflected in the price she fetched. Throughout the period of slavery, this was only marginally less than that paid for an able-bodied man. Ligon quoted £30 for a male negro and £25 to £27 for a female. Before the abolition of the slave trade in 1807, the approximate purchase price of a new male slave was between £50 to £70, while a healthy female sold for between £50 and £60. Prices for creole slaves were roughly 20 per cent higher, although Bryan Edwards asserted that these slaves were sometimes twice as expensive as 'salt-water' Africans,* depending on their particular skills. Men and women were often sold together in 'jobbing gangs'. A Jamaican advertisement in 1827, for instance, offered a 'small gang of effective and well-disposed males, 17 males and 17 females'.[7]

Before 1807 there is no indication that fertility increased the worth of women – women of similar ages, with or without children, generally cost the

*New slaves fresh from the transatlantic crossing.

same. After the abolition of the slave trade, an able-bodied field slave cost approximately £180 sterling and Stewart noted that a female slave with a healthy infant was 'at least twenty per cent more valuable than she was before it was born',[8] a reflection of a change in attitude towards the woman slave on the part of the planter. The decline in slave numbers after 1807 encouraged a much greater interest in the childbearing potentialities of women slaves, in addition to raising the value of infant slaves to a fifth that of a healthy adult.

Controversial debates still rage, particularly among quantitative historians, as to whether slavery remained profitable after abolition of the slave trade or whether slave conditions improved or deteriorated over time. But one important aspect of the slaves' existence remained constant; labour was extracted via coercion and punishment from the beginnings of sugar cultivation. Work in the fields was hard, monotonous and degrading, with the result that slaves, men or women, gave their labour unwillingly and inefficiently. This often resulted in low productivity linked to various forms of resistance to the regime (discussed in Chapter 5) from individual shirking and malingering to sabotage, arson and more collective discontents in the gang which rendered control over productivity difficult. Michael Craton has estimated that Jamaican slaves at the end of the eighteenth century cut only one-fifth as much cane per day at crop time than equivalent modern-day wage earners (Craton and Walvin, 1970). Sheridan disagrees and argues that productivity was good, especially in the case of cane-hole digging where workers were forced to wield hoes in equal time and with equal effect irrespective of sex, age or physical strength (Sheridan, 1985). This debate aside, labour was undoubtedly extracted in the main through coercion. Planters could only squeeze a respectable profit out of their slaves by literally beating it out of them, an unsavoury practice, used on men and women alike, which inspired strong resistance on the part of the slaves. The need to keep the slaves in line and suppress insubordination hence became the slave owner's main justification for habitual physical maltreatment, such as whippings and confinement in the stocks. Sir Hans Sloane, a relatively detached observer, wrote that these punishments 'were sometimes merited by the Blacks who are a very perverse Generation of people, and though they appear harsh, yet are scarce equal to some of their crimes'.[9] Edward Long, in defending allegations of the inhumanity of the planters, asserted that the planter's authority could be equated with that of an 'ancient patriarch'. There was not a great deal of punishment and cruelty, he wrote, but added that:

> Amongst 3 or 4000 blacks, there must be some who are not to be reclaimed from a savage, intractable humour and acts of violence, without the coercion of punishment.[10]

Long did admit, however, that odd planters did at times exhibit 'inhuman tempers'.

The vehement denials of the planters apart, punishment and, not infrequently, unwarranted cruelty were an integral part of plantation life from the

CRUELTY EXTRAORDINARY,

COMMITTED ON A

FEMALE SLAVE of the name of YAMBA

IN THE ISLAND OF JAMAICA.

In Jamaica's distant isle,
Still with Afric's love I burn ;
Parted many a thousand mile,
Never, never to return.

Come kind death and give release,
Yamba has no friend but thee ;
Thou canst ease my throbbing breast,
Thou canst set the pris'ner free.

Down my cheeks the tears are dropping
Broken is my heart with grief,
Mangled my poor flesh with weeping,
Come kind death and give relief.

Born on Afric's golden coast,
Once I was as blest as you,
Parents tender I could boast,
Husband dear and children too.

White man he came from afar,
Sailing o'er the briny flood ;
Who with help of British tar,
Buys my human flesh and blood.

With the baby at my breast,
Other two where sleeping by,
In my cot i slept at rest,
With no thought of danger nigh.

From the bush at even tide,
Rush'd the fierce man-stealing crew ;
They seized the children by my side,
And seized the wretched Yamba too.

Then for love of filthy gold,
Straight they bore me to the seas,
Cramm'd me down the slave ship's hold
Where were hundreds stole like me.

Naked on the platform lying,
Now we cross the tumbling wave,
Shrieking, sinking, fainting, crying,
Deed of shame to Britons brave.

Nauseous horse beans they bring nigh
Sick and sad we cannot eat ;
The whip must cure the sulks they
cry,   meat,
And down our throats they force the

I in groaning past the night,
And did roll my aching head ;
At the break of morning light,
My poor child was cold and dead.

Driven like cattle to a fair,
See they sell us young and old ;
Child from mother too they tear,
All for love of filthy gold.

4.2 *'Cruelty Extraordinary'. The propaganda message of this poem is self-evident and typical of abolitionist poetry of the period. The African slave woman is depicted as an innocent victim of a brutal and mercenary trade which has no respect for family bonds. A graphic picture of the cruelties of the ship-board passage to Jamaica is provided.*

41

earliest days of slavery. Sir Hans Sloane wrote that for 'Negligence' slaves were usually 'whipt by the Overseers with Lance Wood Switches, till they be bloody . . . being first tied up by their hands in the Mill-houses'. After these floggings, slave masters sometimes used 'several very exquisite Torments' such as rubbing pepper and salt or dropping melted wax on the slave's skin. William Beckford remarked that the 'instrument of correction' was to be heard throughout Jamaica, and the Reverend John Riland, despite his Christian views, had to own that his own Jamaican estate 'was not worked without the whip'. Slaves, both men and women, were thus caught up in a vicious circle. When they reacted to the harsh work conditions with non-cooperation or outright insubordination, they were punished. This punishment only served to make them more resentful of their condition and thus the cycle of non-cooperation, resistance and punishment was indefinitely repeated. As Beckford astutely observed, 'the whip . . . does not correct, but multiply faults'.

Women slaves were no less immune to physical punishment than male slaves. There is no hard evidence to suggest that they were more compliant than men. As will be shown in the following section, resistance to slavery was an integral part of the life of the woman slave. The whip constituted an important element in her life. When the first legislation forbidding the whipping of black women was introduced in Trinidad in 1823, it was strongly objected to by planters who felt that women slaves were 'notoriously insolent' and only kept in some 'tolerable order' through the fear of punishment. One colonial official stated that female slaves 'more frequently merited punishment than males'. The general consensus of opinion amongst Trinidadian slave owners on the 1823 law was that insolence among women slaves was checked only by the dreaded whip (Brereton, 1974).

Under the overseer's whip neither age nor sex found any favour. 'Whether the offender be male or female, precisely the same course is pursued,' observed a critic of slavery in 1824, describing the procedure for formal punishment thus:

> The posterior is made bare and the offender is extended prone on the ground, the hands and feet being firmly extended by other slaves; when the driver, with his long and heavy whip, inflicts under the eye of the overseer, the number of lashes, which he may order.[11]

In the case of women slaves in particular, the degradation inflicted by this act was compounded by the fact that frequently a black driver was appointed to carry out the punishment; as his privileged position depended on his ability to conform, overtly at least, to the system, he showed no lenience. John Stedman visited one estate in Surinam where he was appalled by the sight of 'a beautiful samboe girl of eighteen' who was tied up by both arms to a tree, naked and 'lacerated in such a shocking manner' by the whips of two negro drivers. Although conditions on plantations in Surinam were notoriously harsh, a similar pattern of cruelty undoubtedly existed throughout the British Caribbean.

In respect of physical maltreatments, female domestic slaves were perhaps

Flagellation of a Female Samboe Slave

4.3 *'Flagellation of a Female Samboe Slave'. A 'Samboe' was a slave with one black and one white parent, which may account for this woman's Europeanised features. This type of punishment was undoubtedly inflicted until whipping of women was banned in the last years of slavery, when there was greater concern about the childbearing potential of female slaves and increasing abolitionist pressure to make the system more humane.*

in a more vulnerable position than the ordinary field slaves. Because of their close proximity to their masters, they were far more frequently the victim of sadistic whims and personal caprice. Henry Coor, giving evidence to the House of Commons enquiry into the slave trade in 1790, recalled how one evening, as a house guest at a Jamaican plantation, he saw the master of the house nail the ear of a house wench to a tree post because she had broken a plate. In the morning the woman had gone, 'having torn the head of the nail through the ear'. When found, she was severely flogged. During his sojourn in Surinam, John Stedman noted several incidences of cruelty towards female domestics, who were often expected to perform sexual duties in addition to their official duties. The underlying sexual jealousy this aroused in their white mistresses often resulted in acts of unwarranted cruel treatment. In many ways, then, the apparent comforts and privileges of the domestic slave were cancelled out by the precarious nature of her position. Moreover, unlike the ordinary woman slave, the domestic slave could be punished by relegation to field work.

Pregnancy did not guarantee either a lighter work burden or a reprieve from physical punishment. Women were expected to work in the fields until at least six weeks before delivery and return to work no later than three weeks afterwards. In theory, during the early period of slavery a woman was exempted from flogging until after the delivery of her child. In practice little special consideration was paid to the pregnant slave woman. The prime consideration of the planter was the pursuit of profit, not procreation.

As negro prices began to rise in the late eighteenth century, planters introduced measures designed to give better care to pregnant women and slave mothers. However, these measures were often negated by the planter's exploitation of the female slave as a worker. For example, on most large Jamaican plantations in the 1790s, a woman could technically get release from work by producing a large number of children; in effect she usually received little credit for this activity.

When slave owners became increasingly anxious about the threat of the abolition of the slave trade, the slave woman's potential as a breeder of new slaves gained a greater significance. From the end of the eighteenth century, ameliorative laws were passed which, in theory, afforded pregnant women some protection. For instance, women were entitled to perform less arduous labour whilst pregnant. In reality, however, they were expected to work as normal, for a slump in sugar prices motivated planters to extract the maximum profit from their slave work-force. If pregnant women complained about their conditions of labour, they risked a flogging. One abolitionist observer recalled the following incident on a Jamaican plantation in the 1820s:

> Two women, who were pregnant, desired to quit the field during the rain . . . The overseer refused them permission. They went to complain . . . to a magistrate, but were stopped on their way by a neighbouring overseer and by him thrown in the stocks until he sent them back to their own overseer who put them again in the stocks and had them flogged.[12]

Accounting for the propaganda motives of this anecdote, and given that slave women maintained an excessively low fertility rate after the introduction of ameliorative legislation (Chapter 7), the above passage indicates that, even during the so-called ameliorative period, pregnant women were no less immune to heavy labour, harsh conditions and physical punishments than other groups of slaves.

After 1807 some provisions were made to exempt pregnant women from floggings, but, even as late as 1826, in Jamaica at least, legislation limiting the number of lashes which could be inflicted upon an individual slave made no special provision for the woman slave, whether or not she was pregnant. Under the 1826 Jamaican law, punishment was 'restricted' to 10 lashes, except in the presence of the owner or overseer, when a maximum of 39 lashes could be administered. A second punishment could not be given until 'the culprit' was 'entirely recovered' from the former one, under a penalty of £20.

In general, the treatment of pregnant slaves, even during the penultimate years of slavery, left much to be desired. Pregnant women were unnecessarily flogged or confined in the stocks, punishments which jeopardised not only the lives of their unborn children but also their own lives. One critic of slavery, Dr John Williamson, writing of Jamaica in 1817, related the salutary tale of a pregnant woman who was 'confined to the stocks for misconduct' and liberated only a few days before delivery. After giving birth, she subsequently died of puerperal fever.

As slave owners and overseers had little regard for women slaves in their reproductive capacity, it is hardly surprising that they suffered from so many gynaecological disorders. Hard work and cruel treatment took its toll on their health. 'Monk' Lewis, who was genuinely concerned about the welfare of his female slaves, commented strongly on the general atmosphere of callous indifference to the female slaves. Having received several reports of white book-keepers and overseers kicking women in the womb, often crippling them or their unborn children, he felt entitled to state that white overseers and book-keepers 'kick black women in the belly from one end of Jamaica to another'. Some planters, like Lewis, were without doubt genuinely concerned about the well-being of their female slaves, but, in general, a woman slave, pregnant or not, was too valuable a labour unit to be accorded preferential treatment.

Despite the constant threat of punishment and the additional burden of pregnancy, slave women were far from submissive as workers. Their relative independence as field workers, noted by Beckford, had important implications for resistance, collective and individual. As will be shown in the next chapter, female slaves took their revenge on their owners through shirking work, shamming illness, lying, stealing and even openly defying and abusing overseers. These forms of slave resistance, often interpreted by slave owners as evidence of the inferiority of blacks, were harshly dealt with by the whites. 'The indolent only and the ill-disposed, encounter punishments,' remarked William Beckford.

Resistance to punishment itself demanded much courage. Little hard evidence exists to show that slave women in the Caribbean protested against brutal punishment. Thomas Cooper did refer to one particular woman who, when placed in the stocks by her overseer, subsequently complained to the attorney and in consequence received 39 lashes from the same overseer. Such insights into the reactions of slave women, though rare, suggest that similar incidents may not have been as isolated as the absence of evidence indicates. If we can believe John Stedman, slaves in general were 'spirited and brave', they met death with 'the most undaunted fortitude'; if they believed their punishment unmerited, 'immediate suicide' was too often the fatal consequence 'especially among the Coromantyn Negroes'.* Unfortunately it is difficult to substantiate this observation in the context of West Indian slave women. In terms of less dramatic reactions, however, it is possible to glean some useful comparative information from the American South, where a number of references are made in slave narratives to slave women resisting floggings. According to Eugene Genovese, it was not uncommon for women slaves to fight against physical punishment (Genovese, 1974). Slave conditions in the old South were in many respects superior to those in the West Indies, where sugar planting was regarded by one contemporary critic as 'not a very slow species of murder'. Unless we conclude that female slaves in the Caribbean were more submissive than their American counterparts, it is reasonable to assume that, as well as showing their resentment through more convenient modes of non-cooperation, slave women, if sufficiently provoked, would have resisted actual punishment itself.

Informal economic activities: the provision ground and the slave market

In the words of Lucille Mathurin (1975), in West Indian slave society, 'the black women produced, the brown woman served and the white woman consumed'. But not only did the ordinary black slave woman make an indispensable contribution to the external economy of the sugar islands, she also participated in the internal marketing system which developed in the slave islands.** Arguably it constituted a positive and creative area of the slave's existence. The reluctance of West Indian planters to provide their slaves with sufficient food led to the establishment, at a very early date, of provision grounds on marginal lands from which slaves were encouraged to supply their own food. Paradoxically, this failure on the part of West Indian planters to supply their slaves with the basic material necessities of life was

---

*Ashanti or Akan-speaking slaves originating in the Gold Coast (modern Ghana) who had a reputation as proud and rebellious slaves.
**That is, a parallel sector to the formal production of cash crops for export which was controlled by Europeans. It produced goods for internal production and was organised on a loosely structured, small-scale basis by blacks and coloureds separate from but complementing the formal sector.

instrumental in the development of a resilience and independence among the slaves which gave their otherwise depressing lives meaning and purpose.

The provision ground was everywhere more important than the master's store with the exception of Barbados, St Kitts, Nevis, Antigua, Demerara-Essequibo and Berbice (Higman, 1984). In Jamaica, provision grounds came under greater regulation in the Consolidated Slave Act of 1788 and subsequent amendments. Except in crop time slaves were allowed one day per fortnight exclusive of Sundays and public holidays to cultivate their plots. According to Higman, the vast majority of slaves, in the Windward Islands and Jamaica relied heavily on produce of their provision grounds for sustenance although there were some localities, for instance the parish of Vere in Jamaica, where slaves had limited grounds and had to depend on rations provided by slave owners. Under the Jamaican Slave Law of 1816 planters were required to provide rations where no suitable land was available for slaves to cultivate or where drought had caused crop failure. However, as a rule, the only rations provided by planters were salt and pickled fish (Higman, 1984). Internal organisation of provision grounds was left largely to the slaves themselves and they were worked by individuals or family groups with men, women and children all performing labour. Planter involvement was limited to the occasional inspections stipulated by the slave laws.

For one and a half days a week, including Sundays, the slave was thus freed from plantation labour to work his or her provision grounds. The slaves took advantage of this free time to engage in other enterprises such as raising poultry or traditional handicrafts. This was customary from the earliest days of slavery. Sir Hans Sloane noted that:

> [the slaves] have Saturdays in the Afternoon and Sundays . . . allowed them for the culture of their own plantations to feed themselves from . . . [the] ground allow'd them by their masters.[13]

Whole slave families were involved in the cultivation of these grounds. They, not their masters, reaped the benefit of their labours. Thus the slaves expended an amazing amount of energy on their 'polinks' or provision grounds. On these 'polinks' (distinct from the tiny plots, kitchen gardens or yards close to their houses) slaves produced a variety of crops and herbs for medicinal purposes. Crops produced varied with locality but root crops predominated with corn and plantain as subsidiaries. European green vegetable crops were also produced, primarily for sale in the public markets. Pigs and poultry were kept in the slaves' garden plots. Higman argues that slaves in the Windwards and Jamaica played an important part in supplying internal markets but that it is impossible to know how much produce of ground or garden entered the slaves' diet directly or was exchanged at the market for other items, food and non-food, or accumulated as cash (which provided opportunities to buy freedom). The provision ground system was said to be preferred by slaves themselves and created a framework for independent economic activity (Higman, 1984).

Although technically the land which they cultivated belonged to their master, in effect the slaves passed it on as family property, as they did any other possessions they may have had, so that Dallas could note, 'Their right of property in what they acquire is never questioned, but seems completely established by custom.' Bryan Edwards agreed with Dallas that slaves could dispose at their deaths of 'what little property they possess' and 'even bequeath their grounds or gardens'.

If owners disrespected these customary rights it could elicit a strong response from the individual slave concerned. John Jeremie, a legal expert arguing against the practice of selling slaves off separately when plantations changed ownership, wrote:

> The slave becomes attached to his plantation, to his garden, and to his cottage; but when the strip of land is taken from him, which he has cultivated with care, he becomes discontented and often contracts habits of heedlessness and indolence which render him worthless even to his owner.[14]

John Parry (1955) argues that the origins of the Caribbean peasantry can be traced to slavery when blacks were made to provide their own food. He has argued that the system gave slaves a better diet and a small, independent income, and made them less likely to run away or rebel (although this last point may be disputed in the light of evidence presented in the following chapter). Sheridan (1985) is more circumspect and, although he broadly agrees about the origins of the free peasantry, he points out that questions still remain concerning the performance of the provision-ground system. Were slaves given enough time to cultivate grounds? Did they have enough energy and will? How much time was needed to walk to the provision ground or market (the distance could vary from a few to thirty-five miles)? He is dubious about the impact of produce from provision grounds on slave diet and argues that Caribbean slaves were poorly fed in terms of calorie intake, which was far less than that provided by the typical diet of slaves in the USA on the eve of the Civil War. There was also a serious threat of crop failure through drought or hurricane. Hall also concedes that, although Jamaican slaves grew more food than their counterparts in the Lesser Antilles, for instance, their needs were seldom fully met without imported supplies (Hall, 1962). Controversy over the economic contribution of slave provision grounds and plots still needs to be resolved (Mintz, 1983). But this should not detract from their undoubted importance to the slaves themselves, which was recognised by contemporary observers.

Although contemporary plantocratic and abolitionist sources referred to the fact that it was the duty of all 'adult males' to provide for their families, this emphasis on patriarchal family structures reflects a middle-class European perception of gender roles with man as the 'provider'. On the slave plantation, however, many women were single or providing for children (see Chapter 6). More importantly, economic organisation of slave provision grounds was arguably based on a traditional African rather than European division of labour.

Women in traditional African societies make a significant and indispensable contribution to food production and, in West Africa in particular, gain

48

a degree of economic independence from men (even within marriage) through marketing activities. They thus exhibit a high degree of entrepreneurial skills. Although women are still subordinate to men in social terms, they are not simply the passive drudges of plantocratic mythology. Women carried these skills with them to the Caribbean and, in addition to participating fully in the cultivation of provision grounds, they became prominent as market sellers and 'higglers' or commercial intermediaries who sold the crop surplus of other slaves for a small profit. The latter occupation was particularly connected with urban slaves. A runaway slave advertisement in the Jamaican *Royal Gazette*, October 1827, alludes to a whole family of Kingston-based female higglers – Sarah Christian and her daughters Rosetta and Amelia, who also had a female child, Mary. They were described as 'very artful and likely to attempt to pass as free persons'. Arlette Gautier writes that in the French Caribbean, which developed a slave economy very similar to that of the British Caribbean, women sold agricultural products as they had done in Africa and this gave them a high degree of autonomy. The Sunday markets were dominated by free creoles and slave women as it was difficult for male slaves to get passes (Gautier, 1983).

The public Sunday market was an important institution in the West Indian sugar colonies from the very beginnings of slavery and was later to become anathema to religious abolitionists, who wished to stop it in order that slaves and masters could keep the sabbath. Indeed abolitionists like Thomas Cooper were the main critics of the provision-ground system on the grounds that slaves worked too hard to cultivate their crops adequately and were forced to spend their only day of leisure – Sunday – in cultivation and marketing. However, slaves were not noticeably enthusiastic about Christianity until the last years of slavery and such commentators may have misread the degree to which cultivation of provision grounds was an added burden, reluctantly taken up out of necessity. Other contemporary writers, such as Edwards, have noted that slaves approached this extra work with enthusiasm as it was they, not planters, who reaped the benefits.

It is debatable whether the importance of the slave woman in the internal marketing system of the British slave colonies was a direct African retention or a result of the new roles she was forced to adopt as a result of enslavement. Mintz and Hall (1970) suggest, however, that through these activities (which are still dominated by women in West Africa and the modern Caribbean), the woman slave contributed significantly to the integration of creole society. In visiting the market, for instance, women could disseminate information amongst the slaves and facilitate communication between different plantations, for, despite the general stringency of the laws regarding the mobility of slaves, this sharp vigilance was relaxed where marketing activities were concerned. For instance, one clause in the Laws of Jamaica, 1826, stated that 'no slave except when going to market shall travel about without a ticket, specially worded and signed by his owner'. This is perhaps an indication of the importance of the slave market to the entire population of the sugar islands, an importance noted by Bryan Edwards who, reflecting general plantocratic opinion, wrote that the gardening and marketing activities of the slaves were beneficial to both slave and planter, as the former earned extra money and the latter did not have to feed the slaves.

Allowing slaves to grow their own food, then, was an easy way out for the planters. In effect, this lax attitude meant that slaves came to dominate the internal economy of the colonies. Although, as Gautier (1983) notes, more research is needed to establish the extent women were involved in provision-ground cultivation and marketing and the degree to which this represents African retentions, it is certain that they were not only vital to the formal economy of the West Indies but also the informal sector. In her work as a field slave, the individual woman had more autonomy and independence than the elite slaves and this was reinforced by the resourcefulness and individual enterprise she developed in the cultivation of her 'polinks' and her visits to the market. These unofficial economic activities benefited both the slave community and the white society. Despite the harsh realities of the plantation, the woman slave energetically used her precious free time to cultivate her individual or family 'polink'. The internal marketing activities of the slave woman represented a valuable contribution on her part to the creation, in the midst of hardship and oppression, of a positive underlife for herself and her fellow slaves.

Further reading

William Beckford,
A Descriptive Account of the Island of Jamaica
(London, 1790), 2 vols.
C. and R. Bridenbaugh (1972)
Craton (1978)
Goveia (1965)
Higman (1984)
Leith Ross (1939)
Mathurin Mair (1974, 1975)
Sheridan (1974, 1985)

5

The Woman Slave and Slave Resistance

Richard Ligon declared that slaves were a 'happy people whom so little contents'. Contentment implies acceptance of slavery but there is strong evidence which suggests that, from the earliest days of slavery, slaves, both male and female, were indisputably 'troublesome property', and far from content. The record of slave revolts in the British West Indies is, in itself, an indication of the extent of rejection of slavery. On a more mundane level, however, the slaves found many ways during their everyday lives to frustrate their masters. Negroes, remarked Edward Long, were always trying to 'overreach' their overseers, by thwarting their plans, misunderstanding their orders and even attempting to secure their dismissal by filing constant complaints against them to the attorney. Creolisation, despite contemporary allegations to the contrary, did not ensure greater docility, for West Indian-born slaves were judged by Long to be 'irrascible, conceited, proud, indolent . . . and very artful'.

Contemporary writers often alluded to the idleness and dishonesty of slaves. According to John Stewart, for instance, they were 'crafty, artful and plausible, little ashamed of falsehood and strongly addicted to theft'. The generally sympathetic John Stedman also had to admit that plantation slaves were 'commonly thieves, plundering whatever they can lay their hands on with impunity'. But Stedman, unlike other plantocratic commentators, qualified his observation by arguing that it was logical that slaves who suffered 'the most flagrant violations of everyday right' should be disposed to retaliate. Such retaliation involved not only theft and a more generalised rejection of European codes of morality but also many subtle forms of everyday resistance to the harsh conditions under which the slaves lived and laboured. Men and women alike exasperated their masters in countless ways – shirking work, damaging crops, dissembling, feigning illness. Unlike outright revolt, these unspectacular routine acts of non-cooperation did not involve actual violence against whites but persistently chipped away against the whole fabric of slavery. Occasionally, individual acts of violence such as

51

arson, poisoning and murder were carried out by slaves, and planters arguably feared secret poisoning more than collective revolt as they could not be protected from it by the militia.

Since 1975 there have been significant developments in the study of slave resistance and rebellion. Studies by Michael Craton (1982), Barry Gaspar (1985) and Hilary Beckles (1982, 1986) developed a considerably more sophisticated approach to slave resistance and have filled crucial gaps in our understanding of organised slave rebellions. Important new research on maronage and slave runaways has also been carried out (Heuman, 1986). But, with the exception of Lucille Mathurin Mair's monograph *The Rebel Woman in the British West Indies During Slavery* (1975), little else has been published on the contribution slave women made to Caribbean slave resistance in *all* its forms. As Elizabeth Fox-Genovese notes, there is still a lack of works on women in slave resistance in New World societies although new trends in the historiography of slavery are beginning to address this (Fox-Genovese, 1986).

The major emphasis in the new histories of slave resistance in the Caribbean has been on slave revolts but, as Gad Heuman points out, if we are looking for forms of resistance which impinged directly on the lives of slave owners, it is everyday resistance (including cultural and psychological resistance) on which we must focus. This is still a relatively under-researched area (Heuman, 1986). This discussion, then, will examine all aspects of resistance from collectively organised revolts and 'discontents' in the field to individual acts of resistance including running away. The unifying thread is the African cultural heritage of the slave woman which fired her rebellious spirit, frequently bringing her into conflict with the laws and values of the master-class.

Day-to-day resistance

Early historical works on slavery perpetuated and consolidated adverse contemporary images of blacks. The 'massa'/slave relationship involved a high degree of stereotyping which assumed that slaves possessed ascribed, inferior racial traits. This one-dimensional view of the slave ignored his essential individuality and ultimately developed into the composite stereotype of the 'Sambo'/'Quashee' figure. 'Sambo' was the 'typical' slave of the American Old South, 'Quashee' was his West Indian equivalent. The name Quashee derived from Kwasi, a popular name among Akan-speaking slaves of Ghanaian origin which was in common currency in the West Indies and therefore was a suitable tag with which to flesh out the stereotype and give it some human credibility. Other Akan names such as Cudjoe also acquired pejorative associations in the nineteenth century. Slaves were also given ludicrous and demeaning classical names – Hercules, Phibia – which stripped them of their African identity. Such names were important symbolic rituals of enslavement (Patterson, 1982). In the American Old South the Massa/Sambo charade was linked to the idealistic paternalism of the Southern 'gentleman', a domestic mythology centred on the 'father/son' relationship of master to slave (Freehling, 1986). In the Caribbean, with a tiny white minority and high degrees of absenteeism, there was arguably less psychological manipulation of slaves and more brute force. Idealisation of slavery was only found in comfortable surroundings of the English country estate, in the bucolic pastoral paintings of Caribbean plantations. But adverse stereotyping of slaves remained an essential ingredient of social relations in slave society. Although the 'Quashee' stereotype of the lying, lazy, thieving male slave was most dominant, slave women were also stereotyped as licentious, treacherous and scheming.

Orlando Patterson has argued that such denigration of slaves was essential if the master's honour and power was to be retained. In all slave societies, the personality of the slave is portrayed as the opposite of the master to induce a servile mentality typified by seeming dependent and childish behaviour in front of masters (Patterson, 1982). Planters needed the security of these essentially racist stereotypes to define their own reality as a master-class but what Europeans saw as negative traits may have been forms of subtle resistance. This point was first made in early pioneering studies of the Old South by Raymond and Alice Bauer (1942) and Kenneth Stampp (1956), who termed such resistance 'passive' as opposed to the overt, 'active' resistance of slave revolt. Such studies have now been considerably amended and refined. Patterson, for instance, has examined the complex psycho-cultural processes in slave society which inspired slaves with an 'irrepressible yearning for dignity and recognition', arguing that slaves wore 'masks' to deceive masters. To illustrate this he quotes the Jamaican proverb 'play fool to catch wise'. However, Patterson falls into the trap of many historians of referring primarily to male slaves, with the exception of discussions relating to women's sexual role. Thus, while Quashee has been restored some of his human dignity and integrity, Quasheba has remained in the shadows, although there is sufficient contemporary evidence to indicate that she, too, did not live up to her unfavourable stereotype. To discover more about Quasheba's contribution to everyday resistance to slavery, therefore, it is essential to find out more about the behaviour of women slaves in general as recorded through the eyes of contemporary observers.

Many Europeans in the West Indies declared women slaves to be more troublesome than men. Mrs Carmichael, the wife of a plantation owner, felt this to be so, as did the Trinidadian planters who protested against the law of 1823 which banned the whipping of female slaves on the ground that it deprived them of the only means of keeping these women in 'tolerable' order. Matthew Lewis, the liberal Jamaican planter, also reluctantly attested to the insubordinate nature of female slaves. Having tried every means to satisfy his negroes and 'render them happy and secure' he had not found it necessary to punish any of his slaves, with the exception of 'two female demons' for their aggressive and uncooperative behaviour. Although these comments refer to the later period of slavery, 'female demons' as well as the more common but less picturesque 'bothersome'

BRANDING SLAVES PREVIOUS TO EMBARKATION.

5.1 *'Branding slaves previous to embarkation'. An abolitionist water-colour showing a female slave in the foreground being branded by a sailor. In the background is a slave coffle (gang) being brought from the interior. Note the African guard, indicating the involvement of Africans in recruiting slaves for the Atlantic slave trade. Branding was characteristically carried out on the plantations and has probably been included here to enhance the dramatic effect as part of the abolitionist propaganda campaign against the slave trade.*

slave women registered their discontent in numerous ways from the earliest days of slavery.

Resistance to enslavement on the part of Africans began from the moment of their capture (Rathbone, 1986). During the middle passage, for example, the suicide rate was high, especially among Ibos. Slaves frequently died from a 'fixed melancholy' or a refusal to eat and drink; non-accidental drownings were common. Suicide was not merely a succumbing to apathy and despair but a positive means of attaining freedom, according to West African religious-mystical belief. As Sir Hans Sloane observed:

> The Negroes from some countries think they return to their own Country when they die . . . and therefore regard death but little, imagining they shall change their condition by that means from servile to free, and so for this reason often cut their throats.[1]

Women and men alike sought freedom through death on the middle passage. Failed suicides were severely punished. An abolitionist poet writing in 1798 described his encounter, as a sailor on a 'Guineaman', with one determined woman slave:

> But some were sulky of the slaves,
> And would not take their meat;
> So therefore we were forc'd, by threats
> And blows, to make them eat.
> One woman, sulkier than the rest,
> Would still refuse her food –
> Hark! Hark! e'en now I hear her cries!
> I see her in her blood!
>
> The captain made me tie her up,
> And flog, while he stood by:
> And then he curs'd me if I stayed
> My hand, to hear her cry.[2]

Suicide, especially among the 'Coromantine' negroes (Akan-speaking slaves from the area that is now modern Ghana), was sometimes a form of mass resistance against enslavement, both on the slave ship (where 'Coromantines' were also often the leaders of mutinies), and on arrival in the West Indies. Snelgrave recorded how these negroes 'despised Punishment and even Death itself' and noted that:

> in Barbadoes and other Islands . . . on their being anyways hardly dealt with, to break them of their Stubbornness [*sic*] in refusing to work, twenty or more have hang'd themselves at a time in a Plantation.[3]

Although women were regarded by slave traders as less dangerous than men and hence given more spacious quarters and kept in irons only if they were rebellious, evidence suggests that they strongly resented their confinement. The Reverend John Riland, a planter converted to the abolitionist cause, sailed in 1801 from Liverpool to Jamaica in a slave ship. On 7 May he recorded in his diary that he had seen a woman handcuffed because she had attempted to drown herself. She later received severe punishment. Riland further observed that, when the women were made to dance upon the deck, they always maintained their dignity; they 'kept themselves aloof' and 'seemed to feel an indignation which long continued habit could not suppress when forced to behave childishly'. Men and women alike were reluctant to 'dance' and hence often flogged. They were also compelled to sing, though their songs were generally 'melancholy lamentations'.

Because the slave trade generated strong emotions within the British abolitionist movement, much of the information about the behaviour of slaves on the middle passage comes from distinctly biased sources. What information there is indicates, however, that the ways in which slaves expressed resentment of their condition was determined by the oppressive environment of the slave ship. The extremity of the situation, the misery and overcrowding, the total disorientation and transient nature of the middle passage, made organised resistance difficult. Spontaneous revolts or 'mutinies' on shipboard were relatively common (men were chained, sometimes fifty or sixty together, to prevent these), but the majority of slaves, both men and women, had to choose to survive by preserving their morale and dignity against the heaviest odds or rejecting the system completely and committing suicide. Sometimes, according to Alexander Falconbridge, Africans, on being purchased by the Europeans, opted out completely by becoming 'raving mad' and many of them died in that state, particularly the women. After their arrival in the West Indian sugar colonies, however, the slaves adopted different forms of resistance as they adapted to their new and more permanent environment.

As they became established in monotonous work roles on the plantation, women slaves did not succumb to apathy and resignation (an additional problem faced by planters). They often proved difficult and awkward to manage. 'Monk' Lewis, who was frequently castigated by his fellow planters for overindulging his slaves, makes a number of references in his journal to the intransigence of his female slaves. One domestic servant failed to open the jalousies (outside shutters with slats) properly despite being repeatedly instructed in the correct way. Other women refused to carry out their set tasks:

> It seems that this morning the women, one and all, refused to carry away the trash, which is one of the easiest tasks to be set, and that without the slightest pretence: in consequence the mill was obliged to be stopped and when the driver on that station insisted on their doing their duty, a fierce young devil of a Miss Whaunica flew at his throat and endeavoured to strangle him.[4]

Lewis was by no means the only West Indian planter to be plagued by female insubordination. Accounts of plantation life from varied sources relate how women slaves shirked work, verbally abused overseers, feigned illness, stole and lied. Women were even accused of wilfully infecting their children with yaws 'that they might be released for a time from labour'* and

---

*According to Bryan Edwards this was a form of inoculation against yaws practised by female Coromantine slaves. Kiple's evidence confirms that slaves from the Gold Coast knew of inoculations against yaws (Kiple, 1984).

5.2 *'The Abolition of the Slave Trade'. Subtitled 'On the Inhumanity of Dealers in human flesh, exemplified by Captain Kimbers treatment of a Young Negro Girl of 15 for her Virgin Modesty', this cartoon suggests that the girl resisted the captain's sexual advances and is thus being punished. It alludes to the widespread sexual exploitation of female slaves. The sailor walking away to the right is saying 'My eyes, Jack, our girls in Wapping are never flogged for their modesty', suggesting different standards applied to black and to white women. The second sailor comments, 'By G-d, that's too bad; if he had taken her to bed to him it should be well enough. Split me, I'm almost sick of this Black Business', hinting at a growing revulsion against the cruelty of the slave trade. In contrast, the cruel captain is laughing. The sailor holding the rope seems unhappy. His caption reads, 'Damn me if I like it. I have a good mind to let go.' Note the other female slaves on the deck, watching apprehensively.*

were viewed therefore as instrumental in perpetuating this disease (a reflection perhaps more of plantocratic attitudes towards slaves than reality!).

An invaluable source of information about ordinary women field workers and their reactions to servitude are plantation journals and punishment lists. Thomas and William King, merchants of London, owned plantations in Grenada, Demerara-Essequibo (British Guiana after 1831) and Dominica, and as absentee landlords left the day-to-day running of their estates to attorney/managers who were required to keep meticulous records for the benefit of their employers covering the period from the 1820s to 1830s.[5] Such plantation records show that, during the late period of slavery at least, women slaves were frequently accused of insolence, shamming sickness, excessive laziness, disorderly conduct, disobedience and quarrelling. But perhaps the outstanding value of these records is the wealth of detailed information they yield about the defiant behaviour of individual women. For instance, the Plantation Punishment Book of Plantation Friendship, 1827, reveals that Katherine was punished on 11 and 30 November for insolence to the overseer and quarrelling in the field respectively; Henrietta was punished on 27 December for 'continually omitting to comply with her task' and had to spend a day and a night in the stocks.

Data from the records kept on the Kings' various plantations confirm the deep level of everyday resistance to slavery sustained by women slaves. In plantation journals, managers had to enter down all punishments meted out to individual slaves, the reasons why they were carried out, the names of the individuals who administered and witnessed them, and the place and date. One particularly relevant column in these record books specified 'the nature and extent of punishment' if female. It indicates that, whilst male offenders received on an average 15 to 20 'stripes', the common punishment for female offenders was a varying period of time in the stocks or, alternatively, solitary confinement and may reflect, therefore, compliance with ameliorative legislation passed throughout the Caribbean in the 1820s which banned the whipping of female slaves.

On the Kings' Success Plantation in Demerara-Essequibo, where, out of 211 slaves, 93 were female, there appear to have been a number of consistently troublesome women. From January to June 1830, for example, Quasheba was punished repeatedly for 'refusing to go to work when ordered by the doctor' and on 4 May Caroline was punished for 'abusing the manager and overseer and defying the former to do his worst'. During the same period, one woman, Clarissa, is mentioned three times in connection with poor work and malingering. On the first instance she was punished together with another female slave, Lavinia, for 'leaving . . . work unfinished and assigning no cause for so doing'. In the second instance, having a 'seration [*sic*] on her finger', she refused to do any work even when ordered to by the doctor. She also used 'abusive language' to the manager. Finally, she was again punished for 'leaving three fourths of her day's work unfinished'. In Clarissa's case particularly, although her punishments

Bartolozzi Sculp

1. Female Negro Slave, with a Weight chained to her Ancle.

5.3 *'A Female Negro Slave with a Weight chained to her Ancle'. A variety of punishments was imposed on male and female slaves alike. There is no evidence that female slaves were more 'docile'. Ankle chains were used, although this particular pose hints at the symbolic 'weight' of slavery. The nakedness of the woman is arguably used to enhance artistic effect. Evidence suggests male and female slaves were scantily clad at work (see the naked male in the background) but clues about the dress of female slaves, written or visual, are sparse and inconclusive. They are frequently portrayed wearing the clothes of European peasant women (see 'A Negroe Dance', p. 159).*

increased in severity from 12 hours in solitary confinement to 60 hours in the stocks, her resistance to work remained undiminished.

In all the above-mentioned incidents, punishment excluded the whip but there is some evidence that, despite legislation and abolitionist pressure to ban its use on females, it was still employed on certain plantations. Under 'general observations' for 1823, for instance, John Wells the attorney/manager of Baillies Bacolet Plantation in Grenada, notes that 'Eliza received 20 stripes for violent behaviour in the field . . . and for excessive insolence to myself when reprimanding her in the presence of the gang'. As late as 1833, after emancipation, women were still liable to be whipped on the same plantation. The Record of Punishment for that year notes that on 19 February Germaine was given 15 'stripes' for 'wilfully destroying canes in the field and general neglect of duty'.

Official records may have conveniently overlooked harsher punishments inflicted on women, although this cannot be substantiated. Certainly, the temptation to use them must have been there, for the complaints of planters about the unruly behaviour of slave women is amply supported by evidence from the Kings' estates. Women, if anything, were more trouble than men. The Punishment Record Book of Sarah Essequibo, for instance, shows that, in the six-month period from January to June 1827, 34 slaves (out of a total of 171 for the plantation as a whole) were punished, of whom 21 were women. The women, moreover, tended to be more persistent offenders than men and several of them were punished three times and one woman four times during the period noted. (The Jamaican diaries of Thomas Thistlewood, however, show that men were most likely to be punished for cane-breaking and stealing provisions.[5a])

As the threat of punishment proved little or no deterrent to these defiant slave women, perhaps the planters were right in their defence of the whip as the only viable means of keeping females in order and forcing them to work. But there is no guarantee that the whip would have had any greater effect on breaking this spirited resistance than other common and allegedly more humane forms of punishment. In lieu of the whip, women still had to suffer the humiliation and discomfort of the 'hand and foot' stocks or solitary confinement, sometimes with the additional degradation of wearing a collar. If the whip was short and sharp, alternative punishment lasted anything from a few hours up to three days and in very serious cases a longer period was recommended. Sunday was a favourite day for confinement and, as such, may have made this punishment an effective deterrent, interfering as it did with the slaves' one free day and their vital marketing activities. In all cases, punishment was administered by slaves and witnessed by white employees and most commonly took place 'before the House' or in the 'Hospital'. The degradation of women under punishment was compounded by their near nakedness.

Whip or no whip, a significant proportion of women slaves continued to risk the wrath of their white masters, most commonly by refusing to work and engaging in verbal abuse and insolence. Sometimes individual women were accused of the more serious crime of 'exciting discontent in the gang':

others were punished for leaving the estate without permission, some actually running away for long periods. This rebellious behaviour testifies to a refusal on the part of ordinary field hands to accept the harsh conditions of their servitude but domestic servants, who, in theory at least, led an easier and more privileged life, seldom proved more contented and obedient. They, too, refused to acquiesce gracefully to white authority though the methods they used to frustrate their masters and mistresses may have been more subtle and devious.

Female domestic servants were a constant source of irritation, particularly to white women, whose job it was to supervise them. John Stewart argued they were so 'vicious and indolent' that, in managing the household, the white woman was 'a greater slave' than they were. Emma Carmichael, despite the rose-tinted glasses through which she viewed creole society, was forced to admit that she was sorely tried by the bad behaviour of her female slaves. Minor occurrences, such as the theft of a thimble or the lies she received on questioning female domestics suspected of various minor offences, became a constant source of irritation. Her washerwomen never carried out their work properly and used 'generally more than twice the quantity of soap, blue and starch required by washerwomen at home'. They also had a tendency to 'lose' articles of clothing. Of all her 'troublesome establishment', she felt the washerwomen were the 'most discontented, unmanageable and idle'.

From her arrival in Trinidad, Mrs Carmichael was harassed by the grumblings of female slaves with whom she came into contact and complained frequently of their lies and deceit. When the Carmichaels sold their estate just before the abolition of slavery, they cited the insubordination of slaves as the main reason for their departure. It could be argued that this author's observations reflect a certain intrasexual antagonism; however, her complaints about domestic servants are well corroborated by other West Indian commentators.

Domestic servants in the West Indies (the majority of whom were women) were frequently cited as being particularly difficult. Long felt that the 'propensity to laziness' was chiefly conspicuous amongst house servants. 'Monk' Lewis complained of their inefficiency and wrote that attempts to make them correct a fault were 'quite fruitless'. According to John Stewart, although domestic servants were in general well treated, they 'seldom scruple to disobey [or] do their duty without being obliged to do it by their masters'. Of all slaves, domestics probably exhibited the greatest degree of duality of behaviour. Outwardly they conformed and adopted white culture to a greater degree than the more autonomous field slaves, while covertly they rejected the system. Paradoxically, the most favoured slaves, the house slaves and the skilled elite, were often in the vanguard of slave resistance at all levels.

In general, women slaves of all classes used many ploys to frustrate their masters and avoid work. Sometimes they feigned sickness (a strategem with which Kenneth Stampp (1956) believes female slaves in the USA, where childbearing was more highly valued, had great success as they could plead a

61

multitude of female complaints and pseudo-pregnancies. One enterprising female slave on the Carmichael plantation miraculously exhibited a different coloured tongue each time she visited the plantation doctor. At last she came under suspicion: her tongue was wiped clean with a damp cloth and revealed to be 'completely clean and healthy'. Needless to say, she received a flogging, which, as in Grenada, appears to have still been used on the Carmichaels' plantation as the standard punishment for such 'shamming and idling'.

Occasionally, women went so far as actually to mutilate themselves in order to avoid work. When a female slave belonging to Lewis was victimised by two other women slaves and injured, she turned her injuries to good usage. After spending a week recovering in the estate hospital she 'went up to the mountains' for the weekend. Ordered by the doctors to return on the Monday she duly obeyed but was found to be still unfit for work, for, according to Lewis:

> as her wounds were almost well, she had tied pack thread around them so as to cut deep into the flesh, had rubbed dirt into them, and in short, had played such tricks as nearly to produce mortification in one of her fingers.[6]

Individual women sometimes carried their aversion to enslavement to such lengths as to risk severe punishment or even death. For instance, on a visit to the Slave Court, Lewis witnessed the trial of a black servant girl accused of attempting to poison her master. Her name was Minetta and she was fifteen. She acknowledged that she had 'infused corrosive sublimate' into some brandy and asserted that she had taken it from the medicine chest without knowledge of it being poison and had given it to her master on her grandmother's orders. According to Lewis, the grandmother was innocent and Minetta's story a total fabrication. He was appalled by her 'hardened conduct' throughout the trial. Condemned to death, Lewis observed that she heard the sentence pronounced 'without the least emotion' and 'was seen to laugh' as she was escorted down the court-house steps.

Lack of repentance on the slave's part, like ingratitude, was anathema to the planters, for it emphasised the fact that no person can ever be completely controlled by another human being. Again, it was frequently the house slaves, like Minetta, who showed the least gratitude or respect for their masters. 'Negroes are not grateful . . . ,' wrote William Beckford, 'those who have been most indulged are those who will be first delinquent.'[7] This 'delinquency' galled the planters for it was crucial to their own credibility that their human property should appear content and amenable. For this reason, penalties for insubordination (in reality an exercise of free will incompatible with an enslaved condition) were severe. Slaves like Minetta, who laughed in the face of white justice, must have possessed a good deal of resolution and courage.

But the exercise of free will did not always jeopardise a slave's life. Mrs Carmichael gives a detailed account of how one individual woman slave complemented her strong resistance to slavery with her energy and enterprise outside her formal ascribed role. The reaction of this particular woman to enslavement is significant for it illustrates the importance of the

African cultural heritage in determining the role female slaves played in slave resistance, especially the cultural resistance of the slave community against an aggressive and arrogant white culture. G, who, like Minetta, was a domestic servant, was 'a personage next to impossible to manage' although she appeared to be 'a clever and superior person, with not a disagreeable countenance'. Relegated to the field work for insubordination, she one day made such a commotion that she was placed in the stocks. When this failed to subdue her rage, the driver was obliged to admit to Mr Carmichael that she would never work for him 'or any other Massa'.[8]

G is an excellent example of the dual role adopted by many women slaves in slave society. In her work role she was intransigent and negative; in her private domestic life she was energetic and positive, owning extensive provision grounds kept in 'beautiful order' and running 'a complete huckster's shop' on the estate. She held dances at her house from which she made 'a great deal of money'; supper, liquor and music were provided by her and each slave paid 'half a dollar' admission. In view of her profitable and independent existence, it is hardly surprising that she refused to share her enterprises with a husband.

In the writings of Emma Carmichael and 'Monk' Lewis, the individuality of slave women, relegated to obscurity in many other contemporary works, emerges strongly. Both authors, for different reasons, showed an interest in and had close contact with their female slaves. Lewis was much concerned with improving conditions of maternity and childcare on his plantation. Emma Carmichael, as a planter's wife, was in daily contact with household slaves in particular and has given us one of the rare accounts of plantation life from a European woman's point of view. Minetta and G had, perhaps, exceptionally strong personalities which influenced their reaction to slavery. In a less spectacular manner women slaves, in general, showed resentment towards their masters many times and in many ways during their day-to-day existence on the plantation and, arguably, were more troublesome than men, despite the 'peculiar burdens' of their sex.

Female slave runaways

One area of slave resistance where women were noticeably less prominent than men was in individual acts of running away. Running away was different from maronage (where large numbers of slaves, men and women, ran away from plantations, frequently before they had been 'seasoned' into plantation life, and established free autonomous 'maroon' communities). Most slaves were individual runaways and did not aspire to join maroon communities and, after suicide, running away was the only other outlet for individual escape. Because of its random nature, running away does not lend itself easily to a theoretical framework. As Ulrich Phillips, who looked at the runaways listed in the quarterly reports of parish authorities in Jamaica between 1793 and 1796, concluded:

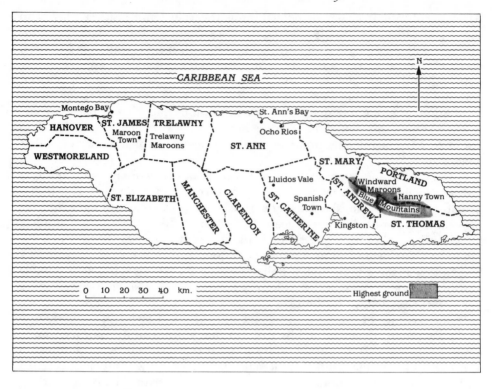

2 *Jamaica* c. *1790, showing the location of maroons and main settlements*

the impulse to run away was not confined to either sex nor any age or class. The fugitives were utterly miscellaneous and their flights apparently not organised but sporadic. (Phillips, 1914)

Recently, however, historians have carried out more detailed studies of runaways which reveal certain broad patterns. In his introduction to a collection of articles about runaways, Heuman notes, for instance, that Africans tended to run away in groups (most maroons were African-born) whereas creoles fled as individuals. Many such individuals were skilled slaves, and creoles and coloureds had more chance of eluding capture. Slaves ran away for a variety of reasons – to put pressure on masters to sell them or improve conditions, to visit kin or friends. Many attempted to merge in the free black and urban communities, where they often found employment. Frequently they were harboured by kin. Heuman suggests that runaways were less concerned about freedom than with preserving some sort of autonomy within slavery itself, which raises the question of the degree to which slaves could control and affect aspects of the masters' world (Heuman, 1986).

Young males without family ties predominated among runaways, but even males who were tied to families ran away with greater frequency than females in the same category. Estimates vary but generally over 60 per cent of runaways were men. Gautier suggests that women may not have had less desire to run away, simply less opportunity. Female slaves took their children with them far more frequently than did men. If caught, both mothers and children were forced to wear collars and running away with children meant that they were more likely to be caught (Gautier, 1983). Women tended to escape to visit kin rather than remain away permanently.

Advertisements for slave runaways provide some useful insights into the lives of slaves and evidence of extensive kinship links. For Heuman, they are an important source because they are not noticeably biased. As they were not written for pro- or anti-slavery advocates, they can contain interesting information (not simply about runaways but about the internal economy and slave sales) which is unavailable elsewhere. In Jamaica, during late slavery, runaway slaves were advertised in the local press, which also published lists of runaways held in the Kingston and Portland gaols and local workhouses. If slaves were not removed from these institutions by their owners before a certain date, they were sold to the highest bidder.

The *Jamaica Mercury* and *Kingston Weekly Advertiser* (the *Royal Gazette* after 1790) give useful information about the slaves' family connections and their status and value. A number of slave women ran away with their children or other close relatives, an indication of strong familial bonds. Other runaways of both sexes were suspected of having fled to join spouses or other kin from whom they had been separated, and often the advertisers alleged that their runaway slaves were being harboured by kin or friends in distant parts of Jamaica. (See Appendix for detailed advertisements.) Thus a significant minority of women, African and creole, were found among the lists of runaways. More importantly, perhaps, the fact that women refrained from running away in larger numbers because of kin ties on the plantation lends support to the view that they had a seminal role in recreating and sustaining kin bonds – a prime area of cultural resistance discussed more fully in the following chapter.

Traitor or amazon? Women in slave uprisings

The specific contribution women slaves made to organised slave uprisings is a contentious area of study. As most recorded history is male-biased, contemporary descriptions of slave rebellions focus largely on the individual male slaves who were their titular leaders; the mass of slaves are depicted as a faceless and genderless mob. From contemporary evidence, it cannot be disputed that the ringleaders of slave uprisings were, in general, men. For instance, after a slave conspiracy was exposed in Antigua in 1736, out of forty-seven slaves, only one woman, Joan, was executed.[9] In a paper on this particular rebellion, David Barry Gaspar observes that a number of slave women were willing to fight in the revolt and cites Councillor Vallentine Morris, who claimed that even slave women 'by their Insolent behaviour and

5.4 *Advertisements from the* Jamaica Mercury, *September 1779, referring to female slave runaways. It was common to advertise runaway slaves in this fashion, frequently with rewards offered reflecting the value of the slave. Local newspapers also provide insight into the pattern of slave sales, the strength of family bonds and the use of slaves in the local economy.*

Expressions had the utter Extirpation of the White as much at heart, as the Men, and would undoubtedly have done as much Mischief' (Gaspar, 1978).

But absence of the names of female slaves from official records and contemporary accounts of slave uprisings and conspiracies does not constitute proof that they played no active part. The historical invisibility of women in descriptions of slave revolts may be merely a result of the cultural conditioning of the authors.* This invisibility makes it difficult to determine the true role slave women played in slave uprisings. Moreover, the rare contemporary references to women, apropos slave revolts, frequently portray them as informants against fellow slaves. The conspiracy in Antigua in 1736 was disclosed by a female slave and likewise a slave plot in Monserrat in 1768. Later accounts also allude to this informant role of women slaves, for example, the official report on the 1816 Barbados uprising.

It could be argued that because of their close proximity to the white man as domestic servants and/or sexual partners, some slave women were more likely to betray than to actively support the conspiracies of fellow slaves. However, given the dubious nature of the evidence, there is no sound reason to suppose that women betrayed their fellow slaves any more frequently than did their male counterparts, or that information, when given, was given voluntarily. The 1736 slave conspiracy in Antigua was allegedly discovered as a result of 'voluntary information' given by one Phillida who was 'taken up on suspicion of some virulent Expressions, used upon her Brother's Account', and subsequently revealed the existence of secret Saturday-night meetings. The anonymous author of the report later revealed that torture was used upon some slaves to extract information, which may explain why a woman seemingly committed to the cause suddenly turned traitor. Women may even have been singled out for torture because of their assumed vulnerability and lack of physical endurance. Thus a more balanced and realistic appraisal of the woman's role in slave uprisings cannot be based solely on biased contemporary accounts. Other important factors must be examined; for instance the African cultural heritage of the slave woman may have significantly influenced her contribution to slave uprisings.

The spirit of revolt amongst slaves did not develop sporadically on a spontaneous basis but was part of a continuum of resistance which linked Africa and the West Indies. In the context of traditional West African culture, African women slaves would have been able and willing to engage in armed confrontation with whites. Olaudah Equiano (*c.* 1745–97), a freed Ibo slave who promoted the abolitionist cause in Britain, reminiscing upon his West African childhood, wrote that the women of his tribe were also warriors and 'march boldly out to fight along with the men'. In one hostile attack on his home village he recalled that there were many women as well as

---

*Eighteenth-century middle-class European women were culturally restricted from invol⌐ ⌐ent in political or military activities. They were expected to be passive and physically weak, and ⌐ ⌐e barred from all areas regarded as 'men's business'.

men on both sides, including his own mother, 'armed with a broad sword'. Although Equiano indulged in a certain artistic licence, his observations are supported by Captain John Adams, who noted that, among the 'Ibibios' (Ibo) of the early nineteenth century, women were 'equally mischievous and ferocious' as men. The Ibibios, he wrote, were generally the ringleaders of shipboard insurrections at Bonny and the women took as active a part as the men. Later Victorian works also allude to the martial role of women in West Africa. Sir Richard Burton, for instance, described in great detail the 'Illustrious Viragoes' of the Amazon Guard of the King of Dahomey and remarked on the fierce, warlike nature of women of other West African tribes, especially the Yoruba. He believed that the women soldiers of Dahomey were braver than men. In more recent times, the ability of West African women to engage in physical confrontation was manifested during the Aba riots or 'Women's War' of 1929 in Nigeria, when a number of Ibo women were killed protesting against a tax imposed upon them by the British colonial government. Women have also fought alongside men in liberation struggles against colonial rule.

Women in West Africa thus have a tradition of active participation in communal resistance against outside aggression. Moreover, although many tribes are nominally patriarchal, women, especially older women, often play an important part in village affairs. Women's political organisations are as important as the men's and, when any major village decisions are made, women are consulted and allowed a significant part in the decision-making process (Van Allen, 1972). In some tribes, for example the Mende of Sierra Leone, women wield great power and influence and are eligible to become village headmen and chiefs (Little, 1967). Matrilineal tribes such as the Ashanti exhibit 'a high degree of equality' between men and women in matters of state and the head of the lineage is always assisted by a senior woman, the *obaa panin* (Forde, 1956). The social organisation of the modern-day Djuka or Bush Negroes of Surinam, descendants of runaway slaves who established African societies in the New World (which remain in many ways typical of eighteenth-century as opposed to twentieth-century West African societies), focuses on a council or *bosseia*. This council is formed of three or four of the most mature men and women of the town and the women members have as much power as the men (Kahn, 1931). The importance of examining black women's contribution to resistance from this cross-cultural perspective has been stressed by Rosalyn Terborg-Penn (1986) and is becoming an increasing focus of research. Thus, the woman's role in slave uprisings must be analysed from three perspectives: her African background, her experience as a slave, and finally the dynamics of slave revolts in the West Indies.

With the exception of the French island of St Domingue (which became Haiti after a war of liberation led by Toussaint l'Ouverture) the greatest slave rebellions in the western hemisphere were in Jamaica and Demerara-Essequibo (the Guianas). There averaged one significant revolt every two years from 1731 to 1823. Some colonies such as Trinidad and Barbados had few big revolts but conspiracies and general disorders occurred. Ornate discussions of the causes of slave revolt have engaged historians over the past few years but fundamentally, as Herbert Aptheker (1943) first observed, the major cause of slave revolt was slavery itself. There was, however, a high incidence of revolt in the Caribbean because absenteeism led to a high degree of depersonalisation of slaves and greater cultural estrangement of whites and blacks than in the Southern USA. Slave revolts were also more common where African slaves outnumbered creole, where the social organisation of the slave regime permitted the emergence of autonomous black leadership, male and female, and where large-scale slave-owning units existed (Genovese, 1979).

The aims and nature of slave revolts and rebellions changed as slave society developed. Slave revolts in the West Indies can be broadly categorised on a chronological basis into maronage, African-led revolts and the creole-led revolts of the later period of slavery which were linked in to the broader economic and political developments in Europe – the French Revolution and the transition to capitalism which ultimately rendered slavery an anachronism. Early slave revolts have been typified by Eugene Genovese as 'restorationist', that is they sought to restore the African slaves' own culture. Where geographical conditions allowed this sometimes led to 'particularism' or withdrawal into maroon societies. Such societies frequently signed treaties with the colonial authorities. In return for helping whites 'police' slave runaways, maroons were allowed to preserve their traditional African way of life (Genovese, 1979). Maronage may have been more common in the early days because of the different languages of various slaves, which hindered communication and thus the organisation of revolts (Price, 1973). Ligon suggested that slaves were unable to face whites openly because they had no access to weapons and hence resorted to running away to escape oppression. There is thus some dispute as to whether maronage was a form of revolt; Orlando Patterson maintains that it was (Patterson, 1973). However, maroons did carry out guerrilla warfare against whites and sometimes were involved in serious slave rebellions, as, for instance, in Demerara-Essequibo and Jamaica before the 1739 treaty was signed with the British.

Unfortunately, source material relating to the role women played in maronage and early slave revolts is scarce, but the story of the legendary Jamaican Windward maroon, Nanny, sheds light upon one function certain women may have had. Nanny was an obeah woman after whom two maroon settlements were named. A junior army officer sent out to fight the maroons, Phillip Thicknesse (who accused her of sentencing a white emissary to death), described this formidable woman thus:

> The old Hagg . . . had a girdle round her waste, with (I speak within compass) nine or ten different knives hanging in sheaths to it, many of which I doubt not had been plunged into human flesh and blood.[10]

Although Thicknesse undoubtedly exaggerated the fierceness of the maroons (he was accused of cowardice by a fellow officer), the little contemporary evidence about Nanny which exists suggests she held considerable political influence, even though she did not displace the headman. At the end of the First Maroon Wars in 1739, Quao, the leader of the Windward maroons, unlike Cudjoe, the head of the Leeward group, reputedly refused to accept Governor Trelawney's terms of treaty on the advice of Nanny, who opposed the measure. Legend has it that she slew English soldiers taken captive with impunity and her supernatural feats are still discussed by Windward maroons.

The attitude of the British colonial authorities towards Nanny after the signing of the First Maroon Treaty in 1739 perhaps explains, to some extent, why so little documentation exists which refers to the active participation of women in slave revolts. The British refused to accept spiritual leaders such as Nanny, recognising only the authority of the headmen. Commenting on this discrimination, Barbara Kopytoff (1976) writes:

> [Nanny] was given no role in the post-treaty organisation with which the British dealt. It was the headman to whom they looked, and they may have expected him to perform duties that in the past fell to her; the fact that the British did not recognise a religious leader may be the reason that none ever again rose to Nanny's prominence and power.

Nanny now exists more in legend than fact but, as Orlando Patterson (1973) stresses, there can be little doubt that she existed. The role she played was crucial to the success of the maroons. Not only was she a tactician and political adviser, but as a spiritual leader she assured communal loyalty and upheld the morale of the maroons.

On a more mundane and widespread level, maroon women in general may have played an important part in promoting and maintaining the spirit of resistance. Thicknesse observed how maroon 'pecananes' were bred to feel detestation towards white men. The children he came in contact with 'could not refrain from striking their pointed fingers as they would knives' against his chest and shouted '*becara . . . becara* [white man]' at him in derision. Maroon mothers must have been largely responsible for transmitting to their children this animosity towards whites, which, according to Thicknesse, they themselves openly flaunted, wearing the teeth of slain white soldiers as ankle and wrist bracelets. Dallas, who wrote his history of the Jamaican maroons at a much later date, also mentioned the contempt maroon women showed towards whites.

Whether maroon women actually fought against the whites in any significant numbers is difficult to determine as evidence is scanty. Some insight may be gleaned from comparative evidence from French and Dutch possessions. One rare reference to the fighting role of maroon women is found in the testimony of Louis, a fifteen-year-old slave who was captured when French troops attacked the maroons of West Cayenne in 1748. Louis informed his captors that 'all the Negroes and Negresses' in the maroon band were equipped with axes and machetes. If maroon women in Cayenne were willing to take up arms, it is highly probable that women in maroon communities in the British Caribbean showed an equal willingness.

If caught as rebels, women were executed in the same brutal manner as men. In Surinam in 1728, a large group of 'fugitive negroes' known as Seramica rebels took refuge in the woods and for two years pillaged estates 'with lances and firelocks'. According to John Stedman, of eleven 'unhappy negroe captives' executed in 1730 for their participation in this unrest, eight were female. One man was hanged alive by an iron hook through his ribs, two men were chained to stakes and burnt alive. The six women were broken alive on the rack and two young girls were decapitated; but 'such was their resolution under these tortures' that they endured them 'without uttering a sigh'. In French Guiana in 1748, the leaders of the maroon rebels were a man and woman, Copena and Claire. On capture, Claire, 'convicted of the crime of maronage and complicity with maroon negroes', was tortured and hung from the public gallows until dead; her children were forced to witness this execution.[11]

Evidence indicates that where slaves established maroon settlements women were as eager to join them as men, despite the heavy penalties they suffered if caught as active rebels. Stedman recorded that, in Surinam in 1772, men, women and children ran away from the plantations to join the Cottica rebels (so named because of their association with a region bordering on the Cottica River). Bonny, their famous chief, was in fact a mulatto. This was accounted for by the fact that his mother had run away to the woods to escape ill-treatment from her master by whom she was pregnant.

Women were obviously prepared to endure the hardships and insecurity which characterised maroon life. Dallas described how after a crushing attack by the whites in 1735, during the First Maroon War referred to above, the Windward maroons of Jamaica retreated from their main town, Nanny Town, and split into two parties. One of these groups, about 300 strong, including men, women and children, marched 100 miles over densely wooded and precipitous mountains to join Cudjoe's Leeward band. The colonial authorities found out about the march and sent out parties to 'disperse and destroy' but the marchers 'fought and forced their way on' and succeeded in their objectives.

If maroon women did not actually bear arms, they certainly made an indispensable contribution to the survival of maroon settlements. They were largely responsible for the cultivation of provision grounds which helped to sustain the rebel communities. Despite Bryan Edwards's assertions that they were used in this respect as mere drudges, this labour was probably given voluntarily as a major co-operative contribution to the community. This supportive but none the less vital role played by women in both a moral and economic sense was perhaps a fundamental factor in the survival of maroon communities.

As in maroon uprisings, women's participation in the African-led rebellions of the eighteenth century was significantly influenced by West African cultural traditions. But, whereas maroons were largely successful in their struggles against the whites, the African-led revolts, characterised by an aura of 'heroic impossibility', had little chance of success. The leaders of these abortive uprisings were often strong charismatic personalities whose power was firmly based in their African cultural heritage. The aim of these rebellions, which were often dominated by one specific African ethnic group with a clear sense of identity, was a reversion to African norms and the establishment of African kingdoms in the New World (Schuler, 1970).

The African-led rebellions of the middle period of slavery, when there was a heavy influx of new African slaves, were often inspired by the example of the maroons – a factor of which contemporary whites were not unaware. Long, for instance, believed that the 1760 rebellion in Jamaica was influenced by the experiences of the maroons. Dallas wrote that during the Second Maroon War of 1795 the Council of Assembly was called to discuss 'the most daring acts of unprovoked rebellion on the part of Maroons'. The maroons were accused of inciting slaves to rebel, despite the fact that, in the treaty signed after the First Maroon War, they had agreed to hunt down and return fugitive slaves and assist in suppressing slave revolts – tasks which Dallas and Long confirmed were generally executed with ruthless precision.

The persistence of African cultural forms is a feature of rebellions of the middle period of slavery. In Edward Long's account of the serious rebellion in Jamaica in 1760, which was perhaps the last true African-led uprising in its purest and most savage form, a curious anecdote about a woman slave named Cubah gives a brief glimpse at one possible function certain women may have had in these events. During this rebellion, a wooden sword was found in Kingston. Long described it as 'of a peculiar nature, with a red feather stuck into the handle' and said it was used among Coromantines as a signal for war. It was subsequently revealed that:

> the Coromantins had raised one Cubah, a female slave belonging to a Jewess, to the rank of royalty and dubbed her Queen of Kingston; at their meetings she sat in state under a canopy, with a sort of robe on her shoulders and a crown on her head.[12]

'Her Majesty' was seized and ordered for transportation* but, 'prevailing on the Captain of the transport to put her ashore again on the leeward part of the island', she remained there for some time, but at length was re-arrested and executed.

Long saw Cubah as a frivolous carnival character not to be taken seriously, a reflection of his own attitudes and thus highly questionable. She may indeed have been only a symbolic figurehead but it was a significant factor that she was elected as one of the leaders of such an important rebellion. Her return to the island under certain threat of execution, if captured, indicates that she was seriously committed to the rebellion.

In the account of the slave conspiracy in Antigua in 1737, a similar figurehead is mentioned, a Coromantine male slave named Court. He was said to have 'a good sabre by his side with a red scabbard' and a 'peculiar

---

*This was used for the most intransigent troublemakers. They were transported to Nova Scotia (Craton, 1982) and even Australia, which became a convict settlement at the end of the eighteenth century (Duffield, 1985).

cap' made of green silk. According to the anonymous author, Court was dressed in accordance with Coromantine rites performed when a king had resolved upon war and, like Cubah (who was dressed in a similar fashion), conducted his affairs 'under an umbrella or canopy of state'. Rattray (1927) recorded the use of similar ceremonial apparel at the courts of the Ashanti (Coromantine) kings. Given the matrilineal structure of Ashanti society and the high degree of equality between men and women in affairs of state, it is possible that Cubah, far from being merely a colourful figurehead, was one of the true leaders of the 1760 rebellion.

In the context of contemporary accounts, Cubah was a unique personality. Most women, however, characteristically supported rebels and maintained a strong loyalty to the slave cause. It was reported that, during the above-mentioned 1760 Jamaican rebellion, slaves of all ages and sexes joined the uprising. Originating at William Beckford's Esher Estate, the rebellion quickly spread to other plantations until, in Long's estimation, the whole party, including women, had increased to about 400, whereupon the group 'retired to the woods and began to carouze'.

According to Monica Schuler (1970), the records relating to armed revolt amongst slaves in the eighteenth century indicate a broad spectrum of participants – male, female, young and old, plantation slave and urban slave. The common denominator was that they were all, in the main, African-born. In the dual context of the African cultural heritage of the slave woman and her experience as a slave, it is far more credible to assume her active participation in African-led slave uprisings, than the passive non-involvement or more damning role as traitor implied by contemporary sources. Moreover, as many early and middle revolts were inspired and led by African religious leaders – obeah, myal and vôdun (voodoo) priests and even Nañigos (Muslim teachers) in St Domingue and Surinam – women's spiritual power in traditional African societies is arguably of paramount significance in analysing slave resistance and demands fuller discussion.

African religion and slave resistance

'An Obeah man or woman (for it is practised by both sexes) is a very wicked and dangerous person on a plantation,' observed John Stewart. Obeah was a term used by contemporaries to describe the 'pagan' religious practices of the slaves. In reality, these practices fell into two distinct categories, obeah and myalism. Obeah was worked by individual priests who dealt in magic, poisons, herbs and folk medicine and were highly secretive. Myalism was concerned more with group worship. It was used as an antidote against the harmful aspects of obeah. Both obeah and myalism were directly African in origin. Planters like Long stressed a strong association between slaves of Ashanti origin, myalism and slave revolts. Obeah was connected particularly with the Popo from Dahomey. Although contemporary whites rarely distinguished between obeah and myalism, the latter, which involved group activities such as the myal dance, was probably the major subversive 'obeah' element in slave rebellions.

The word 'obeah' is almost certainly of African derivation, possibly from the Twi word 'obeye', a minor god (Patterson, 1969) although it may also be of Ashanti origin, from 'Obboney' or malicious deity (Beckwith, 1929). Practitioners of this art, of whom a significant proportion were women, were believed by the whites to wield a great influence over their fellow slaves and were hence accused of many subversive activities including incitement to revolt. Commenting upon the pernicious role of obeah in the Jamaican slave rebellions, Bryan Edwards wrote that, in the 1760 revolt, the influence of 'the professors of the Obeah Art' was such, as to 'induce a great many of the negro slaves in Jamaica to engage in a rebellion'.

As Monica Schuler (1970) has pointed out, traditional African religious practice lent itself quite well to organised rebellion; it was a unifying element to those who believed in it and also provided an acceptable excuse for the gathering of slaves. At these gatherings, in an aura of spirit possession, orders to rebel could be given. John Stedman described in vivid detail how slave spiritual leaders, in this case women, subverted the slaves through the medium of 'pagan' ceremonies:

> [The slaves] also have amongst them a kind of Sybils, who deal in oracles; these sage matrons [are found] dancing and whirling round in the middle of an assembly with amazing rapidity until they foam at the mouth and drop down convulsed. Whatever the prophetess orders to be done, during this paroxysm is most sacredly performed by the surrounding multitude which renders these meetings extremely dangerous, as she frequently enjoins them to murder their masters, or desert to the woods.[13]

There are similar reports from the French Caribbean, where grand voodoo priestesses had an important ritual role and gave 'superhuman courage' to insurgents (Gautier, 1983).

The subversive influence of obeah was probably most marked in the African-led revolts of the eighteenth century. During this period the obeah man or woman may have been less of a magician and more of a priest. Because of their powerful status within the slave community, however, spiritual leaders often risked severe penalties. As John Stedman emphasised, the 'fanaticism' associated with the practice of obeah was forbidden by law and its advocates subject to rigorous punishment. British West Indian slave laws likewise incorporated clauses aimed at the suppression of these dangerous and alarming activities. Under the Consolidated Slave Act of Jamaica of 1792, it was stipulated that:

> in order to prevent the many mischiefs that may hereafter arise from the wicked art of Negroes going under the appellation of obeah men and women . . . Be it therefore enacted [that] any slave who shall pretend to any supernatural power, in order to promote the purposes of rebellion, shall, upon conviction thereof suffer death, transportation, or such other punishment.[14]

This law also extended to slaves administering poisons 'during the practice of Obeah or otherwise'.

The whites feared obeah, not only because it was a potentially subversive element and held a sinister association with poison and the secret, deliberate murder of both white and black, but also because it was incomprehensible to them. Much of West African religion focuses upon a belief in a 'hidden, mysterious, supersensible, pervading energy', powers, potencies and forces – *Nyama* (Parrinder, 1935). This power can be used for destructive or constructive purposes. In traditional African society, the life of the individual is immersed in a world of spirit and religion is part of his everyday, commonplace existence. Europeans in contact with African slaves in the West Indies could conceive of spirituality only in the 'other-worldly' context of European Christianity. They viewed obeah and other mystical beliefs as something to be feared, as something always harmful and destructive. The experience of European witchcraft enhanced this distrust of and aversion to African religion. The planter's fear of poisoning, which sometimes verged on the paranoid, exemplified this irrational and often inaccurate view of African religious practices.

Where actual cases of wilful poisoning did occur, obeah practitioners were frequently implicated. ('Monk' Lewis, for instance, discussed in some detail the connection between obeah and the threat of poisoning.) It was generally believed by planters that certain slaves, particularly old women, had an exclusive knowledge of herbs and plants which could be used as medicine but also for more sinister purposes. Lewis recalled the tale of a white agent 'seemingly in favour' with the negroes, who was, purportedly, obliged to quit his job because of the frequent attempts to poison him. Two book-keepers on the estate had been fatally poisoned when they mistakenly drank his drink. According to Lewis this crime was effected by 'the abominable belief in obeah'. The alleged poisoner was a woman domestic.

Poisoning was an act of individual resistance to slavery. Female domestic servants in particular, because of their close proximity to whites, were able to disguise poison in food and drink with the minimum of personal risk. The poisons used often induced a slow death which was difficult to detect from natural illness. For instance, Sir Hans Sloane referred to a savannah or meadow plant, the *Apocynum erectum fructicosum fiore luteo maximo et speciofissimo*, of which the leaves were highly poisonous. He was informed by a Dr Barham that this poison killed very quickly but could be administered in such a way as to kill a person 'in many Days, Months or Years'. The doctor told Sloane that another 'Practitioner of Physick' was poisoned with this plant by his negro woman 'who had so ordered it, as not to despatch him quickly'. The fact that this same story was cited over one hundred years later by Edward Long is indicative of the strong and often irrational fears about poisoning which were ever-present in white creole society.

Many similar deaths attributed to poisoning may, in effect, have been caused by undiagnosed illnesses, but it is quite feasible that some whites were indeed poisoned by slaves. Richard Madden, writing in the 1830s, described in detail poisons known to West Indian slaves which had very similar effects to those described by Sloane and Long. Madden, a doctor, discussed the various poisons, animal and vegetable, found in the West

Indies, in a letter to a colleague. In Jamaica, he noted, there were many poisonous plants which were 'better known' to the negroes than the whites. The action of these poisons was 'very similar' in its effect 'to the influence of those malign diseases, such as plague, cholera and yellow fever'. Like Sloane, Madden believed such substances were largely undetectable. Long and his slave-owning contemporaries believed poison was used against them frequently by slaves. The former constituted a white minority in an over-whelmingly African-orientated society apparently dominated by incom-prehensible occult practices. They were understandably paranoid and commonly blamed poison for the sudden loss of a number of slaves. Women were often implicated in these alleged mass poisonings, which were characteristically viewed in the context of wider negro conspiracies. V. S. Naipaul cites an example of one such mass poisoning which occurred in Trinidad in 1794. Thisbe, the alleged poisoner, was a nurse in the planta-tion hospital. She confessed to her crimes under torture, when a wider slave plot was revealed (Naipaul, 1973). Edwards recorded a similar case on a Jamaican plantation in 1775 which was blamed on an old woman whose hut was filled with 'material for setting obeah'.

Local whites had long associated such acts of wilful poisoning with individual slaves who possessed specialised knowledge. The Jamaica Committee reported to the 1789 enquiry into the slave trade that 'the skill of some negroes in the art of poisoning has been noticed ever since the colonists became acquainted with them'. Obeah was implicated wherever inexplic-able deaths occurred, even if poison was apparently not involved. One planter, reporting to the Committee, recalled how, when a negro on his plantation was dying, she confessed:

> that her stepmother (a woman of the Popo country, above eighty years old but still hale and active) had put Obi on her as she had done upon those who had lately died, and that the old woman had practised Obi for as many years as she could remember.[15]

Poison and 'sorcery', bolstered by suicide, comprised what Vidia Naipaul has succinctly termed 'a negro atelier in a frenzy'. They were the slaves' secret weapons against slavery. Despite their laws and 'instruments of torture' planters were unable to control such acts. No law, no threat of punishment could suppress the secret and highly influential magical practices of the slaves. Regardless of the severe penalties, obeah consistently played an important part in the lives of the slaves. According to Thomas Atwood, from the earliest days of slavery to emancipation (by which time many slaves were nominally converted to Christianity) slaves were 'addicted to witchcraft' and in great awe of their 'necromancers and conjurers of both sexes'. Such men and women were 'very artful' and had 'a great ascendancy over other negroes'.

African religion, and the magic which constituted one of its fundamental bases, was much misunderstood by whites. Influenced by their beliefs about European witchcraft, they attributed all inexplicable occurrences to the nefarious 'black magic' of the slaves. Correctly or incorrectly, the practice of 'obeah' came to be associated with a wide spectrum of subversive practices. In a wider cultural context, a belief in witchcraft or sorcery may be an indication of tensions in societies undergoing change, where it has a cathartic quality, allowing people to express feelings of hate and anger. Although it can be a source of division and conflict, it frequently restores cohesion and strength.

In Africa, witchcraft was arguably women's response to 'cultural impoverishment' and changes in their position within the family and society during colonial rule (Cutrufelli, 1983). It may thus be viewed as part of the continuum of resistance which linked Africa and the New World. The widespread belief in 'obeah' and similar practices in the modern Caribbean, even among the educated middle classes, is evidence of the durability of such African-derived beliefs. The significance of such beliefs to the cultural survival of Caribbean communities is discussed in more depth in the final chapter. In a more specific historical context, 'obeah' was a catalystic ingredient in slave uprisings, especially in the early and middle period of slavery. John Stedman believed that slave priests or '*gadomen*' used superstitious rites to control slaves and keep them in subjection which were no less effective than those used by the Catholic Church to control the European peasantry. Such power was used to inspire a unified resistance to slavery. The fears of whites were thus not simply paranoid fantasies, as 'obeah' practitioners such as the Jamaican maroon leader, Nanny, were often in the vanguard of resistance until the later period of slavery when slave leadership was taken over by Christian Baptists. Even after Christianity became a more important force, however, myalism became infused into the new black Baptist sects whilst 'obeah' persisted as a strong element of cultural resistance.

The transition to freedom

By the end of the eighteenth century, the character of slave rebellions in the British West Indies had subtly begun to change in response to the increasing creolisation of slave society and the spread of Christianity and literacy. The influence of European demands for the abolition of slavery and the example of the French Revolution were increasingly in evidence in slave unrest. Later slave revolts were arguably part of the upsurge of liberal and democratic values centred on individual rights and liberties which accompanied the transition to capitalism in Europe (Genovese, 1979). With the challenge of abolitionism, planters adapted their mechanisms of control. They no longer relied primarily on force but also on more subtle measures to mitigate resistance and discontent – improvements in slave conditions, promise of manumission and liberal laws on private slave plots (the peculium) allowing them to be passed on to slave children. Together with the practice of allowing certain slaves to hire themselves out, such measures contributed to the development of a more independent proto-peasantry. Slaves had raised expectations, which was arguably the result of a more 'permissive' regime.

SCENE ON A WEST INDIAN PLANTATION—SLAVES RECEIVING THE NEWS OF THEIR EMANCIPATION.

5.5 *'Scene on a West Indian Plantation – slaves receiving news of their emancipation'. Note the European in a benevolent and philanthropic gesture, 'giving' slaves their freedom. In effect, slave resistance and revolt contributed significantly to the abolition of slavery. Note also the windmill in the right-hand corner – a common feature of sugar plantations used in processing the raw cane. The woman in the left foreground also is interesting: the hoe suggests she is a field worker. Her dress, with the traditional Afro-Caribbean head-tie, differs considerably from the portraits of semi-naked black women in Stedman's* Narrative.

Such changes point to a system under pressure and slave resistance was sharpened by this aura of disintegration.

As emancipation became more of a concrete reality, the slaves' concept of freedom changed. No longer did they seek to overthrow the whites and re-establish carbon-copy African societies as they had done during the earlier rebellions; the vast majority of slaves were now creole and envisaged their freedom within the established framework of the existing society. In this respect late slave uprisings could be termed prototype peasant uprisings, and from the scanty evidence that exists it would appear that slave women adopted a role common to women involved in proletarian struggles. They were verbally aggressive, acted as go-betweens, participated in a number of subversive activities, and were prepared to join in physical confrontations with the colonial authorities. Contemporary references to slave conspiracies and uprisings frequently alluded to the verbal and physical aggressiveness of women slaves. For instance, a negro plot was discovered in the vicinity of 'Monk' Lewis's estate. Before the imprisoned offenders were executed, the overseer of a property adjacent to Lewis's had occasion to find fault with a female field hand belonging to a gang hired to perform a particular task. In response to his criticism, 'she flew at him with the greatest fury', grasped him by the throat and cried to her fellow slaves, 'Come here, let's Dunbar him!' (Dunbar was a white overseer killed during the slave unrest upon which Lewis is commenting). The suddenness of this attack 'nearly accomplished her purpose' before the overseer's own slaves came to his assistance. The woman was executed.

As the political ideals of the French revolutionaries diffused throughout the Caribbean, slaves began to articulate their grievances in the context of the egalitarian beliefs of the Revolution. The example of San Domingo (Haiti) was especially influential. This began in 1792 with a slave revolt against the French led by Toussaint L'Ouverture. It soon became part of the extension of the revolutionary wars from Europe to the Caribbean and in 1804 Haiti was established as the first independent black nation. In Trinidad (where many Royalist planters had fled from the French islands, together with their slaves), revolutionary ideals were exceptionally pervasive and greatly disturbed planter complacency. Women were renowned for their vicious tongues and general insubordination. For instance in 1805, when a certain Mr de Gannes was bathing in a stream on his property, twelve black women, balancing plantation baskets on their heads, came along a nearby path. Shaking *chac-chac* pods, they sang a patois song and danced. '*Pain c'est viande beque*' (bread is white flesh), they chanted; the chorus was *San Domingo* –

> *Vin c'est sang beque* (Wine is white blood)
> *San Domingo*
> *Nous va boire sang beque* (We will drink white blood)
> *San Domingo*[16]

It was an old song from another island and, through this picturesque rendition, the women were expressing the revolutionary sentiments felt by many slaves during this period.

Verbal incitement to revolt appears to have been a particular forte of women slaves during the latter decades of slavery. The role a certain woman slave, named Nanny Grigg, played in the slave revolt in Barbados in 1816 (the only major one of its kind on the island) is a striking example of this. According to the confession of Robert, a slave from the Simmon's Plantation, this dangerous woman had informed the blacks that she had read in the newspapers that all the negroes would be freed on New Year's Day; she was 'always talking about it' and told the slaves that they were all 'damned fools' to work. When the blacks had not been freed by New Year, she declared that the only way by which they could achieve freedom was to fight for it by setting fires 'the way they did in Saint Domingo'.[17]

Women also proved troublesome to colonial authorities. For instance, in 1834, during the apprenticeship period* in St Kitts, women used mob action during a general protest against work conditions. A British official who observed this 'turbulent and rebellious' resistance to the law stated that few men were involved in the protest and the mob consisted largely of women and children. After the general unrest was suppressed, sixteen rebels, including two women, were put on trial for 'sedition and mutiny' and inciting others to rebel (Frucht, 1975).

Contemporary accounts of the 1831 Montego Bay rebellion in Jamaica also provide some valuable information relating to the role of women in late slave rebellions. This was also known as the Great Christmas Rising and it involved up to 20,000 slaves. It is perhaps significant that the leader, Sam Sharpe, was a Baptist known as 'Daddy' or 'Ruler', reflecting both the creolisation of slaves and the decline in female power associated with the purer African religions. (As within marriage, Christianisation introduced European-derived gender divisions in church hierarchies.) Another interesting aspect of the revolt is the involvement, for the first time, of Europeans – Baptists whose return to the fundamentals of Christianity inspired slaves to challenge their slave status which the more established Church of England maintained was decreed by God. The uprising gained momentum when the slaves were led to believe that their freedom had, in effect, already been granted by the British Parliament and a vast number joined up with the rebels. An Englishman who helped to suppress the rebels recorded in a biased, but informative, account of this 'Baptist Revolt' that 'not a soul was to be seen on the estates' (excepting the old, disabled, sick or children), all others having fled to the woods 'taking with them whatever weapons, ammunition and food they could collect'. He added that during his sorties with the local militia the women his party encountered prevaricated so much on questioning that, in his opinion, they were evidently concealing information. One such woman even attempted to lead

---

*The period between the emancipation of slaves in July 1833 and the complete abolition of slavery in 1838 when the transitional apprenticeship system, designed to ensure that ex-slaves would continue to work for their former masters, was recognised as a failure and abandoned.

his party straight into a rebel ambush. Another woman apprehended by the militia was discovered to have been sent as a guide with a rebel foraging party as she was well acquainted with provision grounds in the area. As spies and messengers, women would have been additionally aided by their physical mobility as higglers and market-sellers.[18]

As in earlier years, during the late period of slavery, certain women were judged to be highly dangerous slaves and punished commensurately by the planters. For instance, in St Lucia in 1828, some women slaves were charged with 'discontent and mutiny' and subsequently punished. In lieu of the collar (banned by law in 1826) the accused:

> were hung by the arms to a peg, raised so high above their heads, that the toes alone touched the ground, the whole weight of the body resting on the wrists of the arms and tips of the toes.[19]

More individualistic acts of resistance were also punished. One woman, a twenty-five-year-old domestic servant and Baptist, laced the food of her masters' entire family with arsenic (an indication, perhaps, of the persistence of obeah even after slaves had embraced Christianity). After this was detected she was transported to the convict colony of New South Wales, Australia, for poisoning (Duffield, 1985). More detailed analysis of punishment lists and criminal records pertaining to rebel slaves may provide additional and valuable evidence relating to the active participation of women in late slave uprisings, although official contemporary attitudes to women can offset the value of such evidence.

Summary

The theme of resistance was part of the everyday life of slaves from the early period of slavery and was expressed in song and oral tradition and transmitted to children by their mothers. Evidence presented here suggests that women were active at all levels of resistance from everyday non-cooperation to active participation in slave revolts, where they showed as much, if not more courage than men, and were equally prepared to die. Studies of the French Caribbean confirm a similar pattern of resistance to that which existed in the British West Indies.

In their response to slavery and the methods of resistance they adopted, slave women reflected the ever-pervasive influence of African cultural traditions but also the more tangible reality of the brutal circumstances under which they existed. Women, moreover, in their important role within the slave family and wider slave community, contributed significantly to promoting the 'consciousness and practice of resistance' amongst the slaves. Slave women may not have been 'amazons' but neither were they necessarily traitors. In their unwillingness to co-operate, in raising their voices in satirical or subversive song, in verbally abusing their masters and refusing to behave submissively, as well as in their participation in slave revolts, they showed much courage and strength. Women slaves had as deep a commitment to 'putting down massa' and the continuing struggle for human dignity and freedom, as any of their male counterparts.

Further reading

Craton (1982)
Gaspar (1985, 1986)
Genovese (1979)
Heuman, ed. (1986)
Mathurin Mair (1975)
Okihiro, ed. (1986)
Price (1973)
Turner (1982)

6

'The Family Tree is Not Cut'

The Domestic Life of the Woman Slave

In the preceding chapters, the major focus has been the formal economic role of the woman slave; the emphasis is now shifted on to her less historically visible although no less important domestic life and thus involves primarily the role of the woman slave in the slave family. Because of the complex nature of human relationships, love and codes of morality, the specific contribution of the woman slave as mother, wife and kinswoman to the domestic life of the slaves must be viewed from the broader perspective of interpersonal bonds within the slave community as a total entity.

There has been important new research on the composition of the slave family since the 1960s by, for instance, Barry Higman (1976, 1984) and Michael Craton (1978, 1979) but it remains a controversial area of study (Proctor, 1982) in which differences between rural and urban regimes, small- and large-scale plantations, African and creole slaves must be considered. The main focus here is to re-evaluate the woman's contribution to family life, with the emphasis on the larger, rural plantation unit. This involves a broader discussion of studies of black family life and definitions of family and marriage, a reassessment of negative stereotypes of slave immorality, and an examination of the diversity of slave family and household structure. Evidence will be presented for the existence of strong family and kinship bonds but the forces which constantly threatened to undermine these bonds – the work regime, slave sales and the sexual power of white men – will also be considered with the emphasis on how slaves adapted to or resisted such forces to ensure that, in the words of the old Ashanti proverb, the 'family tree' was not cut.

The black family reassessed

Marriage and morality amongst slaves, according to contemporary observers, either did not exist, or existed only in unstable, 'uncivilised' forms such as 'polygamy';* slaves were not just immoral but amoral. In the opinion of abolitionists such as John Riland, the miseries and toils of her everyday labour left the slave woman too exhausted to 'promote the comfort of her household'; the nature of her work as a field slave precluded the existence of 'the pure and enlightened' institution of marriage.

Much evidence exists in contemporary literature which indicates that slave masters were, in effect, more aware of the significance of the slave family and the existence of marriage forms which did not conform to the modern European model than a superficial examination of their writings would suggest. Until the radical historiographic developments of the 1970s, studies perpetuated the overt negative approach to the slave family promulgated by plantocratic writers, frequently in justification of their position as slave masters. Historians, anthropologists and sociologists, with subtle differences in emphasis, accepted the general thesis that African slaves suffered cultural dislocation and total severance from their traditional kinship ties. Slave society was thus characterised by unstable personal, sexual and familial relationships and an atmosphere of cultural and social anomie. The anthropologist M. G. Smith (1953) suggested that it would have been impossible for slaves to establish stable marriage in slavery because they 'lacked the kinship and lineage groups' to sanction and give permanence to unions. Marriage in Africa was accompanied by a transfer in property but slaves had no property and hence 'mating' of slaves was unstable, with some islands – Jamaica, St Vincent – lacking marriage altogether. This line of argument perpetuated negative contemporary images of sexual instability but, whereas planters linked promiscuity (a word commonly used to define any sexual behaviour which deviates from the narrow limitations of lifelong monogamy) to inherent African traits, modern analysts who adopted Smith's approach saw it as a consequence of the peculiar conditions of slavery, actively encouraged by planters.

Such negative interpretations of the slave experience informed studies of modern black family structures, portraying them as 'pathological' or an unhealthy and inadequate deviation from the norm. Conversely, modern Afro-Caribbean or Afro-American families were too readily used as models for slave family life – an illustration of the pitfalls of reading history backwards. We cannot assume that codes of morality in the modern Caribbean differ only marginally from those which obtained in slave society and vice versa. Since emancipation changes in the economic and social infrastructure of West Indian societies have occurred which have had important ramifications on black family structure. For instance, the de-emphasis of the father role amongst some segments of society, which has often been cited in support of matrifocal theories of black family organi-

*The misuse of this term has been discussed in Chapter 2.

sation,* rather than being a direct result of the weakening of the father role during the days of slavery, is far more plausibly the result of the migrant labour system which developed after slavery ended (Clarke, 1957). Whilst it cannot be denied that Caribbean societies, past and present, are strongly linked in a cultural sense, in a socio-historical context they are not strictly comparable, an important factor which must be borne in mind in any study of the family in slavery.

In the 1970s there was a surge of interest in the domestic life of slaves which led to a revised view of family life. This began when American historians challenged the 1965 Moynihan report on black family life in the modern USA, which reiterated conventional views that Afro-American families were typically unstable and 'pathological' and that this was part of a pattern inherited from slavery. New research material in the registration lists from the Freedman's Bureau and detailed plantation lists enabled quantitative historians such as Stanley Engerman and R. Fogel (1974) and Herbert Gutman (1976) to produce convincing empirical data relevant to the stability of slave family structures.

Sidney Mintz, in a critical reappraisal of socio-anthropological works on the black family, has outlined the major theoretical flaws involved in studies of Afro-Caribbean marriage forms and family structures. He argues that models used in modern industrial society are not applicable to the study of slave families; 'family' cannot be equated with 'household' and marriage does not necessarily imply a religious or civil service (Mintz, 1975). Unfortunately, most definitions of slave morals and marriages have relied on the narrow context of modern western marriage forms, although they are a relatively recent development. Thus, as Mintz has shown, multiple divorce in modern western society, for instance, is accepted by scholars as a normal, legally sanctioned institution, whereas serial unions amongst West Indians, which are characterised by a succession of 'marriage' partners, are cited as evidence of moral and social instability. This ethnocentric perspective has ignored the fact that, although slaves apparently rejected western norms, they may have had their own strong and no less viable normative system. As Barry Higman stresses, any fresh analysis of family life in slave society demands a reorientation of perspective and redefinition of terms (Higman, 1975). Thus, before commencing an examination of the specific role of the slave woman in the slave family, it is necessary, first, to define exactly what is implied by nebulous words such as family, second, to illustrate how the modern concept of family is a relatively recent development, and third, to show how slave family forms can be linked positively to parallel institutions in West Africa.

The 'convention of monogamy', which defines the family as an elementary or nuclear, co-residential unit, comprising two legally married partners, with or without children, has until very recently, been recognised as the norm against which differing family patterns in widely diverse societies have

---

*These point to the disproportionate number of mother-headed families with no co-residential male and are used to stress the unstable nature of black family life and the high rate of 'illegitimacy'.

been examined. Although in many ways – in their own moral behaviour and in the rare candid and perceptive comments they made about slave behaviour – planters acknowledged a degree of deviance from the common norm, the majority of contemporary writings supported the prevailing European bourgeois ideal of the sacredness of monogamous Christian marriage. Whilst this form of family organisation undoubtedly existed amongst slaves, possibly (as will subsequently be shown) to a greater degree than has hitherto been assumed, any study which aims to enlarge upon the more positive features of slave family life requires a more flexible definition of family.

The tendency for black Caribbean family forms, past and present, to be described largely in terms of illegitimacy, common-law marriage and matrifocal family organisation equates 'family' with 'household'; the classical concept of the nuclear family is applied to slave society, which results in a number of serious misconceptions. A household which does not conform to this conventional definition and is grouped, for instance, around a grandmother–mother–child structure containing no conjugal (married) pair is none the less a viable co-residential domestic household unit. This distinction is highly relevant to slave society where the extended (consanguine), co-residential family unit is of as much, if not greater, importance for purposes of definition as the nuclear (conjugal) unit.

If the extended rather than the nuclear family was of primary importance in slave society, a further distinction must be made between the extended family household which is a co-residential unit and the true extended family which forms a complex non-co-residential kinship network. In slave society complex family relationships existed between non-co-residential as well as co-residential kin: in some cases, however, 'family' was represented by fictive kin. In the absence of blood kin, non-related slaves were 'adopted' to reconstitute traditional kinship-based relationships. Quite simply, where absent, slaves created 'brothers', 'sisters', 'aunts', 'uncles' and 'parents'. Thus the narrow scope of anthropological definitions of family and household outlined above, while useful in themselves as primary definitions, are insufficient for the purposes of this study. A more flexible concept of family is indicated to attain a fuller understanding of the complexities of slave domestic life.

A similar lack of conceptual flexibility occurs in relation to slave marriages. The majority of scholars involved in research into slavery refer to the modern western norm of the lifelong monogamous union entered into by legally sanctioned civil or religious contract. A much broader definition will be employed here whereby marriage will imply a stable though not necessarily lifelong partnership between two adults who may live in a co-residential nuclear unit, but who may also be incorporated into a wider extended family arrangement or not even be continuously co-residential, as in the case of polygynous marriage. The complex nature of slave society and the diverse cultural backgrounds of the slaves ensured that different marital and family forms existed side by side. The opposing cultures of Europe and Africa were continuously juxtaposed in situations of conflict and assimila-

86

tion. The slaves, by sheer force of circumstances, had to adapt their traditional cultural patterns to their new social situation. This resulted in what Melville Herskovits termed a certain 'elasticity of the marriage concept' amongst New World blacks (Herskovits, 1941). Yet, wherever possible, the slaves strove to re-establish African patterns of marriage and retain traditional attitudes to family, children and kin, even where this involved resistance to European cultural impositions, as in the case of Christian marriage.

The family patterns which the slaves established often corresponded much more closely to the family structures of pre-industrial Europe than the modern nuclear model. It is perhaps interesting to note that early West Indian commentators such as Richard Ligon and Sir Hans Sloane were more favourable in their comments on slave marriages and morality than were the later eighteenth-century writers. At the time they were writing, the modern concept of marriage, founded upon an essentially bourgeois code of morality, had not as yet become an established ideal in European society. Philippe Ariès has shown that, before the seventeenth century in Europe, 'family' implied a far looser and flexible institution than it does today. The wider kinship unit predominated over the conjugal marriage unit and communities were cohered by non-family age-group structures as in many West African societies. The wider community was of more importance to the individual than the nuclear family unit; little personal privacy was expected or attainable and hence the concept of modesty and the code of sexual morals differed considerably from those which prevailed in later industrial societies (Ariès, 1962).

As Peter Laslett points out, the development of the family has not been one of a simple evolution from the large multi-generational household of the pre-industrial age to the nuclear family of the industrial era, but a complex process involving a shift of emphasis and redefining the values relating to family and kinship structures. The nuclear family has probably existed in most societies during all periods of history, not as the pre-eminent domestic unit it is today, but as a sub-unit enmeshed in a much wider and complex network of familial and social relationships (Laslett, 1971).

The status of woman and the conceptualisation of love in pre-industrial society differed correspondingly, as did attitudes to children. Relations between marriage partners were 'instrumental' rather than romantic; that is, they were based on practical considerations related to work and reproduction, although this did not imply a lack of affection. Romantic love as the prime bonding element in marriage was arguably an upper-class ideal derived from 'courtly love' which was eventually to permeate, via the new middle classes, the entire social strata of European society (Shorter, 1975). In pre-industrial Europe men *and* women made an equally vital and indispensable social contribution to the marital partnership and, despite the overall public subjugation of women, within their own particular domains, women were all-powerful. 'Mothering' in the modern sense of the word did not exist, for women had vital work to do in the house and fields and could not devote all their time to their children. The high infant mortality rate

CHAP. XXVI. ought to be treated; and this mode of conduct might ftill be more general, by amending the laws, which ought not corruptly to inveft human nature with what it is certain to abufe—an authority completely defpotic. No mafter furely ought to be entrufted with the dangerous power of taking away the life of his flaves with impunity; and it ought to be confidered an equal crime in the eye of the law to kill a negro or a white man, as it is equally murder in the fight of God.

I fhall now introduce to the reader's acquaintance a negro family in that ftate of tranquil happinefs, which they always enjoy under a humane and indulgent mafter. The figures in the plate are fuppofed to be of the *Loango nation*, by the marks on the man's body, while on his breaft may be feen *J. G. S.* in a cypher, by which his owner may afcertain his property. He carries a bafket with fmall fifh, and a net upon his head, with a large fifh in his hand, caught by himfelf in the river. His wife, who is pregnant, is employed in carrying different kinds of fruit, fpinning a thread of cotton upon her diftaff, and comfortably fmoking her pipe of tobacco. Befides all this, fhe has a boy upon her back, and another playing by her fide. Thus, under a mild mafter and an honeft overfeer, a negro's labour is no more than a healthy exercife, which ends at the fetting-fun, and the remaining time is his own, which he employs in hunting, fifhing, cultivating his garden, or making bafkets and

and fifh-nets for fale; with this money he buys a hog CHAP. XXVI. or two, fometimes fowls or ducks, all which he fattens upon the fpontaneous growth of the foil, without expence, and very little trouble, and, in the end, they afford him confiderable profit. Thus pleafantly fituated, he is exempt from every anxiety, and pays no taxes, but looks up to his mafter as the only protector of him and his family. He adores him, not from fear, but from a conviction that he is indebted to his goodnefs for all the comforts he enjoys. He breathes in a luxurious warm climate, like his own, which renders clothes unneceffary, and he finds himfelf more healthy, as well as more at his eafe, by going naked. His houfe he may build after his own fancy. The foreft affords him every neceffary material for the cutting. His bed is a hammock, or a mat called *papaya*. His pots he manufactures himfelf, and his difhes are gourds, which grow in his garden. He never lives with a wife he does not love, exchanging for another the moment either he or fhe becomes tired, though this feparation happens lefs frequently here than divorces do in Europe. Befides the regular allowance given him by his mafter weekly, his female friend has the art of making many favoury difhes; fuch as *braf*, or a hodge-podge of plantains and yams boiled with falt meat, barbacued fifh, and Cayenne pepper. *Tom-tom* is a very good pudding, compofed of the flour of Indian corn, boiled with flefh,

VOL. II.   O o   fowl,

6.1 *Extract from Stedman's* Narrative of a Five Years Expedition [to] Surinam, *1772–1777, describing the 'Family of Negro Slaves from Loango' (see p. 89). John Stedman was a soldier who went out to help fight the maroons (rebel slaves who ran away in large numbers) in Surinam, where conditions were notoriously harsh. He was there from 1772 to 1777, and formed a close and loving relationship with a female slave, Joanna (p. 16), who bore him a son. As a temporary resident, Stedman had no particular stake in the slave system, and, although his account is undoubtedly Eurocentric, it provides a detailed and vivid insight into slavery, and one which is unusually sensitive to the depth of slave family and marriage bonds.*

Family of Negro Slaves from Loango.

6.2 *'Family of Negro Slaves from Loango'. Loango is the modern-day coastline of Gabon; and the Congo Republic in Central West Africa. This illustration is accompanied by a commentary by Stedman (p. 88). It provides a romanticised and paternalistic view of slavery, but does draw attention to the survival of family bonds in the slave community. It also affords a rare insight into the daily life of slaves. The wife is portrayed as pregnant, the children compounding the image of fecundity. However, with the threat of the abolition of the slave trade, slave masters became increasingly anxious about the failure of slave women to bear children in sufficient numbers to replace the slave population.*

resulted in a certain degree of 'indifference to a too-fragile childhood'. As Ariès observes, this did not imply a lack of care but was simply a recognition that the contribution which children made to the family was primarily a social and communal rather than a sentimental reality. Children were thus valued for the contribution they made to household production and the concept of childhood as a special phase in the life of the individual did not exist before the cultural, demographic and economic changes which resulted from industrialisation in the nineteenth century (Ariès, 1962).

Modern conceptions of family and marriage developed during the seventeenth and eighteenth centuries with the growth of modern capitalism. This view of family life remained essentially a preserve of the bourgeoisie until well into the nineteenth century. Although it is far too simplistic to imply that attitudes to family, marriage and children in West Africa and slave society corresponded exactly to those in pre-industrial European society, African social institutions centring on the family and marriage related far more closely to parallel institutions in pre-industrial Europe than to the modern western ideal which has come to be recognised as the norm. Like slaves, the European urban poor of the eighteenth century were accused of promiscuity and 'shameless' freedom of the sexes (Medick, 1976) and it was only towards the latter part of the nineteenth century that they conformed more noticeably to 'respectable' Christian morality. The system of marriage and morality adhered to by slaves and the European proletariat differed considerably from that which prevailed amongst the middle and upper classes of eighteenth-century Europe, and this factor should be borne in mind when any analysis of the slave family is made, for it places slave morality in the context of the world historical picture.

As Hans Medick points out, writing in the context of his study (1976) of European peasants:

> The historian of the family must, in his conceptual approach, in the questions which he asks and in the course material which he scrutinises, reassess history, as it too often has been retold by historians and sociologists of the family even today. Ruling class perspectives not only determined the way contemporary observers perceived rural artisans; they persisted in the explicit or implicit middle-class bias which still seems enshrined in the conceptual approach and even methodological perspectives of much that is written in contemporary history and sociology of the family.

Unfortunately, in reading contemporary accounts of Caribbean slave society, it is possible only to glean a limited insight into the domestic life of slaves. As John Stewart observed, perhaps with a good deal of justification, the majority of slaves were 'beyond the ken' of their masters' immediate observation. A certain degree of intuition and empathy is therefore necessary when dealing with such an intimate sphere as the domestic life of slaves. Source material relating to the slave family in the Caribbean is far more limited than that available in the United States. Contemporary appraisals of the Caribbean slave family were also skewed by ignorance or misinterpretation of West African social institutions.

The most fundamental social unit in West African society is the kinship unit; this forms the political, social and economic basis of community life. Other interpersonal relationships, such as the nuclear family unit, exist only by definition and not as separate parts of the social structure. Legal, that is communally sanctioned, marriage in Africa is a development process rather than an isolated official ceremony, of which the most important stage is not the actual marriage ceremony but the birth of the first child. The wife is protected by her family from maltreatment by her husband and, although she is expected to perform strictly delimited social and economic functions, she has equal rights with her husband in such matters as divorce. As in pre-industrial Europe, the African woman wields much power in her own sphere of activity. A high degree of influence, autonomy of action and prestige is accorded to her as a mother. This factor enables her to play a strong and important role within the wider community for, as Daryl Forde observed in his study of the Ashanti, the bond between mother and child is regarded as 'the key-stone of all social relationships' (Forde, 1956). Thus any new analysis of slave family life must be preceded by an examination of the notion of matrifocality in the context of the woman's role in traditional African society.

The black matriarch: slave motherhood in the African cultural context

Misinterpretations or ignorance of the position of the woman as daughter, wife and mother in West African society, in addition to the traditional economic independence of women in both matrilineal and patrilineal* societies such as the Ashanti and the Ibo and the authority endowed them over their children, could have contributed to the common misconception that the slave woman was the dominant figure in the slave family. The fact that slave descent was through the female line facilitated these theories. Common law unions with whites, the practice of polygyny, widowhood and separation of married couples through sale would also have resulted in mother-headed slave households. The image of the black woman as dominant within the slave family was further enhanced by the glaring contrast between the roles and functions of black and white women in the contemporary cultural context. In comparison to the relative independence of black women, the white woman in plantation society had a highly subordinate and distinctly unfavourable status, despite the glowing image presented of white womanhood by such plantocratic writers as Thomas Atwood. Independence, however, was not tantamount to sole dominance within the family unit.

Melville Herskovits has observed that the number of 'competent, self-sufficient' women in the Caribbean was as much related to the

*Line of descent through the female and male line respectively.

socio-economic position of African women as it was to the specific conditions of slavery (Herskovits, 1941). In the slave family, women held considerable control over economic resources as they did in the West African family. If the slave women lived in polygynous family units, they would have had even greater control and authority over their children than women in monogamous unions.

In a cultural perspective, family organisation may have retained certain features of the matrilineal organisation of some West African societies such as the Ashanti, remnants of which are still found in isolated black groups in the modern Caribbean, such as the Cottica Djukas of Surinam. Daryl Forde, in his study of the Ashanti, discovered that, in a 'relatively stable Ashanti community', between 40 and 50 per cent of the population lived in matrilineal households under female heads and only about a third of all married women resided with their husbands, the remainder living chiefly with matrilineal kin. In other parts of Africa women have the right to refuse to relinquish control of children in favour of a husband. Even in matrilineal societies, however, men are by no means devoid of power or authority. Under Ashanti custom, for example, every lineage has a male head who is chosen from amongst living male members by consensus of the whole body of members irrespective of sex.

Maria Cutrufelli (1983) has explained the essentially patriarchal basis of African societies, which can result in social oppression of women, despite their relative economic independence. It may thus be argued that the typology of the slave family as matriarchal has been done without any meaningful referral to the slaves' African cultural inheritance within which all forms of slave family organisation, including mother-headed families, must be examined. As will be subsequently shown, the oversimplified contrast made by historians like Richard Dunn (1977) between the dominant slave matriarch and the weak emasculated male slave is not borne out by either contemporary evidence or a more objective analysis of the slave woman in her cultural context.

Slave women had an alien sexual division of labour enforced upon them which negated and undermined the traditional African division of labour. Arlette Gautier (1983) and Jacqueline Jones (1985) have both argued that female slaves, in the French Caribbean and the USA respectively, reverted to a subordinate position within the black family after they were freed. Jones argues that this was a position aspired to under slavery but not attainable, while Gautier shows that, although women were capable of fighting courageously alongside men in the rebellion in St Domingue, in independent Haiti they reverted to less prestigious roles as cultivators and housewives. Sheridan has made a similar claim for women in the British Caribbean in explaining how the gender composition of the plantation work-force changed after the abolition of slavery, reflecting a withdrawal of women into the home (Sheridan, 1985). Conflicts between the formal economic role of women and their role in the slave family obviously existed and, as will be subsequently shown, there is evidence that women reverted to a traditional African division of labour in the slave community.

In the slave community male authority was far from moribund. The leaders of slave communities, such as the elite slaves and elders who adjudicated at slave disputes, were predominantly men. Furthermore, if the European-imposed official line of descent was through the female slave, according to the custom of slaves, primogeniture was the norm. William Beckford recorded that 'negroes absolutely respect primogeniture and the eldest son takes possession of his father's property immediately after his decease'.[1] Both Long and Edwards described the process whereby personal possessions, rights to provision grounds and houses were passed on by slave fathers to their families. The true importance of the father in the slave family, whatever form it took, was, however, obscured by the practice of slave owners failing to mention slave fathers in plantation lists. It is possible that a study into slave naming practices, similar to that carried out by Herbert Gutman for the Old South, would reveal strong evidence for the importance of the father in the slave family.

The argument presented here, then, does not seek to deny completely the existence of a matrifocal form of family organisation in slave society, but to refute the notion that it was the dominant form of slave family organisation. Certain aspects of slave society outlined above indicate that, except in a few exceptional cases, the matrifocal family, where it existed, was linked to cultural retention, rather than evidence of pathological development reflecting sexual and social instability.

Barry Higman suggests that contemporary allusions to mother-headed families may have been based primarily on female coloured domestics who had children by transient whites and rarely formed stable unions with black or coloured slaves. Adult female labourers were far more likely than domestics to live in family households containing males (which may reflect greater cultural retention among field slaves). Male drivers and tradesmen were more frequently part of such households than field labourers, reflecting male status in the slave hierarchy but also, perhaps, the connection made in traditional African society between male wealth and prestige and ability to marry. Higman thus concludes that it was creole women, not African-born women, who gave the matrifocal tendency to slave society (Higman, 1984). His study of family structures in Trinidad, Barbados and Jamaica indicates that most slaves lived in stable family units and had probably done so since the beginning of slavery. 'It is clear', he writes, that

> the simple family household (here defined as simple nuclear units and what might be described as truncated nuclear families; man and wife, father and children, mother and children) accounted for the greater part of the slave family. (Higman, 1975)

Higman's data are confined largely to the period after the abolition of the slave trade in 1807, which removed in part one significant factor affecting the composition and stability of the slave family. But, as Higman points out, if the sources of the 'chaotic' black family are to be traced to the period of slavery, this pattern should have been apparent in the years after as well as before 1807. More detailed examination of the contemporary evidence effectively supports his observations, refuting allegations of slave immorality and family instability.

The myth of black female promiscuity

According to plantocratic writers, 'promiscuity' began at an early age amongst female slaves, a factor which contributed to the general instability of slave family structures. The Jamaican Assembly, in answer to questions pertaining to the state of slave morals put to them by the parliamentary report into the slave trade in 1789, reported that slave women 'have commerce too early in life and with a multitude of men'. From puberty onwards it was assumed that slave women indulged in promiscuous pre-marital sex and that their subsequent lives were a constant quest for sexual pleasure and satisfaction. To a large extent, these beliefs were merely a continuation of the shallow preconceptions of Europeans about the sexual immorality of Africans in general, which are strongly contradicted by both contemporary and modern evidence. Promiscuity was by no means a natural trait of African women. Equiano wrote:

> our women were . . . uncommonly graceful, alert and modest to a degree of bashfulness; nor do I remember to have heard of an instance of incontinence amongst them before marriage.[2]

Virginity in traditional West African society is highly valued although it is not always rigidly required. Pre-marital sex *is* allowed but only within the bounds of a strictly regulated communal code of behaviour. In Africa, as in other pre-industrial cultures, including certain classes of European society, pre-marital intercourse may have been accepted as a developmental phase in the marriage process. In this context, the birth of a child outside marriage would not necessarily be viewed as a social stigma as it would probably be shortly followed by marriage. In many West African societies a couple are not regarded as truly married until after the birth of the first child.

The many allusions to sexual instability and the incidence of serial unions amongst younger slaves may have represented a distorted, Eurocentric interpretation of African cultural behaviour patterns. Amongst the Ashanti, whose culture was dominant in Jamaican slave society, trial marriages of young persons are allowed, if approved by both sets of parents, and are accepted as a proper marriage for all practical purposes. However, unlike in true marriage, the man has no right to demand adultery damages if his partner has a lover and the couple can separate with ease by mutual consent (Forde, 1956). Herbert Gutman found evidence that similar trial marriages existed in slave society in the USA (Gutman, 1976). Such trial marriage in a communally regulated framework does not constitute promiscuity.

One important factor which may have contributed to the erroneous belief in the sexual precocity of young slaves was perhaps their apparent lack of 'modesty' and shame, especially where nakedness was concerned. (To middle-class Europeans, lack of modesty in women was particularly abhorrent.) Of adolescent slaves in Surinam, John Stedman wrote:

> They swim promiscuously in groups of boys and girls . . . I have not only seen a negro girl beat a hardy youth in swimming . . . but on landing challenge him to a two-mile race and beat him again, naked as they were; while all ideas of shame on one side and of insult on the other are totally unknown.[3]

In their healthy and innocent attitude to nakedness, as in their relative physical equality commented upon by other contemporary authors, the relationship between young male and female slaves must have differed markedly from that of their white counterparts in both the West Indies and Europe. The tacit equality and mutual respect among slaves remarked upon by Stedman would have been socially unacceptable amongst all but the lower echelons of eighteenth-century European society.

Physical closeness of youths and a relative freedom of slave girls (*vis-à-vis* European girls) does not imply that sexual activity began at an early age. Visiting one particular sugar plantation, John Stedman was amazed by the fact that the young woman waiting on table was 'stark naked'. The reason Stedman was given was that:

> it was ordered so by their mothers and matrons to prevent (by such means of protection, said they) their too early intercourse with the males, and child-bearing which would spoil their shapes, weaken their strength and cramp their growth.[4]

Although Stedman's anecdote may have been rather fancifully elaborated upon, in the African cultural context, it is perfectly feasible that too early childbearing and, thus, sexual intercourse would have been 'negatively' sanctioned by slaves. Amongst a number of African tribes, for instance, sexual activity amongst young girls is culturally regulated until they reach a suitable age (Hoffer, 1972). Dallas observed a similar practice amongst the maroons of Jamaica, where a girl was not deemed ready for marriage or childbirth until this was publicly and ceremoniously announced by the parents, who 'killed a hog' for a feast to which neighbours were invited. Dallas believed that this practice was derived from an African custom which was intended as a signal to young men to make an offer of marriage. He maintained that amongst the maroons, even after it was publicly known that a girl 'had killed a hog', she often preferred a state of celibacy for some years after (which may explain the late onset of childbearing of female slaves in the Caribbean discussed in the next chapter). It is thus plausible that some form of community and parental controls operated in slave society which closely regulated and limited the sexual activities of the young. Today in the modern Caribbean if girls are too sexually free in adolescence they are strongly dealt with (Henry and Wilson, 1975).

The notion that slaves, both adolescent and adult, lacked shame and modesty and were sexually 'incontinent' has contributed significantly to the distorted view of slave family life still subscribed to in the present day. Richard Ligon wrote of slaves:

Chaste they are as any people under the sun; for when men and women are together naked they will never cast their eyes towards the parts that ought to be covered, and . . . I never saw so much as a kiss, or embrace, or a wanton glance with their eyes, between them.[5]

Emma Carmichael and John Stedman both made similar comments on the modesty of slaves. Stedman, having failed to notice during several years' residence among them 'even an offer to kiss a woman in public', believed that the 'delicacy' of slaves deserved to be acknowledged. Thus from their own cultural reference point, it would seem that slave men and women were, if anything, more modest and showed greater propriety and reticence in relations between the sexes than the eighteenth-century European peasantry and urban proletariat. Granted, a certain degree of nakedness may have been accepted as the norm by African slaves but, as in West Africa, was probably circumscribed by certain conventions of dress and behaviour which precluded promiscuity. Because of their inhibited attitude to nakedness, however, Europeans would have been unable to comprehend the subtlety of these social conventions. Thus, their conclusions about the sexual life of slaves were partially based on a false logic which deduced promiscuity from nakedness and 'immodesty'.

Late eighteenth-century commentators, however, seemed duty-bound to refer to the promiscuity of slaves if only to contradict themselves subsequently. One plantocratic observer, for instance, having proclaimed that 'chastity' was not classed as 'among the cardinal virtues' of blacks, continued by stating that a 'violation' of this esteemed virtue, even in a woman not contracted to a husband, was viewed as a shameful thing by her fellow slaves. He added that a lapse of virtue in the unmarried woman brought on 'the ridicule of the gang' when detected and in women who were wives 'a want of fidelity' was considered disgraceful.[6]

If the same high premium was not placed upon pre-marital chastity in slave society as it was in middle-class white society, marital fidelity amongst slave wives was highly valued. Of slave husbands, Richard Ligon wrote:

Jealous they are of their wives and hold it for a great injury and scorn, if another man . . . makes the least courtship to his wife.[7]

Sir Hans Sloane also remarked on the high value slaves placed on wifely fidelity. Almost a century later, the Barbados Committee reporting to the 1789 enquiry into the slave trade testified that, although slaves 'had no marriage regulations but such as they make according to their own customs', the women exhibited 'a sense of Decency and Decorum in their Fidelity under this voluntary Connexion'. Slave men, however, were accused of engaging in 'loose amours', following the example of lower whites. According to Dr William Sells, a slave doctor in Jamaica during the same period, adultery among slaves was 'by no means so much more frequent' than it was in England at that time, despite the invidious practice a 'polygamy', an observation with which John Stedman agreed. As in Europe, however, the above evidence implies that a double standard of morality for male and female was in operation in the slave community despite the relative independence of slave women and the apparent gender equality in the formal sphere of plantation society. If we accept the veracity of Equiano's reminiscences, such a double standard also existed in contemporary West African society where 'the men do not preserve the same constancy to their wives as they expect from them'.

Although allegations were made to the contrary, it was usually the men who contracted polygynous unions. Because fidelity in women was the norm, polyandry* was extremely rare. White observers possibly mis-interpreted the important extra-plantation kin networks of the slaves as polygamous. Long, for instance, wrote that the individual slave had 'six or more husbands or wives' in different places but added that 'by this means they find support when their own lands fail them, and houses of call and refreshment, whenever they are on their travels'. Contemporary evidence indicates that, while a minority of men often had more than one wife, slave women were expected to remain monogamous. Ligon noted that, although certain 'brave fellows' of 'extraordinary qualities' were allowed two or three wives, 'no woman was allowed above one husband'. Most men only had one wife.

Because of the confusion over the term polygamy discussed in Chapter 2, discussion on the status of slave women in poylgynous unions is fundamental to any further examination of slave family life. Many serious misinterpretations of the domestic life of slaves cluster around this ubiquitous term. If polygamy was not fostering 'immorality' in slave women, it was rendering her a debased and degraded drudge. In effect, individual wives were often accorded a good deal of respect from their husbands and, as in Africa, the head wife retained certain privileges. Barbadian planters reporting to the 1789 enquiry into the slave trade observed that, although the male slaves were allowed a number of wives, the first wife was still in 'friendship and confidence' with the husband and continued to govern the household, her position being one of 'great respect and influence'. Long maintained that polygynous males had only one true wife; the rest, although called wives, were:

> a sort of occasional concubine . . . whose existence the husband claims in the culture of his land, the sale of his produce and so on, rendering to them reciprocal acts of friendship when they are in want.[8]

Like the majority of his contemporaries Long may have misinterpreted the significance of the head wife in polygynous unions. In most West African societies, the 'great wife' holds a position of especial importance. Indeed, most planters knew very little in general about polygyny. As stressed in Chapter 2, polygynous marriage among slaves was essentially a direct cultural inheritance from Africa. Higman found that where polygynous households existed, they were frequently modelled directly on the African system and both husband and the co-wives were often from the same tribe.

*The practice of women having more than one husband at a time.

In many cases the man was a member of the slave elite and probably would have held a position of authority in his native African community. The polygynous family unit, which on the surface provided evidence that slave families were matrifocal, probably accounted only for a minority of slave marriages. However, its incidence may have varied from plantation to plantation, depending on the tribal composition of the slave population, a factor which may partially explain why, in studies of individual plantations, there is such a high range of fluctuation in estimates of the number of slaves in family groupings (Higman, 1975). As polygyny was not typical of women's domestic lives it must be examined within wider patterns of marriage and divorce in the slave community.

Marriage and divorce

In her private domestic sphere, as a wife and a mother, the woman slave was performing the only labour of the slave community, with perhaps the exception of the cultivation of provision grounds, which could not be claimed directly by the master. In this area of her life, she readopted, wherever possible, the traditional role of the West African woman. As well as putting in a hard day's labour in the fields, she was expected to cook, clean and care for her family in addition to tending her provision grounds. The male slave had a far less onerous domestic burden. When Mrs Carmichael asked a particular slave if he would cook the fish he had just caught, she received the indignant reply that 'he wife cook a vitual, no him'. (Cooking is taboo for many African men.) Although the master provided certain bare necessities of existence, childcare and the creation of a more meaningful home life was largely the province of the female slave. 'A wife and a family', continued Mrs Carmichael, 'have been the greatest possible advantage to a slave . . . his wife works and cooks, the children soon begin to assist the mother and they all work in their gardens and grounds.' Thomas Cooper also commented on the demanding 'double shift' of slave women, remarking that slave men had an easier burden as they did not need to carry out domestic chores when their work for the master was done.

From the earliest days of slavery, slaves valued their marital and family connections highly. Sir Hans Sloane, writing in the late seventeenth century, admitted that plantations were 'kept in good order' only if masters and overseers paid due attention to the marriage ties of slaves and 'bought wives in proportion to their men [slaves]'. Over a century later, Edward Long wrote of Jamaican slaves, 'they are all married [in their way] to a husband and wife', and the Bermuda Assembly, in response to a question put to them by the official enquiry into the slave trade in 1789 on the practice of marriage amongst slaves, replied that the latter were 'fond of domestic lives' and formed 'early connexions'. Reporting to the same committee, the Jamaican Assembly conceded that, although no legal forms of marriage existed, the slaves 'cohabited by mutual consent' and, although they occasionally separated 'without much ceremony', they frequently lived

" Oh! Massa, Massa! no flog Zeka! Zeka only stay see poor Nasa die. Nasa no Zeka wife, but Nasa moder. Zeka poor babies!"

(Slaves are frequently not allowed to marry.)

6.3 *An abolitionist cartoon depicting a male slave being flogged for remaining with his dying wife, Nasa. Opponents of slavery were highly critical of slave masters' lack of respect for family bonds. Slaves had their own marriage bonds, often unrecognised by either abolitionists or supporters of slavery. In the caption to this cartoon, the slave is pleading with his master, saying that, although Nasa was not his legal wife, she was the mother of his children and thus deserved respect in death.*

and grew old together and a 'strong family attachment prevailed amongst them'.

The official plantocratic view of slave marriage sought to deny the slaves any loving bonds or long-standing relationships, thus conveniently rationalising the indiscriminate separation of close kin through sales. John Stedman believed that 'the tender passion' was the slave's only 'solace in affliction' and that even when separated from his loved one he would travel at night just to be with her. The less sympathetic Bryan Edwards, reflecting the plantocratic view, condemned the above author's statement as merely 'the language of poetry'. In reality, he averred, 'the negro had no leisure time to indulge a passion'; love was a 'sentiment refined by delicacy' and hence hardly ever found amongst Africans, the fundamental basis of whose relationships was mere 'animal desire'. Yet William Beckford, a planter himself, came to doubt the prevailing white view of slave emotions, observing that:

> although insensibility appears to be the characteristic of an African negro, yet there are many who have their feelings as exquisitely alive to the melting impressions of tenderness and sorrow, as those who are distinguished by a better fortune.[9]

Similarly, Alexander Falconbridge observed that, together with 'a just sense of the value of liberty', Africans were 'not bereft' of the finer feelings. Writing at a much later date in the 1930s when he travelled in West Africa, the novelist Graham Greene remarked that Africans were tender towards each other in a 'gentle, muffled way', never resorted to shrill speech or blows as did the European poor, and conformed always to a 'high standard of courtesy' (Greene, 1936).

Slave marriages did not correspond to the idealised, sentimental relationship which was believed (somewhat hypocritically in view of the importance of property and wealth) to cement the typical European bourgeois marriage. Hence, loving relationships between slaves were deemed to be of less significance than those between Europeans. The ease of divorce in slave society, in particular, was often cited as evidence of the shallow nature of love bonds between adult slaves. Divorce was rare in eighteenth-century European society; it was against all the teachings of the Christian church and extremely difficult to obtain, especially for women. In contrast, slaves of both sexes apparently viewed divorce as a simple and expedient means of terminating unsatisfactory relationships. 'They laugh at the idea of marriage which ties two people together, indissolubly,' declared Edward Long, and saw love and marriage as 'free and transitory'. But slave divorces did involve some measure of ceremony. A common divorce rite in Jamaica, according to Long, involved the division of the *cotta*, a circular pad of dried, plaited plantain leaves, upon which slaves customarily rested the loads which they carried upon their heads. When a married couple agreed to a voluntary divorce, this object was cut into two and each party retained a half signifying 'the severance of their mutual affection'.

In view of the almost total impossibility of a European woman obtaining a divorce, the fact that the woman slave had equal rights with the male slave in this area would have been difficult for the European observer to comprehend. Divorce was thus cited as further evidence of the instability of slave marriage, although in reality it was derived from traditional West African practice. West African attitudes to divorce reflect the autonomy, independence and relative equality of African women *vis-à-vis* their European counterparts. In most West African societies, both partners have equal rights to divorce, even in those influenced by Islam. Sexual satisfaction, for instance, is, in many societies, an accepted prerequisite of matrimonial harmony under tribal marriage codes; hence failure to provide this is acceptable grounds for divorce. Kahn (1931) found that among the Djuka of Surinam, whose society is modelled closely on the lines of traditional eighteenth-century West African society, divorce was 'instantaneous and easy' and a husband's impotence was an adequate reason for his wife to divorce him. Little change occurred in her social circumstances or economic position when divorce took place; no moral stigma or social penalties were incurred and the status of the woman's children was unaffected. Compare this with the position of English women in the eighteenth and nineteenth century. If divorced or separated from their husbands they were not entitled to the custody of their children as they had no rights in this respect. Wife and children were the property of the husband; moreover they had no rights to their own property, or to income they themselves earned. In this context the apparent ease of divorce for woman slaves, based on traditional African custom, would have been taken by Europeans as further proof of their licentious habits.

In the late era of slavery, religious abolitionists preached that the duties and joys of monogamous Christian marriage would greatly benefit the moral and material welfare of the slaves. However, in Jamaica in 1823, the Reverend Bridges had allegedly married only 187 couples out of 16,000 slaves and John Riland observed that, even after conversion to Christianity, the slaves lived 'in a state of lawless concubinage' and refused to renounce 'the carnal desires of the flesh'. As Dr William Sells cynically noted of the missionaries' attempts to persuade the slaves to accept Christian marriage:

> Sensible negroes have been known to object to it as a solemn contract; saying that they understood that many of the white people, both here and in England, were as bad afterwards as before marriage.[10]

Slaves, it would appear, did not view Christian marriage in the same virtuous, uncritical light as abolitionists such as John Riland.

Planters in both the British and French Caribbean agreed with abolitionists and missionaries on the need to 'moralise' the slaves on the grounds that it would render slaves more docile and increase fertility (see Chapter 7). Such campaigns proved unsuccessful. For women slaves, Christian marriage held few attractions. As had been shown, under the African-derived marriage forms adopted by the slaves, women retained an independence of action and equality in status, especially with respect to divorce, denied the vast majority of European women. Thus women slaves had strong reasons to resist Christian marriage with its creed of lifelong fidelity and total submission to a husband's authority. An English observer, writing towards the end of slavery when the creolisation of slaves, according to some scholars, resulted in greater acceptance of Christian marriage, commented on the difficulties which faced one Jamaican planter in his efforts to promote 'true' marriage amongst his slaves. Only one pair of slaves put themselves forward. They were 'daily instructed in the various responsibilities of the married state' and clearly shown 'the consequences of deviation from their duty'. Unfortunately, this 'instruction' acted as a strong deterrent in the case of the prospective bride who failed to appear next to her 'forelorn bridegroom' on the appointed day. She was subsequently discovered hiding, 'fixed and immoveable' in her determination to continue living in the same manner she had lived with her 'husband' for many years in 'peace and comfort'; legal, Christian marriage, she feared, would give him licence to beat and ill-treat her (strong grounds for divorce in African cultures).[11]

Christianity was believed to have a civilising but also a subduing influence on slaves. Creole slaves, especially the elite, appeared superficially to accept Christian marriage forms more readily than African slaves and were thus viewed as more 'civilised' and 'intelligent' than the latter. Thomas Atwood wrote that there were many good negroes amongst the creoles who were 'very industrious' and made 'good husbands, wives, tender parents and diligent servants'. Christian marriage was 'respectable' as opposed to African-derived marriage forms, and creoles would have been more heavily indoctrinated into notions of white respectability than African slaves. However, overt acceptance of imposed values does not imply a complete commitment. The dichotomy between respectability and reputation which the anthropologist Peter Wilson (1973) noted in the modern Caribbean may have existed in slave society. Respectability implied an internalisation of European cultural norms which 'bettered' the individual's social position in the formal slave hierarchy. Yet in the slave village a counter-culture existed which exercised its own communal sanctions and formulated its own codes of moral behaviour independent of the external codes of law and morality to which Europeans subscribed.

In the later days of slavery especially, slaves may have paid lip-service to the notion of respectability but within the slave community it was reputation (adherence to the norms of the Afro-orientated code of morality) which established their recognition and worth in the eyes of their fellow slaves. This seeming schizophrenic attitude on the part of slaves to European codes of morality was part of a general pattern in all areas of slave life. Overt acceptance of the role ascribed to them by the whites often disguised a continual rejection of, and resistance to, slavery. In accepting European moral codes, slaves could establish their respectability in the eyes of the whites, but, in essence, it was reputation which retrieved them from the 'social death' and degradation of their slave status, established their position within the slave community, and gave meaning to their existence. Hence, in both the French and British Caribbean, slaves refused to cede their right to divorce and common-law marriage remained popular, being generally stable and enduring (Higman, 1975). Christian marriage merely subjected slave women to a dual patriarchy, as Christian values of male power were grafted on to existing African patriarchial structures.

Parenthood

Not only were adult slaves regarded as sexually feckless, they were also judged to be bad parents. As the slave mother was viewed as the principal parent, she became the especial target of plantocratic criticism. If her alleged 'promiscuity' was one of the major causes of lack of marital stability in slave societies, it was also seen as the reason, in the words of Bryan Edwards, for 'that neglect, and want of maternal affection towards children produced by former connections, observable in many of the Black females'.[12]

Because the slave woman, as a mother, did not conform to the romanticised view of motherhood subscribed to by the middle and upper classes of eighteenth-century Europe, she was often accused of cruelty and negligence. Mrs Carmichael, for instance, felt that slave women were 'cruelly harsh' to their children and often shirked their maternal responsibilities for such trivial pleasures as dancing through the night. They enjoyed 'the gossip and fun of the field' and felt that to stay at home and nurse their children was 'too monotonous'. 'Monk' Lewis, in many ways sympathetic towards women slaves, also felt that, at times, mothers put pleasure before duty where the care of their children was involved.

Sir Hans Sloane, however, perceptively drew attention to the difficulties of parenthood in slave society:

> The Negroes are usually thought to be haters of their own children and therefore 'tis believed that they sell and dispose of them to strangers for money. But the Parents, here, although their Children are Slaves, for ever, yet have a great love for them, that no master dare sell or give away their little ones, unless they care not whether their Parents hang themselves or no.[13]

Slaves did care for and love their children but, as with contemporary European views on slave marriage, comments on attitudes to children were made from the confines of a narrow and ethnocentric cultural perspective. As in their choice of marriage style, the behaviour of slaves towards their children was determined to a significant extent by their African cultural heritage. It is in this context that attitudes of slaves to their children should be examined.

As in other pre-industrial societies, children in West Africa belong to the whole community rather than exclusively to their biological parents. Affection is often tempered by discipline, for children are regarded as part of the general labour force of the village; they have duties and obligations which must be carried out. Children in the Caribbean, as in West African society, were subjected to strict discipline and behaviour codes. Slave parents, wrote Bryan Edwards, exercise a kind of sovereignty over their children, which never ceases during life, chastising them sometimes with much severity; and seeming to hold filial obedience in much higher estimation than conjugal fidelity.[14]

Such 'severity' did not necessarily imply a general lack of affection. Edward Long noticed that, although slave parents treated their children with a 'rigour bordering on cruelty', in general they loved them and their care of them was often 'remarkably exemplary'.

In the case of the slave woman, the retention of her traditional role as a mother represented a feat of cultural resistance. Slave mothers suffered continual frustrations in their everyday life. The nature of their labour was frequently exhausting and, doubtless, slave mothers did beat their children. To be a 'good' mother in the modern sense of the word was not possible, but in this respect she differed very little from, for example, nineteenth-century working-class English women. In situations where mothers work long hours in manual labour, the ideal of romanticised 'motherhood' is unrealistic and a more pragmatic attitude to childrearing is necessary. For similar reasons to those which applied to slave women, working-class mothers in nineteenth-century England were also accused of negligence and cruelty towards children. Despite the rigours of the slave regime, there is evidence that slave mothers tempered necessary strictness with tenderness and affection, especially towards infants. A cameo of one devoted slave mother appears in Richard Ligon's book. Though burdened by her toil in the field, this particular women would still allow her three-year-old 'pickanniny' to cavort on her back whilst she worked 'so glad was she to see him merry'. Later commentators such as William Beckford and John Stewart also remarked on the tenderness of slave mothers and their 'solicitude' towards their infants. On 'Monk' Lewis's estate there were many devoted mothers who cared not only for their own children but for adopted children also. Wrote Lewis:

> There is a woman named Christian, attending two fevered children in the hospital, one of her own and another an adopted infant, whom she reared upon the death of its own mother in childbirth; and there she sits, throwing her eyes from one to the other with such increasing solicitude, that no one would discover which was her own child and which was the orphan.[15]

Because the concept of childhood and the role of the mother differed in slave society from that of eighteenth-century, middle-class European society, contemporary observers accused women slaves of indifference, neglect and cruelty towards their children. In this sense, they presented a distorted view of the slave mother, for, in effect, in many ways she had simply readopted her inherited cultural role. In West African society, as has already been stressed, individual mothers wielded a considerable degree of authority over their children.

In Caribbean slave society, bonds between mothers and children remained strong despite the extenuating circumstances of slavery. 'The affections between mothers and even spurious offspring', wrote one contemporary commentator, 'are very powerful as well as permanent . . . and with respect to black children, nothing is so sure to irritate them and enrage them as cursing their mothers.'[16] This description of the significance of the mother in slave society correlates very closely with those relating to the mother in West African society where identity comes through motherhood and sterility is a terrible stigma (Cutrufelli, 1983). Equiano noted that Africans had a deep attachment for their mothers and in traditional Ashanti society to show disrespect to one's mother was tantamount to sacrilege (Forde, 1956). The authority and respect accorded the slave mother, derived from African custom, is best assessed in relation to the wider extended kinship networks in the slave community, for, as Richard Dunn has stressed, within these kin networks the maternal bond was 'the key element'.

Kinship and community

As in West Africa, the extended kinship group was the integrating social factor in the slave community. Wherever possible the slaves recreated kinship links and adapted them to their specific situation. In the absence of true kin, fictive kinship networks were developed. Herbert Gutman has argued that these were not simply copies of West African systems but had their roots, nevertheless, in the African belief that kinship was the 'normal idiom of social relations' (Gutman, 1976). According to Bryan Edwards, old established negroes of both sexes 'adopted' young Africans, perhaps to replace children lost by death. The newly arrived slaves considered themselves adopted children, called the slaves who cared for them parents, and 'venerated them as such'. In a few months' time the newcomers were fully integrated into slave society and 'well established in their families, their houses and provision grounds'. In accepting strangers so readily as adopted kin, creole slaves in particular must have acquired a certain psychic and emotional satisfaction. In conversation with these newcomers, they could 'revive and retrace the remembrance and ideas of past pleasures and scenes of their youth' and reinforce their bonds with Africa. Adoption of new Africans would hence have been an important element in cultural continuity in slave society.

Long recorded slaves as having 'a strong attachment' to ancestors, kin and lineage which was interconnected by 'the bond of fatherly love on one side and filial obedience on the other'. Family and kin supported the individual slave against the vagaries of plantation life. When, for instance, 'Monk' Lewis tried to demote a skilled slave to the rank of common field hand as a result of a misdemeanour, he received supplications from the man's wife, then his mother, and finally 'his cousin's cousin'.

Respect for parents and veneration for the aged is strong evidence for the importance of kinship links in slave society. According to Dallas, 'Ta Quaco' and 'Ma Quasheba' (my 'father', my 'mother'), were widely used amongst Jamaican slaves to denote filial reverence and fondness. Old men and old women were cared for by the wider community in accordance with 'the universal phenomenon with which old age is treated by the African race'. As in Africa, grandparents played a highly important role in the socialising of slave children, tempering the necessary strictness of slave parents. In slave society a communal approach to the care of children existed, in which elderly slaves in general were involved.

'Warmth and dutiful sentiment' marked relationships between kin to such a degree that William Beckford could write of the slaves in Jamaica:

> they are in general attached to their families . . . the young will work with cheerfulness to maintain the weak and . . . they are much disposed to pay age respect and veneration.[17]

Slaves were also observed to be generally affectionate towards their 'friends, kindred and offspring' and this warmth of feeling for each other was diffused throughout the whole community. The existence of such a strong feeling for kin in slave society belies the negative viewpoint that slave family life was disorganised and lacking strong emotional bonds. Moreover, the fact that parents and grandparents of both sexes had an important role in family and community life constitutes additional evidence against the oversimplified model of the slave family as an isolated unit consisting solely of mother and children.

Contemporary descriptions of slave villages, the focal point of slave communities, in addition to furnishing further evidence relating to the strength of family ties, place kinship links firmly in the context of the slave community as a whole. With respect to their houses and yards, Edwards observed that slaves had a good deal of autonomy and built them 'according to their own fancy' both in size and shape. (There were generally few laws on slave housing.) Descriptions of slave houses correspond quite closely to those of houses in West Africa. In general, contemporary observers noted that they were detached and between 15 and 20 feet in length, oblong in shape and divided into a minimum of two compartments, although the number of rooms varied 'in consequence of the inhabitant' and tradesmen and domestics were reputed to have had larger houses with better furniture. They were generally 'for a man and wife'.

Slave villages were reported to have a 'picturesque appearance' and both Dallas and Edwards alleged that slave houses surpassed those of British peasants 'in structure and comfort'. Such glowing testimonies must be treated cautiously. Slave houses were built mainly on the wattle and daub principle and were thus constructed primarily of wood and mud with cane or grass roofs. They were 'poky and dark', prone to catch fire, and susceptible to hurricanes and rain. Sanitation was poor and houses contained on average three to six slaves (which *might* have compared favourably with the wretched cellar dwellers of Manchester in the first half of the nineteenth century). Yet when planters took more interest in slave housing after 1820 and tried to introduce more planned housing in rows or barracks there is evidence that, in Jamaica at least, slaves objected on the grounds of reduced privacy and loss of yard space.

Slaves were attached to the idea of their own home and, according to Higman, were expected to be housed from puberty onwards. Some individuals thus lodged with others and paid rent in labour on the family provision grounds, for instance. In retaining privacy from whites in their own village, plantation slaves had the edge over domestics, who were often accommodated in rooms attached to the great house. Unfortunately little tangible evidence of slave housing remains today. Barrack-type housing may still be seen in some parts of Trinidad, for instance, but it was built after emancipation to house indentured labourers from the Indian sub-continent. New archaeological investigations now under way may cast fresh light on this aspect of slave life (Higman, 1984).

Whether the basic structure of the individual slave family was polygynous, nuclear or extended, the house and its important extension, the yard, were fundamental to the general integration and cohesion of the slave community. Barry Higman, in his research into the slave family in Jamaica, Trinidad and Barbados, discovered that extended or polygynous households were often based on a series of contiguous units built around a yard and enclosed by a fence. The individual units were occupied by mothers and children in the case of polygynous households and by nuclear units in the case of extended family households, an arrangement which is common in West African societies (Higman, 1975).

The yard became the focal point of family activity, an indication of the strength of kinship ties amongst slaves. The common property of the extended family, it would have been used for many purposes – as a burial ground, for gossip, fighting, dancing and cooking. Together with the family provision ground, it was a symbol of family unity and continuity. In West Indian communities this fierce attachment to family land has survived even to the present day and, in some areas, vestigial communal yards still exist (Wilson, 1973). Household patterns in slave communities also reflected the importance of community ties. The building of individual houses was often a communal concern, as it was in West African society. Mrs Carmichael noted that upon marriage every man had a house to live in with his family and house-building and the feast which occurred on a girl's first mating was maybe the only ceremony involved in slave marriages (Smith, 1953). Given the significance of material continuity to family and community bonding, it is hardly surprising that slaves were 'greatly attached' to their houses and provision grounds and both were passed on from parents to children. Patterson has argued that liberal laws on this private property (peculium) of slaves acted as a mechanism of social control for planters, preventing more widespread unrest (Patterson, 1982).

Family and kin were perhaps the most vital element in the life of an individual slave and the basic social framework of the slave community. On a more pragmatic level, as noted in Chapter 4, the family, including young children, were an indispensable asset to the cultivation of provision grounds. But, more importantly, perhaps, the development of strong intra- and inter-familial relationships amongst slaves helped to shield the individual slave against the alienation and degradation inherent in the slave system. As Terrence des Pres (1976) has pointed out, survival with dignity in adverse situations depends on solidarity and communal action. The extended family in slave society ensured the common concern for fellow bondsmen crucial to survival. In their leisure time slaves displayed this emotional and physical solidarity. 'No people can have more esteem or have a greater friendship for one another than the negro slaves,' observed John Stedman; 'they appear to have an unbounded joy in each other's company.' He was also impressed at the way in which slaves freely shared whatever they had with each other, were 'generous and faithful', and possessed 'so much friendship for one another' that they never needed to be told to 'love their neighbour as themselves' as did many Europeans.

Such was the degree of this community feeling that slaves spent most of their free time with family, kin and friends. Cooking, which invariably took place in the open, was a focal point. Mrs Carmichael wrote that, after work, slaves sat outside their doors in the fine nights of a tropical climate cooking and eating their suppers, telling stories and singing songs. William Beckford made a similar observation. The attitudes of slaves to marriage, children and kin and the strength of their community ties belie the belief that their fundamental societal organisation was weak and disorganised. On the contrary, slaves, far from lacking social or moral order, adhered to a strong code of communal behaviour, cherished family links and preserved these wherever possible. But the slave regime consistently undermined these determined attempts to create a viable family life. Thus negative forces – slave sales and separation, conditions on large-scale plantations, and the predatory sexuality of white men – must also be considered in exploring the private domestic life of women slaves.

Slave sales and enforced separation

Planters were obviously aware of the significance of the slave family and household but often showed little respect for emotional bonds between individual slaves and their immediate and extended families. The threat of the abrogation of kinship ties was constant. From the earliest days of slavery, indiscriminate sales and separation severely disrupted the domestic life of individual slaves. During the late period of slavery, especially, a large proportion of estates were mortgaged and hence frequently sold off with 'stock' to pay outstanding debts. Bryan Edwards severely criticised this practice, arguing that it was bad for men to be torn from wives and children and the 'creation of their own industry', their provision grounds; slaves were attached to the land and should be sold with it.

Some planters were sensitive to the miseries and indignities of the public slave auction. William Beckford wanted sales to be held in private and families to be sold together or kept as near as possible in the same neighbourhood. Although laws were passed in the late period of slavery to prevent the breakup of slave families by sale, as has been stressed in Chapter 3, these laws were frequently ignored and the indignities and miseries of public slave sales continued.

On their part, slaves frequently reacted strongly to enforced severance of their emotional bonds and many gave themselves up to 'sorrow and despair' as a result of separation from 'old attachments'. The Reverend Thomas Cooper, writing of Jamaica in 1820, described the separation of slaves from their loved ones as 'a grievous hardship' which produced at times 'a species of rebellion . . . known to occasion death . . . through the distress of mind it produces'. John Stewart, a less emotional observer, was also touched by the 'affecting scenes' at slave sales, when husbands and wives, mothers and children, clung to each other weeping and 'shrieking piteously'. He declared that, if slaves were forcibly separated from kin or friends, not infrequently the buyer had generally 'cause to regret his inhumanity', for his new purchases were often plunged into such despair that they either 'sank into utter despondency or put period to their lives'.

There is evidence to suggest that slave family relationships were maintained despite physical separation. Long alludes to slaves having 'family connexions' throughout Jamaica and runaway slave advertisements in contemporary Jamaican newspapers reveal the importance and strength of kinship ties amongst slaves which transcended physical separation (see Appendix). Close relatives who had been separated endeavoured to maintain their relationships, despite the hardships involved, using their well-earned rest after the day's labour for travelling. The Barbados Assembly reported to the 1789 enquiry into the slave trade that:

> both sexes are frequently travelling all night, going or returning from a distant connexion, in order, without sleep, to be in due time to go through a hard day's labour after their nocturnal adventures.[18]

Observations on night 'rambling' are recorded for other islands. This was linked to exogamy (marrying outside the community), which was particularly common in heavily populated islands or where there was a large creole population. This resulted in 'visiting unions' where no permanent co-residence was possible (Higman, 1984). In the French Caribbean, slave marriages outside the plantation were refused by masters and slaves were therefore unable to marry whom they chose. This also led to travel to partners off the plantation. Indeed, so strong were bonds between couples that they sometimes ran away together. Edward Brathwaite discovered that the runaways from Jamaica plantations during the period from 1770 to 1830 included a fair number of husband and wife combinations (Brathwaite, 1971).

Slave women, in particular, strongly resisted separation from their children. When a mulatto carpenter at Lewis's estate agreed to purchase a girl from a neighbouring property to obtain his own freedom, the girl's owner refused to sell her child also. The girl promptly disappeared in response to this threat of separation from her infant and was believed to have committed suicide. Only when her owner agreed to sell both herself *and* her child did she agree to return to the estate. John Riland recalled how a recently purchased slave woman on his father's estate became 'desperate with grief' and was a 'most troublesome woman' until his father agreed to purchase her son also.

On a less dramatic level, slave mothers often resisted attempts on the part of the planters to separate them from their infants at too early an age. As in West Africa, female slaves suckled their children for at least two years, during which time the child, wherever possible, was with its mother almost continuously. Mrs Carmichael noted that slave infants were never weaned before they were fifteen or sixteen months and 'rarely so early': they were 'great robust children' and followed their mothers 'all over the estate'. This practice, however, did not always fit into the smooth running of the estate. Owners could not extract the maximum amount of labour from a nursing mother and extended suckling was therefore viewed as merely another form of malingering.

To reduce this suckling period Jamaican planters sought to place infants in 'weaning houses' out of the direct care of their mothers. 'Monk' Lewis, though in favour of this innovation, was none the less forced to comment upon the resistance it elicited from slave mothers. He recalled, for instance, a visit from the attorney of a neighbouring plantation who was accosted by a group of his female slaves complaining that the overseer had demanded that they should wean their children too young. According to Lewis, the reason for their obstinacy in this matter was that they wished 'to retain the leisure and other indulgences annexed to the condition of nursing mothers'. But it is doubtful if this reason alone would have produced such a strong reaction in the women, for when their demands were rejected they went home in 'high discontent', one of them declaring aloud 'with a peculiar emphasis' that, if her child was put in the weaning house against her will, the attorney would 'see it dead' in less than a week.

Despite the planters' callous indifference towards family and kinship ties, there is evidence to suggest that slaves resisted enforced separation from their kin and strove to preserve precious interpersonal bonds under the most adverse circumstances. In the case of women slaves, in their objections to early weaning, they not only were resisting enforced separation, but also preventing the erosion of traditional African-derived practices of childrearing which were part of their cultural heritage. These will be discussed more fully in the following chapter.

'Hot constitution'd ladies': black women, power and sexuality

Despite a tenacious retention of their own marriage forms, slaves could seldom claim respectability or legitimacy for their marriage or their children in the eyes of Europeans, a factor which had important implications for the woman slave. In conjunction with existing sexual stereotypes, the denigration of, and lack of respect for, slave marriages and codes of morality provided white men with a suitable rationale for the sexual exploitation of black women. Slave women did not deserve the 'reputation for lewdness' or 'hot constitutions' which they acquired. Unfortunately, white propaganda in this direction was extremely pervasive. The sexual subordination of slave women represented a natural extension of the general power of white over black, the sex act itself becoming, in Winthrop Jordan's (1968) words, 'a ritualistic re-enactment of the daily pattern of social dominance'. Not surprisingly, perhaps, overseers and black drivers in positions of power and authority sometimes abused their privilege by taking sexual advantage of black women. Arlette Gautier has also suggested that the excess of men over women in the earlier period of slavery up to the end of the eighteenth century may have increased the risk of sexual violence to women from black men in general, a consequence of loneliness and sexual frustration. 'The appropriation of women's sexuality', she argues, 'redoubled women's exploitation as workers.' Male slaves could at least take refuge in the 'fantasies of their sexual power' (Gautier, 1983). But, although exploitation existed, such power over women was not monolithic and operated at a number of levels, not always with negative consequences.

For the French historian Michel Foucault, sexuality constitutes a 'particularly dense transfer point for relations of power', allowing for many varied strategies and proving highly effective in determining the more generalised social and power relations in society. Power is diffuse and comes from below in 'manifold relationships of force in play in the machinery of economic production, families and institutions'. Because this power network forms a 'dense web' which passes through official institutions without being exactly localised in them, there are innumerable, diverse points of resistance which may even involve a temporary inversion of power relations. Such inversion was evident, for instance, in the power white women held over black men, whom they could punish at will. Black women, too, despite their racial and sexual inferiority, could at times manipulate white men to their own advantage.

The ambivalent relationship between black women and white men in terms of power and resistance may be partly explained by Foucault's assertion that sexual power is not purely repressive. For white men, black women were 'forbidden fruit'; sexual relations between black and white could create 'perpetual spirals of power and pleasure' from which white women were excluded. These labyrinths of sexual power served as a basis not only for social control but also for social development (Foucault, 1977, 1978–9).

Black concubinage was regarded as an integral part of plantation life, inextricably woven into the social fabric. Undoubtedly, the scarcity of white women in contrast to the availability of black women contributed to this situation. Long estimates that by the mid-eighteenth century there were only 9 whites to 100 blacks and Dunn's figures show that, despite the balancing of the sexes in the late seventeenth century, by Long's time, white women were at a premium. This was the reason, according to Long, why 'such a number' of young widows, created by the 'intemperance and sensuality' of their husbands, were 'snapped up' when barely out of the widow's weeds. This lack of white women cannot be cited, however, as the sole reason for black concubinage, as this also occurred on a wide scale in the Southern USA where a stable white family structure and an even balance of white men and women existed.

Whilst white men sought their bodily pleasures with black and coloured women, as Atwood testified, by the mid-eighteenth century, sexual relations between black men and white women were strictly proscribed by custom if not by law. Thomas Atwood wrote that white women in the West Indies were 'very strong' on conjugal fidelity, unlike in Europe where it was 'common' for women 'to form connexions with negro men', an arrangement which, was 'very odious' in the eyes of creole women. As Stedman cynically commented, although she had to tolerate her menfolk's blatant peccadilloes, 'should it be known that any European female had an intercourse with a slave of any denomination', the woman is 'forever detested and the slave loses his life without mercy – such are the despotic laws of men over the weaker sex'. This 'peculiar application of the double standard', to quote Kenneth Stampp, was arguably an extension of the moral precepts, based on class/gender distinctions, applied by middle- and upper-class men in contemporary European society, reinforced by the racial element. Indeed obsession with black male sexual potency has been a powerful ingredient of European racism since early times, reinforced by imperialist domination (Rogers, 1944).

In European society, 'respectable' women were demarcated from lower-class 'wenches', who were the prime illicit sexual targets for middle- and upper-class men. In the West Indies, this situation was further distorted by the racial hegemony of white over black. Lower-class men in the islands also had access to women of an inferior class (black women) for illicit sex, while all white women, regardless of class origins, were elevated to a superior 'respectable' status. White men utilised the alleged moral inferiority of black women to firmly establish them in the role of the 'other woman'. Few men, with the exception perhaps of John Stedman and 'Monk' Lewis, openly admitted their attraction to black women.

Of the white male population, the major slave owners were the most wealthy and powerful. However, this group of men was the most distant from the slave population, particularly in the later absentee phase, and their power was mediated through overseers who frequently abused their privilege by taking sexual advantage of black women. According to Higman's data, between 1807 and 1832, transient single white men on absentee plantations fathered large numbers of slave children, particularly on large estates. In Jamaica, for instance, the proportion of coloured births reached a peak in units of between 300 and 400 slaves (Higman, 1984). Because of the high black-to-white ratio and the 'get rich quick' mentality of white men, from the earliest days, white society in the Caribbean was never as 'settled' as that in the Southern USA. Most Europeans believed they were only in the West Indies for a few years to make their fortune, and thus saw matrimony as a 'bar to their expectations'. In the case of the poorer white men marriage was frequently proscribed in their contracts. An influx of these poor but adventurous young men, from Scotland in particular, accompanied the parallel influx of African slaves during the eighteenth century. Some of these more menial whites were described by Long as 'the very dregs of the three kingdoms', who 'had many vices' and were 'heartily despised by the better sort of slave'. It was this section of Caribbean society which planters blamed for the degree of black concubinage and abolitionists for the corruption of the morals of black women, a reflection of middle-class values and their hypocritical application. Although lower-class men thus became the moral scapegoats, in reality, men of all classes, married or unmarried, engaged in sexual liaisons with black women, determining the moral climate of plantation society. The main difference between classes of white men was that richer whites could afford to keep mulatto mistresses and select from the free coloured as well as the slave population.

In their sexual behaviour, white men undoubtedly exhibited a callous disrespect for the marriage bond amongst slaves. Aware of this, Lewis, when he drew up a 'new code of laws' for his estate in Jamaica, ruled that:

> any white person, who can be proved to have had an improper connexion with a woman known publicly to be living as the wife of one of my negroes, is to be discharged immediately.[19]

In Barbados, with the highest white population, many planters tried to prohibit 'improper inte010urse' between white employees and slaves but, generally speaking, unlike in the American slave states or the French Caribbean, few anti-miscegenation* laws were devised until the later period when attempts were made to prevent the worst aspects of sexual abuse of slave women, especially married women. There is little indication, however, that this influenced the behaviour of white men.

Slave men and women reacted strongly to this disregard for their marital bonds and the sexual hegemony of white men. John Stedman wrote:

> but what is peculiarly provoking [to the slaves] is that if a negro and his wife have ever so great an attachment for each other, the woman, if handsome, must yield to the loathsome embrace of an adulterous and licentious manager, or see her husband cut to pieces for endeavouring to prevent it. This in frequent instances has driven them to distraction and been the cause of many murders.[20]

Given the strong marital and family ties in slave communities, sexual violation of slave women *must* have provoked acts of resistance. However, evidence of resistance of slave women to the sexual advances of white men is scarce, though this does not constitute proof that it did not exist. Joanna, John Stedman's mulatto mistress, fiercely reacted to the unwarranted sexual advances of one of his fellow soldiers who 'offered her violence' and received 'the marks of her just resentment on his face'. John Jeremie, who was First President (Chief Justice) of the Royal Court of St Lucia between 1825 and 1831, intimated at one possible reason why the manner in which slave women reacted to the sexual abuses of white men remains largely unrecorded. Angered by the mockery made of justice by white men, Jeremie cited a case reported to him from Jamaica of 'a small plantation owner' who tried to seduce 'from the path of virtue' the natural child of his own father. The girl refused to comply and was placed in the stocks. The man 'renewed his entreaties', which produced no other effect than to induce her to 'more strenuously resist'. Finally, she was 'unmercifully flogged'. After release

*Sexual relations between different races.

from confinement, she complained to the magistrate and her story was authenticated; the man, though guilty, went unpunished. The girl's evidence was subsequently removed from the printed minutes of the Jamaican Assembly, possibly because it reflected upon the morals of white society and had to be 'expunged' for propriety's sake. Censorship of this nature may explain the absence of evidence relating to resistance on the part of slave women to the unwarranted sexual advances of white men. Slave narratives and documents from the American South certainly indicate that black women resisted the advances of white men.

If slave women did try to protect their sexual integrity and resist white men they risked physical cruelty and beatings. In contrast, 'favoured' slave women who accepted liaisons with whites were targets of the jealousy and sexual animosity of white women and were sometimes forced to submit to punishment according to the caprice of an embittered wife. Summing up the precarious position of such women, Stedman wrote:

> I have seen the most cruel tortures inflicted for submitting to the desire of a husband, or for refusing the same to a libidinous master, and more frequently a rascally overseer: nay, even the most innocent, from the false accusations of a lustful [white] woman, prompted alone by jealousy.[21]

White women were themselves an oppressed group, facing competition from black women for the attentions of white men, a factor which arguably made them more brutal (Heuman, 1981). Within these complex sexual dynamics, there was also rivalry between black and white men. In the French Caribbean, black African female slaves who had relations with whites were also reputed to have a 'hidden yearning' ('un penchant invisible') for African men (Gautier, 1983). These ideas fed the myth of enhanced black male sexuality but also unwittingly testified to the strong bonds between African men and women. There appear to have been few instances of sexual relations between black men and white women, in contrast to the USA (a factor which J. A. Rogers (1944) attributes to the African's distaste for such sexual contact).

The sexual exploitation of black women in slave society was, and still is, a highly emotive topic around which cluster innumerable misconceptions and myths which militate against any objective appraisal of the intimate life of slaves. Abolitionist writers, such as Thomas Cooper, reflecting their own sexual prudery, talked in terms of the 'general profligacy' in evidence on plantations, arguing that slave women became mere 'instruments of gratification' at an early age. Basing their conclusions on dubious contemporary accounts, some modern authors have condemned all concubinage as callous sexual exploitation of black women, characterised by rape, seduction and 'heinous forms of sexual torture'. Such scenarios seem more appropriate to a steamy novel which exploits inter-racial sex taboos. A more balanced appraisal of the *modus vivendi* of both black and white reveals a subtle and complex framework of sexual relations. Although without doubt sexual exploitation did exist, many white men from all social ranks had fond and enduring relations with black and coloured women. If higher-ranking men had their coloured mistresses, as Maria Nugent noted, in Jamaica, no 'vulgar Scotch Sultan' or lowly overseer was without his black 'chère amie'. John Stedman's unceasing devotion to his mulatto mistress, Joanna, is a particularly striking example of such relationships. He married Joanna and, although she refused to return to Holland with him, he secured the freedom of their son who was brought up as his legal heir. After many unsuccessful attempts he also succeeded in buying Joanna her freedom.

Wealthier white men often bequeathed their estates to black or coloured 'wives' and their offspring or made provisions for manumission in their wills. Despite the harsh, unequal and callous nature of slave society, close, loving bonds between black and white did exist and the degree of money and property left by whites to mulattoes was a cause for concern and controversy in plantocratic circles. According to Edward Long, upon enquiry in 1762 into recent wills made out to mulatto children, the Jamaican Assembly noted the value to be between two and three thousand pounds and included 'four sugar estates, seven pennes, thirteen houses and other unspecified lands'. After 'duly weighing the ill-consequences that might befall the colony' as a result of such wills, a law was passed 'to prevent the inconveniences arising from exorbitant grants and to restrain and limit such grants and devises'. The law therefore declared void any such sum over £2000. Long adds, though, that many people objected 'with great warmth' to this law, declaring it 'oppressive', depriving men of the right to dispose of their own possessions in a manner 'most agreeable to their inclinations'.

Long himself was strongly convinced that it would be better for Britain and Jamaica if white men in the colony would abate of their infatuated attachments to black women and perform the 'duty incumbent on every good citizen by raising in honourable wedlock a race of unadulterated beings' but no abatement was apparent. White men remained 'infatuated', particularly with lighter-skinned coloured women. This preference was rewarded by the great 'attachment and devotedness' of coloured women to the white men who chose them as 'companions' or 'housekeepers'.

In view of the prevailing attitudes to inter-racial sex, it is hardly surprising that slave women were often portrayed in contemporary literature as scarlet temptresses, willing, even desiring, relationships with white men and vying with each other for the latter's favours. The abolitionist James Ramsay castigated 'that legion of harlots and their children, with which the plantation abounds', adding that, when a female slave had become the 'new object' of a white man's attachment, she immediately became the target of envy of 'those that have gone before her' and would be lucky if she did not have to pay with her life 'the forfeit of her attentions'. Slave women were accused of being scheming and mercenary. Thomas Atwood decried the fact that white men appeared content with negro or mulatto mistresses, producing a 'spurious race of children' whose maintenance, together with 'the extravagance of their sable mothers', dissipated the men's savings. Long accused higher-status men, 'indolent and inactive', of being almost entirely 'under the dominion' of their mulatto favourites. Atwood felt that this state of affairs contributed towards a 'great aversion to matrimonial connexions', which 'impeded' colonisation.

This popular image of the 'easy' black slave woman contrasts unfavourably with descriptions of free coloured women who entered into liaisons with wealthier white men. Both Lewis and Maria Nugent commented that the favours of the mulatto women were 'extremely difficult' to obtain and many of them held respected positions as 'housekeepers' or cherished mistresses. Prolonged unions with whites led to a rise in status for coloured women, slave and free, and could help a small minority to establish themselves more firmly in the mainstream of Caribbean society. One such woman, Rachael Pringle Polgreen, built up a lucrative tavern business in Barbados by means of securing two white protectors and benefactors, Pringle and Polgreen. On her death her will revealed that the social relations to which she attached most attention were to whites to whom she left most of her money. In view of her position in creole society she was paid the homage of being called 'Miss Rachael', a title rarely given to coloured women (Handler, 1981).

In the social cauldron of the Caribbean, some coloureds, particularly free coloureds, would have transferred their cultural allegiances to white society, distancing themselves from blacks. Similarly, a minority of slave women would have voluntarily, even eagerly, entered into relationships with white men. Some writers, Orlando Patterson, for instance, have even suggested that some creole women would save themselves for whites, avoiding having children in order not to lose their figures (Patterson, 1969). However, as Long notes, such women often risked isolation from the rest of the black community, and, given the importance of family and community ties, this raises the question as to their motives. Long blamed the devious wiles of black mistresses, ambitious for themselves and their relatives, for the heartless exploitation of their protectors. Berating one such woman, he writes:

> All her kindred and most commonly her very paramours are fastened upon her keeper like so many leeches, while she, the chief leech, conspires to bleed him [the white man] *usque ad deliquium* . . . the quintessence of her dexterity consists in persuading the man she detests to believe she is most violently smitten with the beauty of his person.[22]

Thus, her 'seeming affection' was cunningly used for her own material benefit and she frequently stole from her 'trusting' master. Similarly, in the French Caribbean, black 'coquines' were blamed for seducing white men and ruining their purses. As Arlette Gautier notes, the powerful have always blamed the oppressed for their weaknesses (Gautier, 1983).

This image of the conniving black woman conforms perfectly to the popular notion that blacks were lying, deceitful and immoral. Looked at from another perspective it is also an example of how the individual black woman, by outwardly conforming to the sexual demands of the white man, could exploit the situation to the fullest and thus covertly help her own family and kin. It is difficult to believe, for instance, that the black 'chère amie' with whom Maria Nugent conversed on her travels was truly enamoured of the 'vulgar, ugly Scotch Sultan' of an overseer whom the diarist described in such scathing tones, but it is possible that she felt that her 'three yellow children' would have a better chance in the world than those of her fellow slaves. Mulattos did indeed have a greater opportunity of upward mobility than did black slaves. Although having a white parent was no guarantee of manumission, it certainly helped. Higman's data from the late period of slavery indicate that manumitted slaves were concentrated in small-holdings and towns and tended to be female, creole, young and coloured, predominantly working as domestics – precisely the type of female slave most likely to enter into a long-term liaison with whites. Indeed, females in the sugar colonies were generally twice as likely to be manumitted than males before 1820 and were commonly manumitted through sexual relations with whites or freedmen (Higman, 1984). The only other way women could attain freedom was through accumulating cash from higgling and selling or through being bought out of bondage by freed children (also more likely if their father was white). A similar pattern of manumission existed in the French Caribbean. Manumission had its benefits but it also placed women in a contradictory position between black and white society.

The sexual exploitation of slave women has been viewed by historians like Richard Dunn (1977) as one of the major impediments to stable family life on the plantation. But, as was shown in the preceding section, slaves maintained strong marital and family bonds *despite* such impediments. Thus, although all women were sexually at risk, the number of slave women involved in sexual relationships with whites most likely was limited to a small percentage of the total population of slave women. Exploitation undoubtedly occurred but the worst forms of this, particularly casual sexual encounters, probably provoked strong resentment and open resistance on the part of slaves of both sexes. Where slave women did enter into long-term unions with whites they may have been exhibiting a form of what Genovese (1944) has termed 'resistance within accommodation' or, in Terrence des Pres's (1976) words, 'the duality of behaviour' essential to survival in any unnatural and extreme situation, including slavery. The heterogeneity of modern Caribbean populations testifies to the fact that sexual intermixing between black and white occurred during slavery (although later influxes of population – East Asian and Chinese – and post-slavery social conditions are important here). Yet there are also incidences where exclusivity has been maintained, as for instance in Bequia in the Grenadines where poor blacks and whites live next to each other but are separate to the extent that there are obvious signs of inbreeding.

Undoubtedly, a small minority of black women may have entered into unions with, or sold sexual favours to, white men to no other end than pure self-interest and material gain. Such individual decisions were understandable, given the opportunities for manumission. But their behaviour would have been at odds with the communal sentiment and well-defined codes of behaviour which existed in the slave community. In many inter-racial unions, however, an element of genuine mutual affection existed and they were often long-lasting and stable. Given the potential for social and sexual chaos ever-present in slave society, it is indeed a tribute to slave women that, even in their relations with white men, they, in general, did *not* succumb to promiscuity and immorality. Subjected to many indignities and hardships, they were still able to make a valuable contribution to the stability and survival of the slave family and wider community in a situation where, in Winthrop Jordan's (1968) words, anything *but* promiscuity represented tenacious cultural conservation, or, more significantly in the long run, a triumph of cultural adaptivity.

Summary

Every aspect of the Caribbean slave regime worked against the stability of the slave family. Yet, although the production of sugar on large-scale planta- tions undoubtedly caused some family disorganisation, Higman's evidence suggests that elaborated or extended families were most common on large plantations where the availability of potential mates was greatest. Women and children units accounted for a smaller proportion of slaves living on sugar estates than on other plantations, and slaves attached to large holdings suffered separation by sale or transfer less often than those on other estates. Generally, the proportion of matrifocal families declined steadily with increased holding size and the proportion of nuclear families rose. The African-born slaves were more likely to be in nuclear families than creoles. Types of families other than matrifocal and nuclear accounted for much smaller numbers of slaves, but extended and polygynous units as well as families of more than two generations were more common among urban rather than rural populations. Higman concludes:

> There is no doubt that the slave system disorganised patterns of family and kinship organisation, particularly through its narrow emphasis on the mother–child link, the separation of kin by sale and transfer, the large scale restriction of residential mobility and the authoritarian role of the master and overseer, most obviously symbolised by sexual intervention. At the same time there is evidence of strong family bonds within the slave community of parent–child affection and of subtle variations of family patterns having their origin in Africa. (Higman, 1984)

This discussion of the domestic life of the woman slave has confirmed Higman's comments. It has emphasised that no environment, no matter how appalling the quality of life, can destroy family and community bonds. Where kin was absent, bonds were formed with shipmates or people from the same tribe, and a sense of community developed, based on a well-defined code of morality and order; slaves did not become promiscuous or exist only in a chaotic and unstable social environment. Wherever possible they recreated a meaningful family life based largely on their African cultural heritage. It was the existence of this stable family life which gave the individ- ual slave, as well as the slave community as a whole, the strength and will to endure and survive the experience of slavery. And, because of the traditional importance of the African woman to family bonding and stability, the woman slave played a crucial and indispensable part in the creation and defence of these precious family and community values.

Further reading

Ariès (1962)
Bush (1981)
Craton (1982)
Cutrufelli (1983)
Genovese (1974)
Gutman (1976)
Heuman (1981)
Higman (1976; 1984)
Jones (1985)
Laslett (1971)
Laslett and Wall, eds (1972)
Radcliffe-Brown and Forde, eds (1956)
Sabeen (1983)

7

Slave Motherhood

Childbirth and Infant Death in a Cross-Cultural Perspective

> It has been a matter of surprise to some, that the Negroes in our colonies do not increase in that natural proportion which is observed among mankind in other countries, and to a remarkable degree among the Blacks in Africa.[1]

With the ending of the slave trade in 1807, the failure of the slave population to reproduce itself became of paramount importance to West Indian planters. 'The old Africans are daily wearing out,' remarked Thomas Roughly; 'our duty is to support the present stock.'[2] In the contemporary arena of opinion, solutions to this crucial problem hinged largely upon improving the treatment of pregnant women and eradicating 'undesirable' African cultural practices. The slaves' 'propensity to vice and cabalistic or obea arts' was also believed by the planters to hinder significantly the 'healthy propagation' of their property. Thus, as a solution to the problem of low fertility, they advocated an improvement in the moral timbre of the slave community, better living conditions, conversion to Christianity and 'creolisation', that is Europeanisation, of the slaves. 'Intelligent creole mothers' were reputed to bear more children and care for them better than their African sisters.

In the last decade, modern historians have concerned themselves increasingly with the low rate of natural increase of West Indian slave populations. During all periods of slavery, in most slave-owning areas of the British Caribbean, the fundamental factor affecting the slaves' ability to reproduce themselves was the low fertility rate of slave women. Planters were very much preoccupied with this low birth rate and it has recently proved an interesting dilemma for modern historians. As yet, however, no satisfactory explanation for this demographic anomaly has been agreed upon. Recently compiled statistical data have furnished historians with important new evidence and given the study of slave fertility a sound empirical basis. Unfortunately, modern academic discussions on what has become essentially a statistical problem render the woman an anonymous object, often to a greater degree than contemporary accounts. The individual slave woman's own attitudes to childbearing, the control she retained over her own reproductive potential, have seldomly been taken into account.

For the woman slave to emerge from the historical obscurity to which she has been condemned, the whole question of childbearing in slave communities must be looked at afresh, from the inside, from the slave woman's viewpoint, rather than the analytical stance of the historical demographers. Existing reasons put forward in explanation of the low fertility of women slaves need to be critically re-examined. The possibility that abortion and contraceptive techniques, even infanticide, were practised in slave society (a possibility to which, as yet, little serious thought has been given) needs to be explored in far greater depth. The crucial question is how much control the individual slave woman exercised over her own body and what impact her attitudes to childbearing had on the fertility rate of slave communities in the British West Indies. Thus this chapter will focus on a critical examination of contemporary and modern explanations of low fertility, the slave woman's experience of childbirth, arguments for abortion and infanticide, and the positive interventions in reproductive processes by slave women as mothers and midwives. This does not demand a detailed debate with quantitative historians but a closer examination of the complex relationship between cultural resistance and material conditions as they affected slave women's attitudes to childbirth. As Higman notes, variations in levels of slave fertility were determined not only by work regimes but also the cultural forms of slaves and attempts of masters and missionaries to alter those forms (Higman, 1984).

Patterns of slave reproduction: contemporary explanations re-examined

Sir Hans Sloane wrote of the female slaves he encountered on his travels through the West Indies in the early years of the eighteenth century: 'They are fruitful and go after the birth of their children to work in the fields, with their little ones tied to their Backs.' Apart from this brief image of fecundity, a low rate of natural increase appears to have existed from the early days of slavery and was not restricted to the later 'absentee' phase. In discussing the financial details of plantation management, for instance, Richard Ligon observed that 'though we breed both Negroes, Horses and Cattle, yet that increase will not supply the moderate decayes which we find in all those'.

As slavery intensified, plantation conditions deteriorated. The threat of the abolition of the slave trade forced planters to realise that, without the continuous replenishment from Africa, the numbers of their slaves would soon seriously decline. This would drastically affect the profitability of their estates. Leading questions such as 'how many children were born to negro slaves' were put to representatives of island assemblies by the Lords of Trade enquiry into the slave trade in 1789. The consensus of opinion among planters was gloomy. The Barbados Committee replied that births were not so frequent among the negroes as among the peasantry of Great Britain and not so many children were born to slaves 'as might be reasonably expected in proportion to the number of male and female'. The Jamaican planters replied in a similar vein.

Planter anxiety over the disastrous consequences which the ending of the slave trade would have on slave numbers was not empty scaremongering. Bryan Edwards estimated that in 1794 the 'present Annual Decrease' of negroes in the British West Indies was $2\frac{1}{2}$ per cent. In Surinam, where conditions were equally harsh, Stedman noted there was also an 'excess' of deaths over births 'tho' each man negro has a wife or two if he chuses'. French planters exhibited a similar panic over slave numbers. In most of the sugar islands, the heavy influx of new slaves was quickly counteracted by the extremely high mortality rate of 'salt water' negroes* during the 'seasoning period'. The low fertility rate of women slaves failed to compensate for this loss and is now generally recognised as the prime reason why West Indian slave populations did not naturally reproduce themselves. Other contributory reasons commonly put forward by contemporary observers were the adverse sex ratio amongst slaves, unstable mating patterns and (heavily related) the practice of 'polygamy' and promiscuity. The abolitionists favoured factors such as hard labour, poor living conditions and the maltreatment of pregnant women. To a minor degree, the adverse effects of African childbearing habits, such as the late weaning of infants, were also cited as influential in determining the childbearing potential of female slaves.

The existence of an adverse sex ratio on slave plantations was perhaps one of the most popular plantocratic rationales of low fertility. According to Bryan Edwards, male slaves were preferred to females and the sex ratio on some Jamaican plantations was purported to be as high as five men to every one female. This situation was blamed on the failure of the slave traders to balance their cargoes suitably. On 'unquestionable authority' Edwards was informed that 'only one third' were females. Long went even further, stating that 'of the slaves shipped from the [Guinea] Coast not a sixth part are women'. Edwards estimated that in 1789 there was an excess of 3000 males in Jamaica and concluded that the failure of the slaves to reproduce themselves resulted from this numerical imbalance between the sexes and not excessive harsh treatment on the part of the planters.

Plantocratic commentators, of course, were writing in defence of slavery and the slave trade when abolitionists were trying to prove these institutions cruel, inhuman and, quite simply, unnecessary. Thus the numerical imbalance between the sexes and the subsequent low rate of natural increase were emphasised for propaganda purposes to provide an adequate *raison d'être* for the continuation of the trade in human flesh upon which their

*Slaves newly arrived by boat from Africa.

profits depended. Modern quantitative analyses provide more realistic estimates. Michael Craton (1978) has calculated that towards the end of the eighteenth century, British slave cargoes contained a more realistic average of 60 per cent males and the high sex ratio of males to females alluded to by Long and Edwards is not reflected in the numerical analyses of individual plantations included in the evidence given to the 1789 enquiry into the slave trade (Table 1). If a high sex ratio had existed in the mid-eighteenth century, by the time the concern over the low rate of natural increase of slaves was voiced by planters it had probably balanced out.

Table 1   A numerical comparison of two Barbadian plantations in 1787
The gender breakdown indicates women's equal participation in work gangs, which suggests that their productive role was paramount to their reproductive role.

	Anno, 1787		Males	Females	Males and females	Total on both estates
First Class, including all ages from 20 to 97	Plantation K 1st Gang		78	80	158	222
	Plantation B 1st Gang		36	28	64	
Second Class from 13 to 19	Plantation K 2nd Gang		19	15	34	44
	Plantation B 2nd Gang		8	2	10	
Third Class, ages from 6–12	Plantation K 3rd Gang		10	16	26	31
	Plantation B 3rd Gang			5	5	
Fourth Class, ages from 2–5	Plantation K Playing children		6	12	18	26
	Plantation B Playing children		3	5	8	
Fifth Class, ages from under 2 years	Plantation K Plantation B	Sucking & weaning children	4 2	7 2	11 4	15
			166	172	338	338

Source: 'Report of the Lords of Trade into the Slave Trade', *British Parliamentary Papers*, Commons, vol. XXVI (1789), 646a, Part 111, Barbados, Ans. No. 3b.

Higman's extensive data for the period 1817–32 indicate that by this time there were actually more women than men (Higman, 1984). As Richard Dunn (1977) notes, planters may actually have continued to exaggerate the adverse sex ratio that undoubtedly existed in the first half of the eighteenth century (Galenson, 1986) to conceal the economic exploitation of women as field workers. There is thus insufficient evidence to link the low birth rate solely to the sex ratio on plantations. Both Ligon and Sloane noted that West Indian planters in the early period of slavery strove to maintain equal numbers between the sexes. Yet Ligon noted that, in Barbados at least, owners failed to replace the 'moderate decayes' of slaves except by reliance on fresh imports. On his own plantation, for instance, he maintains that there were 100 males to 100 females.

Planters believed the adverse sex ratio on plantations was further aggravated by the practice of 'polygamy' in the slave community. Contemporary myths and misconceptions about this African institution have already been explored in Chapters 2 and 6. 'Polygamy' and the promiscuity with which it became associated in the minds of planter and abolitionist alike were cited by contemporary writers as one of the principal causes of the low fertility rate of women slaves. The Jamaican Committee, giving evidence to the enquiry into the slave trade in 1789, reported that negroes committed 'such foul acts of sensuality and Intemperance' as to bring on 'the most foul distempers'. Women caught colds at 'nocturnal assemblies' and thus their 'natural periods' were obstructed. The Committee believed that the venereal disease resulting from this promiscuity 'did perhaps more to impede the natural increase of slaves than any other cause'.

To contemporary observers, the 'barbaric' mating patterns of slaves contributed significantly to the general lack of morality on the plantation. Simultaneously, women slaves were regarded as the instigators *and* the principal victims of this 'immorality', as it caused women to become barren. Thus women were 'rendered unprolific' by their own 'bad practices'. Furthermore, the medicines they took to rid themselves of the resultant 'venereal taint', in addition to inducing sterility, allegedly killed their unborn children. In fact, as Sheridan notes, African-derived herbal remedies were arguably less likely to kill than the mercury and arsenic-based preparations administered by frequently inexperienced European 'quack' doctors (Sheridan, 1985).

Venereal disease was frequently cited as a reason for the high incidence of sterility among women slaves. Planters believed it afflicted large numbers of slaves. Long felt that slaves would enjoy 'robust good health' if not 'prone to debauch' and hence venereal infection and the Jamaican Assembly testifying to the 1789 enquiry accused slaves of both sexes of 'studiously concealing' this disease as they considered 'abstaining from pleasure' during treatment as an 'intolerable punishment'. However, the planters' moral diatribes against venereal disease were a logical corollary to their belief in the natural promiscuity of Africans, a belief largely based on myth. The linkage made by planters between promiscuity and infertility echoed the ideas on population of the influential Reverend Thomas Malthus and the Christian morality which was effectively employed by the ascendant bourgeoisie in Europe to consolidate their power. To quote Malthus:

> Promiscuous intercourse, unnatural passions, violations of the marriage bed and improper arts to conceal the consequences of irregular connexions are preventative checks [on population] which come under the heading of vice.[3]

It is difficult to determine to what extent venereal disease, with its harmful effect on women's fertility, afflicted slaves. Contemporary medical opinion on the subject is contradictory. Sir Hans Sloane wrote that in the West Indies, 'Gonorrheas of all sorts amongst Men and Women are very common . . . especially in plantations amongst Negroes.' He believed that gonorrhea and 'pox' (syphilis) were transmitted in the same way and 'had the same symptoms and course amongst Europeans, Indians and Negroes'. Conversely, Thomas Dancer (1755?–1811), a versatile doctor–scientist practising in Jamaica at the end of the eighteenth century, believed (as did many of Sloane's contemporaries) that, in the West Indies, venereal disease took a much more benign form than it did in Europe and was hence more difficult to detect. Dancer observed that:

> Among Negroes, who are principally the subjects of it, [venereal disease] is sometimes latent for a long time before it is discovered . . . the disease being mild they linger under it, sometimes to old age, having families of children to whom they communicate the taint.[4]

Symptoms occurred in children 'before they can be possibly suspected of having got the disease by sexual intercourse' and induced pains, swelling of the bones, the collapse of the bridge of the nose and infected tonsils.

Such statements illustrate the confusion over definitions of diseases and diagnosis commonplace in the field of tropical medicine at this time. The symptoms cited by Dancer could relate to a wide range of diseases which afflicted slaves such as yaws, tuberculosis or even leprosy. Kiple notes that there was confusion over the diagnosis of syphilis and yaws in the Spanish islands and modern research has confirmed a cross-immunity between the two diseases. It was widely believed that syphilis was a 'white man's disease' and yaws a black disease. 'Pure' blacks were allegedly never stricken by syphilis and Kiple argues that this disease only became a problem for Caribbean blacks when yaws disappeared in the twentieth century. He also maintains that tuberculosis of the urinary tract was frequently diagnosed as gonorrhoea (Kiple, 1984). Certainly the alleged high incidence of death from venereal disease is not reflected in contemporary mortality lists. Sheridan's and Higman's data on mortality indicate that the death rate from venereal disease was much lower than that for yaws or TB (Sheridan, 1985; Higman, 1984).

The notion of promiscuity as the root cause of venereal disease was little more than a popular and highly tenacious myth. There is no firm evidence to support the planters' belief that the 'veneral taint' was of epidemic proportions in the slave community. In his study of slaves in the Southern

USA, Eugene Genovese argues along similar lines (Genovese, 1974). Slaves probably suffered no more and no less from venereal disease than did the inhabitants of any given European city in the eighteenth century. Yet at this time, although cities in Europe were allegedly rife with prostitution and 'immorality', the birth rate was booming. In this context, venereal disease as a major cause of infertility in slave women loses its validity.

In the light of evidence presented in the previous chapter most of the explanations for the low fertility of slave women based on the sexual habits of the slave have little credibility. Polygynous unions constituted only a minority of slave marriages and, although it would have resulted in an imbalance of sorts between the sexes, this would not have had a marked impact on birth rates. Discussing the customs of the peoples of the Guinea Coast, Edward Long declared that in West Africa 'Polygamy universally prevails and contributes greatly to populousness', thus contradicting his own views on the practice of this marriage form by Jamaican slaves.

In seeking a rationale for low fertility in slave behaviour, planters also criticised African-derived childbearing practices, particularly the late weaning of slave infants. More recent research by Klein and Engerman (1978) and Handler and Corrucini (1986) also suggests that lactation practices may explain fertility differentials between American and Caribbean slaves. Late weaning found among Caribbean slaves, absent in slave society in the Old South, was related to the two-year postnatal taboo on intercourse common to many African societies and, Klein and Engerman argue, may also have acted as limited contraceptive protection.

Contemporary evidence exists which both supports and queries these arguments. Slave women transported to Africa were already heavily immersed in their own cultural traditions and, in the West Indies, they most certainly continued African childrearing practices. John Stedman observed of women slaves in Surinam:

> In general, during the two years which they usually suckle [their infants], they never cohabit with their husbands; this is considered unnatural and prejudicial to the infants.[5]

The slaves continued this practice, however, because they believed that children died 'if born too close together'. This suggests it may have had a beneficial, not an adverse, effect on population increase. Long suckling did result in the wide spacing of births, but also effectively improved infant and maternal well-being in the absence of other adverse influences. Genovese (1974) and Gutman (1976) both cite evidence of prolonged nursing among nineteenth-century slave mothers in the American Old South where a healthy rate of natural increase existed.

Another argument against 'long suckling' explanations of low fertility is that the postnatal taboo on intercourse with which it is commonly associated does not exist in all West African societies. Daryl Forde observed that the Ashanti (from whom a large number of Jamaican slaves were descended) only prohibit intercourse for eighty days after delivery and children follow 'in rapid succession' (Forde, 1956). Moreover, this custom of prolonged lactation was not confined to African-born women and was also practised by creoles, thus, Kiple (1984) reasons, eliminating it as a factor to account for perceived differences in fertility between the two groups. Late weaning was arguably a strong area of cultural persistence and resistance to planter pro-natalist policies (Kiple suggests that there is evidence to show that it persisted in the Caribbean well into the twentieth century). Planters viewed it as another form of shamming and idling, for women were frequently accused of citing a multitude of 'female complaints' to avoid work. When weaning houses were introduced in Jamaica to cut down on extended suckling, women strongly resisted this early separation from their infants. For instance, the planter John Baillie failed to get a single mother during the period from 1808 to 1832 to accept the premium of two dollars which he offered women if they would wean their children in twelve months (Sheridan, 1985).

Women's reluctance to return to the plantation work regime and resistance to forcible separation from their infants were arguably a rational response to the problems associated with childbirth, including high infant mortality. Long suckling did undoubtedly result in wide birth spacing and, in the absence of adverse influences, can improve infant and maternal well-being but, as an explanation of low fertility, it is inadequate. As modern West African fertility rates remain very high despite long periods of breast feeding, restrictions on intercourse, high foetal and infant mortality and early sterility of women, Kiple (1984) argues we must seek other reasons. For him these are located in the high infant mortality and diet and disease patterns of Caribbean slavery, whilst Richard Dunn (1977), who also rejects the long suckling explanations, argues that 'eccentric' birth intervals are better explained by sexual abstinence, miscarriages and abortions, which suggests a more active role for slaves in determining fertility.

While planters blamed the slaves, in explaining low fertility abolitionists, predictably, indicted the regime of slavery itself. In their opinion the harsh working conditions and the cruel punishments to which women were daily subjected affected their physical constitution and were the cause of numerous gynaecological complaints. Certain planters were also aware of the correlation between ill-treatment of women slaves and low fertility. Evidence was presented to the parliamentary enquiry into the slave trade in 1789, to show that, as punishments were reduced and conditions on the plantation generally improved, birth rates rose correspondingly. The Barbados Committee cited one such example:

> On a plantation of 288 slaves in June 1780 . . . by the exertions of an able and honest manager, there were only fifteen births and no less than fifty-seven deaths in three years and three months. An alteration was made in the mode of governing the slaves; the whips were taken from all white servants and arbitrary punishments were abolished . . . in four years and three months . . . there were fourty-four births and only forty-one deaths.[6]

Contemporary observers noted that women whose tasks were lightest had more and healthier children than their less fortunate sisters. Long, for instance, agreed with the Barbados Committee that 'good management' was fundamental to improving slave fertility rates and commented:

> I will not deny that those Negroes breed best, whose labour is least or easiest. Thus the domestic Negroes have more children in proportion than those on the pennes; and the latter, than those who are employed on sugar plantations.[7]

Richard Sheridan (1985) agrees with Long here, arguing that respective figures for early nineteenth-century Jamaica indicate that coffee plantations and cattle ranches (pens), where better conditions prevailed, showed a reasonable rate of natural increase.

Abolitionist writers were particularly strong on the harmful effects of punishment. They stressed how a reduction in punishment resulted in a normal natural increase. John Jeremie, writing of St Lucia in the period after 1815, observed that as a result of the amelioration laws 'as births are increasing and deaths diminishing, so punishments have diminished by one half'. Jeremie had first-hand Caribbean experience, but all too frequently abolitionist statements were based not on fact, but sweeping generalisations designed for their propaganda impact. The equation between punishment and fertility was not always applicable. On 'Monk' Lewis's estate, for instance, all punishment was stopped but little improvement in the fertility rate of his female slaves ensued.

As the experience of paternalist planters like Lewis confirms, the correlation between harsh conditions and low fertility did not always apply. The Barbados Committee reporting to the 1789 enquiry into the slave trade admitted that, on most estates, there were some hard-working females 'who breed very fast' while many others who laboured less 'do not breed at all'. Higman has noted that in some cases field labourers had a higher fertility rate as they tended to be more concentrated in the childbearing ages. However, he concludes that occupational differentials in fertility were not really significant. Contrary to analyses both contemporary and modern which tend to focus on the low fertility on sugar plantations, Higman's data suggest that fertility was relatively high on large-scale sugar estates, almost the same as on cocoa estates, and exceeded rates for coffee and cotton (Higman, 1984).

The causes of low fertility are obviously more complex than would appear on superficial examination of evidence. As Higman concludes, harsh regimes on sugar plantations may have had a more direct impact on mortality patterns than fertility (death rates were much higher on large-scale plantations). Planters themselves believed that they had a greater capacity to manipulate mortality than fertility and there is no hard evidence for the conscious breeding of slaves (Lowenthal and Clarke, 1977). Black women in the Caribbean were always work units first and foremost, not breeding units. Because of the controversial nature of this historical demographic problem, there has been considerable interest over the past decade in statistical variables and conditions of health, hygiene and labour. Recently collated data indicate that women on sugar plantations generally arrived later at menarche (the onset of menstruation), had fewer children, more numerous miscarriages, a higher sterility rate and greater birth space, and completed childbearing earlier than women in comparative contemporary societies, including those based on slavery but affording better material conditions.

Pioneer works into the historical demography of slave society have indicated that some West Indian populations, such as that of Jamaica, were demographically atypical. Slave populations which showed normal demographic spreads tended to have healthy average birth rates. In his comparative study of the Rolle slaves of Exuma in the Bahamas and Worthy Park slaves in Jamaica, Michael Craton discovered a marked discrepancy in fertility rates. Exuma, with a normal population composition, showed a healthy natural increase; the fertility rates of Worthy Park slaves were abnormally low. In 1793, for instance, shortly after an influx of new African slaves, the slave population of Worthy Park was predominantly male with 156 men to 90 women in the 20–44 age range. The crude birth rate was under 20 per thousand. In contrast, no new slaves were purchased by the Rolle estate after 1783. A healthy balance of the sexes quickly developed and the birth rate became normal. 'My own work over the last few years', concludes Craton, 'has suggested the importance of the demographic balance of the sexes, ages and creole to African-born in achieving "natural increase" in slave populations' (Craton, 1978).

Craton's well-argued hypothesis, however, does not hold true for all slave communities. Richard Dunn, in a parallel study of Mount Airy, Virginia and Mesopotamia, Jamaica, found that although the age/sex ratio at Mesopotamia was more favourable to a healthy natural increase than it was at Mount Airy (where many women were sold away) the fertility rate remained very low in comparison with that of the American slave women, although there was always a larger number of women of childbearing age at Mesopotamia than at Mount Airy. 'Indeed', observes Dunn 'the age structure at Mesopotamia plantation was seemingly very favourable to high fertility' (Dunn, 1977). Higman suggests alternative reasons for fertility differentials not based solely on variable material conditions. A low fertility rate may be explained by a low frequency of sexual intercourse in 'visiting unions' while a higher fertility rate of field labourers in comparison with domestics may be explained by the latter's lack of opportunity to establish co-residential unions. His data suggest that women living in co-residential unions were significantly more fertile than women with no family or co-residential mates, thus indirectly supporting the contemporary arguments for more stable 'marriage'. As isolated women tended to be African, this could also explain fertility differentials between Africans and creoles (Higman, 1984).

Inbreeding amongst slaves has also been cited as a possible causal factor but this is unlikely to have had much effect because of the existence of strong incest taboos within the slave community. William Sells noted that incest was 'never heard of' among negroes and, in his study of the American South, Herbert Gutman (1976) found that strong sanctions operated in the slave community against marriages between close kin. Herskovits and

Herskovits (1934) found that among the bush negroes of modern-day Surinam, whose societal values are similar to those of West African societies at the time of slavery, incest was one of the worst three crimes (the other two were murder and informing on a negro to a white man).

If demographic data cannot provide clear-cut answers as to why West Indian slave populations showed such a low rate of natural increase, it does provide valuable evidence about the childbearing patterns of women slaves, often confused or distorted by contemporary observers. For instance, it was generally believed that slave girls had an early puberty. Discussing the onset of menstruation, Dr Dancer noted that there were rarely any instances of 'retardation of the menses' among negro girls in contrast to the poorer white girls whose inactive and sedentary life rendered them 'obstructed and chlorotic'. This observation is flatly contradicted by Edward Long, who wrote that the white women of Jamaica often married young and were mothers 'at twelve years of age' but declined earlier than women in 'Northern climes'. To conform to the contemporary notions of white womanhood, young girls often led an unhealthy and sedentary life, suffering from psychosomatic and gynaecological maladies such as 'retardation of the menses' which commonly afflict repressed women living in enforced idleness. In contrast, black girls were far more active. Swimming and exercising on an equal basis with male adolescents, they may have had a healthier puberty and onset of menstruation. However, the heavy work load of black women in later life took its toll and it is highly debatable whether their later experiences of childbirth were 'easier' than those of white women. Of slaves in Surinam, John Stedman noted that 'their females arrived early at the age of puberty, but as in the fruits of this climate, this early maturity is succeeded by a sudden decay'. The Barbados Committee reporting to the enquiry into the slave trade in 1789 made similar remarks.

Recently collected quantitative data relating to Jamaican slavery indicate that slave women on sugar plantations generally had fewer children, more numerous miscarriages and a higher sterility rate and finished childbearing at an earlier date than women in comparative societies. Despite accusations of sexual precocity levelled at them, black women were in fact slower to arrive at sexual maturity than European women. According to Dunn's figures, women at Mesopotamia entered into their first pregnancy at least a year later than women at Mount Airy, while women on the Worthy Park plantation apparently reached their peak of fecundity at a later period (some five years) than comparative sectors of the female population of the modern West Indies.

Demographic analyses can also cast light on the high sterility of slave women. This high sterility rate, especially in newly arrived African slave women, reflects the marked incompatibility of the West Indian system of slavery with a healthy pattern of reproduction. In 1789, the Barbados Committee observed that women slaves were 'very prone' to contract disorders of the reproductive system 'which will often last for their lives'. Most black women, wrote Edward Long, 'are subject to obstructions from what cause I will not presume to say'; Ibo women, he maintained, were particularly prone to 'obstructions of the menstrua', often associated with sterility and 'incurable'.

In West Africa sterility in a mature woman is regarded as a terrible stigma and prolific childbearing is honoured. Yet as Michael Craton has observed, despite the fact that most African females were in the fertile age range when first brought to the West Indies, their average actual fertility was no more than half that of creole females in the same age range. The incidence of sterility among them was abnormally high (Craton, 1978). A similar differential in fertility rates between African and creole also existed in the American South (Gutman, 1976). When Rose Price of Worthy Park plantation looked into the fertility of his slaves for the year 1793, he recorded that out of a total of 240 females slaves, only 89 were mothers, 34 of whom had suffered miscarriages; only 19 had children still alive. Of the 19 women whose children survived, 15 delivered only one child. Michael Craton estimates that a high proportion of female slaves in Jamaica were sterile and cites how a census taken by Rose Price in 1795 indicated that probably more than half the female slaves at Worthy Park never gave birth at all (Craton, 1978). Dunn's (1977) study of Mesopotamia plantation revealed a similar pattern in contrast to the buoyant birth rates at Mount Airy, Virginia. The infant mortality rate was roughly equal for both plantations, indicating the significance of the low fertility rate to population growth at Mesopotamia.

Kiple (1984) suggests that an inability to bear a child may have been a criterion for selection for the slave trade in West Africa. This is not an unreasonable suggestion given the high premium placed on female fertility in traditional African culture, but more evidence is necessary to confirm the hypothesis. New quantitative data relating to the demographic performance of the African population between 1730 and 1850 indicate a fall of 3 to 7 million from a base of 25 million in 1730. A major reason for this was arguably loss of females in the crucial reproductive years (Manning and Griffiths, 1988). Hence, the presence of African-born women in itself is an insufficient explanation of low fertility. Most African-born women were in the fertile age range when they arrived in the Caribbean but the incidence of sterility was abnormally high, although, in African cultures, social identity for women comes solely through motherhood and new-born children are greeted with joy and celebration. A childless couple will explore every possible means to overcome sterility. (According to Maria Cutrufelli (1983) African women characteristically have a high sterility rate.) Demographic data alone cannot thus resolve the question of sterility and the significance of this in relation to cultural factors will be discussed shortly.

Such data do, however, raise some interesting questions relating to slave fertility and physical conditions. Both Dunn's study of Mesopotamia and Mount Airy and Craton's contrast of Exuma and Worthy Park point to harsh conditions as the prime causal factor in low fertility. However, it is not useful to generalise from such limited studies. For instance, the fecundity of Exuma slaves may have been related to other factors independent of material living conditions, such as the relative 'freedom' allowed them by their liberal, absentee master, Lord Rolle. To substantiate the link between harsh conditions and the low rate of natural increase a more detailed examination of such conditions is required.

With the new biological and medical histories of slave life, there has been an upsurge of interest in nutrition and morbidity (sickness and ill-health) as explanations of low fertility. In her study of slave life in nineteenth-century Rio, Mary Karasch suggests that dietary deficiencies affected the ability of slave women to bear and raise healthy children. Their childbearing potential may have been impaired by diseases such as rickets (Karasch, 1987). Kiple also argues that women may have suffered calcium deficiency leading to rickets (although Dr Thomas Dancer argues that this was 'rarely seen' in Jamaica) and were frequently anaemic. He notes that a high frequency of stillbirths may be linked to malnutrition as well as the high rate of toxaemia in pregnancy associated with female slaves in the Caribbean (Kiple, 1984). Delayed menarche and early menopause are also related to poor nutrition. Sheridan (1985) has shown that slaves were also subjected to periodic famines and there is a well documented medical link between starvation and amenorrhoea (cessation of menstruation leading to temporary sterility). In addition, endemic diseases such as yaws and epidemic diseases like measles and smallpox may have increased the incidence of still births and miscarriages as well as reducing what Michael Craton (1978) terms 'the ability and willingness' to procreate.

Certainly slave nutrition and work practices influenced childbirth patterns, on large plantations in particular. As Higman concludes, few free populations of the New or Old World in the early nineteenth century were subjected to 'such a persistent combination of conditions unfavourable to population growth' (Higman, 1984). However, Higman has convincingly argued that factors affecting fertility are less clearly related to material conditions than those determining mortality differentials, and he concludes that the symbiotic relationship between nutrition, infection and fertility remains a controversial subject, a view supported by Dunn. Indeed, Emmer and Van den Boogaart's study of a model plantation in Surinam shows that the birth rate remained low despite the fact that the food provided was nutritionally excellent (Emmer and Van den Boogaart, 1977). Other factors must be examined in attempting to understand high sterility and miscarriage rates. To unravel such hidden variables the actual experience of women in childbirth must be considered.

To breed or labour? Women, childbirth and the plantation regime

There is evidence from both the French and English Caribbean that in the early days of slavery African slaves were encouraged to marry and reproduce. Equal ratios were maintained and slaves were allowed to keep their own marriage forms. It was believed that such pro-birth (pro-natalist) policies would increase the labour force, improve slave morale and act as an effective means of social control (Sheridan, 1985). Conditions of childbirth, however, remained crude. Ligon records that, during childbirth, the man left his wife alone 'to God' in one room of the cabin. A 'neighbour' came in to help. The woman lay on a 'board' such as those which the slaves slept on and the neighbour made a fire by the woman's feet 'that serves instead of Possets, Broaths, and Caudles'. After two weeks, the woman was back at work. If the overseer was 'discreet' she was suffered to rest a little more than ordinary but if not she was compelled 'to do as others'. Women had 'times . . . of suckling their Children in the fields, and refreshing themselves'.

With the development of sugar monoculture and the large-scale plantation unit, interest in the reproductive potential of female slaves was abandoned and they were increasingly valued solely as work units. As Arlette Gautier notes, the need to make quick profits, combined with a plentiful supply of fresh slaves from the labour reservoir in West Africa, became a major drawback to healthy childbirth; a sharp conflict emerged between women as 'labour units' and 'breeding units' (Gautier, 1982). Conditions of labour and childbirth sharply deteriorated in the eighteenth century (the rigours of the plantation regime have already been discussed in Chapter 3.) Pregnant women were often kept at field work, even during the last months of pregnancy, and suffered from many gynaecological complaints, including early miscarriage and sterility, in addition to general ill-health related to the plantation regime. Research by Lucille Mathurin Mair (1974) and Higman (1984) confirms that women had a higher morbidity rate than men – a factor which has also been used to explain planter preference for male slaves.

In a slave community, pregnancy and childbirth were fraught with many hazards. During pregnancy the slave woman had to endure constant hardships. Her daily existence was one of strenuous labour, frequent punishment and constant fatigue. But, from the early days of slavery, the special needs of the pregnant slave women were generally ignored. This resulted in part from the racialist assumption voiced by planters like Long that African women, being closer to the animal world than white women, gave birth to children 'with little or no difficulty' and in 'rapid succession'. This contemporary myth justified the fact that slave women were profitably put to work throughout pregnancy and were returned to the fields shortly after giving birth. As Sir Hans Sloane noted in the early eighteenth century, 'negroes keep not to their beds over a week after having brought forth [a child] when they return to their ordinary business'.

Slave women allegedly gave birth without pain in contrast to white women, who were believed to have a much more difficult time and exhorted by doctors such as Dancer to avoid all 'acts of exertion' even so light as bending down to pull out a drawer. According to Lady Nugent, it was the 'general opinion' of medical men in Jamaica that white and mulatto women had a far more difficult time in pregnancy than black women. The coloured housekeeper of a Jamaican planter whom she and Governor Nugent once visited had remarked to her that:

it was astonishing how fast . . . black women bred, what healthy children they had, and how soon they recovered after lying-in . . . it was totally different with mulatto women, who were constantly liable to miscarry.[8]

In this intimate area of their lives, both black and white women suffered from male misconceptions and dictums concerning their sexuality and reproductive functions. But, where gender was a common bond, race and class divided them. In white men's eyes, the former were primarily workers and mistresses, the latter 'respectable' mothers and wives. To enforce such distinctions, the two groups were compared and contrasted at the most fundamental level of reproduction to establish their male-defined status in Caribbean society. In reality, more similarities than differences may have existed between black and white women, particularly where childbearing was concerned. Inadequate obstetric knowledge and unhygienic conditions rendered childbirth hazardous for *all* women in Europe and the West Indies alike. The existence of strong patriarchal attitudes to paternity and the lack of satisfactory contraceptive techniques meant that most women's lives involved a succession of often dangerous pregnancies which precipitated numerous gynaecological complaints. In this context, it may be argued that 'privileged' white women, deprived of any concrete economic function, became the victims of male manipulation of their bodies to a far greater extent than poorer working women and female slaves who relied on traditional midwifery and folkloric medicine. The expropriation of the ancient art of midwifery by the new medical men of science and the development of what Foucault has termed 'Scientia Sexualis' (the development of a 'scientific' explanation of sexuality) reduced the control women had over their bodies, particularly middle- and upper-class women (Foucault, 1978–9).

The myth that childbirth was easy for slave women was deep and pervasive and consistently influenced plantocratic attitudes to pregnant women slaves. Yet as Maria Cutrufelli has illustrated, the hazards of childbirth in Africa belie myths, still common today, that 'primitive' women have easy births. In traditional African societies, moreover, women were supported by a 'remarkable degree of female solidarity'. They were exempted from labour for three months, assisted by a mother or elder sister who would stay constantly at their side. How different the experience of slave women! Planters themselves conceded that black women had difficult labours, which was predictably blamed on themselves. Long writes:

Childbirth is not so easy here as in Africa . . . so many children are annually destroyed as well as their mothers by the unskilfulness and absurd management of negro midwives.

Dr Jonathan Troup noted that fewer black women died in childbirth than white women but slave infant mortality was much higher.[9] Maria Cutrufelli (1983), in her study of modern African women, argues that what has been wrongly defined as the insensitivity of black women to, for instance, pain in childbirth is a result of being socialised into stoically bearing pain first experienced in clitoridectomy ('female circumcision') at puberty. Such cultural factors may have affected African slave women's attitudes but do not detract from the fact that childbirth was hazardous and dangerous for *all* women at the time.

Although planters were obviously aware of the incompatibility of the slave regime with a healthy natural increase, during the heyday of slavery scant attention was paid to the welfare of pregnant women. William Beckford reproached his fellow planters for this insouciant attitude. 'I am aware', he wrote, 'that there are many planters who do not wish their women to breed, as thereby so much work is lost in attendance on their infants'; he recommended the better treatment of pregnant and nursing mothers.[10] Such measures to improve slave fertility were introduced after 1790 with the threat of the abolition of the slave trade and the spectre of dwindling slave populations. Individual island assemblies (the legislative bodies of the dominant white population) passed laws to improve breeding and slave conditions in general (hence the term 'ameliorative' legislation). Planters such as Long now recommended 'rewards' for slave mothers and 'gratuities' for slave parents, which would 'endear' the owner to the parents and help them 'to provide better, the several little necessaries wanted to keep the infants cleanly and decent'. There was also a good deal of discussion about the treatment of pregnant and nursing women. Slave doctors became authorities and were more commonly employed by planters. They advocated better care of slave mothers, the building of lying-in houses and the early weaning of infants. Dr William Sells also recommended the keeping of careful records of slave women's childbearing experiences. He also advised careful medical attention, light employment after the fifth month and better education of black midwives, who were often regarded by planters as incompetent or even dangerous. Similar measures were adopted in the French Caribbean.

The slave midwife became a highly important member of the slave community, despite the accusations about negligence. There was a general increase in hospital provision after 1790 (although medical costs per plantation slave remained low in comparison to the cotton belt in the Southern USA). Black nurses, doctors and doctoresses took most of the load in caring for the sick. The head nurse or doctoress on large plantations had to supervise other staff – midwives, cooks and nurses. Midwifery and infant care were of prime concern and midwives were elevated in the slave hierarchy in both the French and British Caribbean, occupying positions just below that of the top slaves, the head overseer and housekeeper. In 1805 there were 7 midwives on the properties of John Tharp, a Jamaican planter, all aged between 30 to 60. Of 51 black medical attendants, 34 were female and 17 male, reflecting perhaps the important contribution made by women in traditional African medicine (discussed below in Chapter 8). Of the combined medical staff, 50 per cent were involved in births or infant care. The high value placed on midwives in some parts of the Caribbean is not reflected, however, in data from the Tharp estates in Jamaica, except when 'able' midwives were valued at slightly less than male hothouse doctors (often creoles). Midwives were often old and weak and valued at less than £50. One midwife was classed as insane and valued at zero (Sheridan, 1985). Moreover, considerable hazards attended the job, as midwives were frequently blamed for infant deaths, and in the French Caribbean if a death occurred both mothers and midwives were sometimes punished by the whip or iron collar until the mother was pregnant again (Gautier, 1983). Midwives and nurses also had to double as prison warders and had unpleasant, isolated lives, in constant contact with diseases such as yaws.

Despite these new measures, there is evidence that women's experience of childbirth remained difficult, as an overriding priority was to get them back to the fields. Dr Sells exhorted planters not to allow 'too much indulgence' to their female slaves. He saw no reason to alter the usual practice of returning women to work after a month or six weeks after delivery, providing 'nothing peculiar' in the state of their health forbade it. Maria Nugent remarked that women worked in the fields until at least six weeks before confinement and returned within *two* weeks. As abolitionists like James Stephen pointed out, absentee proprietorship led to a lack of direct planter involvement and an absence of white women who may have taken an interest in slave births (as did, for example, Fanny Kemble, the English wife of an American planter).

Recently collated demographic data confirm the general failure of pro-natalist policies. Higman's data have shown that, with the exception of Barbados, no British sugar colony showed an absolute increase in the slave population before 1832, and between 1807 and 1834 the total slave population declined from 775,000 to 665,000 at a time when adverse sex ratios of men to women were evening out and the population contained a greater number of creole slaves, supposedly more adapted to plantation life (Higman, 1984). Attempts to creolise slaves may even have had an adverse effect. Gautier suggests, for instance, that imposed Christian marriages in the French islands may actually have worked against fertility. French planters also tried to give slave women the desire to be mothers by promising manumission to mothers of five children, but the birth rate remained sluggish (Gautier, 1983). Similarly the paternalist planter 'Monk' Lewis provided all the 'comforts' and 'requisites' deemed necessary to healthy childbirth by eighteenth-century European medical science yet there was little improvement in the fertility rate on his plantation.

In themselves, neither 'bad African practices' nor promiscuity of slaves, harsh conditions, physical punishment or unfavourable demographic factors are sufficient to explain the abnormally low fertility rate of West Indian women slaves. Creolisation and improved treatment failed to stimulate the natural birth rate. The only variable as yet not considered is the attitude of the slaves themselves. As Dunn notes, psychological as well as physical and economic reasons may have been involved. The feelings of the slave women themselves must be taken into consideration. A puzzling paradox in the history of Jamaica is that, ten years after full emancipation, the black population began to grow although the number of practising doctors declined sharply and material living conditions were in some ways worse than in pre-emancipation times (Sheridan, 1975). What was achieved by better medical care and improved conditions in the 'amelioration' period, concludes Richard Sheridan, must have been partly negated by factors beyond the control of planters, possibly the attitude of female slaves themselves.

Throughout the period of slavery, there remained insuperable difficulties attached to pregnancy and childbearing, on sugar plantations in particular, and there was little incentive for women to bear children despite the importance attached to motherhood in African culture. The 'poor wretches' of slave women in addition to labouring in the fields were now also expected to produce children to add to the value of their master's estate. The threat of separation from the infants they had borne and nurtured was ever-present and, as early as 1789, the Barbados Committee, reporting to the enquiry into the slave trade had recognised that the spectre of sale away from their friends and relatives discouraged women from having children. Under these circumstances it would not have been unnatural for a slave woman to wish to avoid unwanted pregnancies, let alone have children at all when, in the words of one contemporary writer, her situation was

> upheld by no consolation, animated by no hope, her nine months' torment issuing in the production of a being doomed like herself to the rigours of eternal servitude.[11]

This raises the possibility that the conditions of slavery reduced women's desire and ability to have children or may even have resulted in conscious forms of limitation such as abortion, contraception and infanticide.

Reluctant mothers: conscious and unconscious limits on fertility

Under extreme conditions, women's desire and ability to have children is reduced. The classic example here is the concentration camp. Stanley Elkins's analogy between the slave plantation and the concentration camp is not generally acceptable, but it may have some relevance in terms of the effects of stress and dislocation on individuals (Elkins, 1959). Deportees and prisoners in the Second World War suffered terrible psychological conditions, anguish and shock and, as the French historian Le Roy Ladurie notes, amenorrhoea (absence or stoppage of menstruation) was arguably a 'defence mechanism', a reflection of the suppression of the 'luxury function' of reproduction in order to survive (Ladurie, 1979). The effects of physical starvation and hardship thus combined with psychological factors to reduce fertility. Such factors may help to explain the high incidence of amenorrhoea amongst slave women and modern medical opinion confirms that 'emotional amenhorroea' can occur due to psychological disturbance and 'secondary amenhorroea' from illness or a change in environment.

There is evidence of a reluctance to bear children in adverse situations in a number of societies. Early Spanish sources refer to the use of abortion and infanticide by Amerindian tribes of the Caribbean and Latin America as a form of resistance to colonial oppression. One such source observed that, under the harsh regime instituted by the Spaniards, 'the women promised themselves not to bear further children and instead aborted themselves by means of well-known plant poisons', while Fray Juan de la Conception wrote that the women of the Marianas Indians 'made themselves deliberately sterile and threw their own infants into the water . . . which saved them from being overworked and from grief'.[12]

The anthropologist, Herbert Aptekar (1931) cites how the destruction of cultural institutions in Melanesian society resulted in native apathy towards children. Similarly, in Africa in the 1930s in the Congo region there were reputably women who took herbal concoctions to make themselves sterile because they did not want to bring into the world children condemned to a life of slavery. The low birth rate of Africans caused concern to colonial authorities as it potentially affected the recruitment of labour power. Recent research has concluded that this was due largely to self-inflicted abortions and 'psychic alteration' producing a 'dread of motherhood' resulting from the way in which colonialism undermined traditional cultures (Cutrufelli, 1983).

Undoubtedly a complex relationship exists between the individual psyche and culture. The slave trade considerably disrupted African societies and the threat of enslavement could have altered attitudes to childbearing. The psychological disorientation of the 'middle passage' and the rigours of the 'seasoning' period when slaves were initiated into the slave regime may also have deeply influenced attitudes to sexuality and procreation. As Des Pres points out in his study of the concentration camp, much evidence now exists that under 'privation and horror' the need for sex disappears. When men and women are exhausted and starving sex becomes unimportant: 'horror and moral disgust' are the most powerful depressors of sexual drive (Des Pres, 1976). Preoccupation with sex is arguably a bourgeois luxury. What reason do we have to suppose that slave women had the time, energy or inclination to procreate regularly? Women were forced into productive roles on the plantation alien to their traditional cultural practices and were left isolated as individuals when they were used to support from extended families and a clear status which afforded them emotional security. Indeed, a 'psychological' resistance to childbearing is hinted at by Monk Lewis, who declared:

> negresses can produce children at pleasure . . . when they are barren it is just as hens will frequently not lay eggs on shipboard because they do not like the situation.[13]

The notion of 'psychological contraception' may not be as bizarre as it may initially appear. In some pre-literate societies women, though seemingly leading a normal married life, are reputed to fail to conceive simply because 'they no longer wish it'. Lewis's notion of slave women 'producing children at pleasure' could have some truth in it. Moreover, the psychological impact of physical and emotional stress on menstruation (and hence conception) may also be significant.

Slave women in the West Indies had a high incidence of gynaecological illness, notably amenorrhoea. This has been generally attributed by modern historians to the heavy labour performed by women and the poor living conditions they endured. However, as stressed above, menstrual disturbances may have been psychological in origin. Adverse conditions were present on the slave plantation as they were in a more extreme form in the concentration camp, where, as Des Pres notes, a large percentage of female prisoners ceased to menstruate, their periods not reappearing until after liberation.

Contemporary works on Caribbean slavery occasionally intimate that slaves consciously avoided having children in response to the adverse conditions under which they lived. Edward Long, for instance, quoted a 'very reliable' source, a Monsieur Bossue, a French officer stationed in Hispaniola in 1751, who heavily condemned 'the brutal avidity' of some French planters who forced their slaves to such hard labour that they refused to marry 'in order to avoid generating a race of human beings to be enslaved to such masters'.[14]

If the problem of low fertility is looked at in terms of the *desire* rather than the ability of slave women to bear children, it is crucial to allow for the fact that, although enslaved, the individual woman still possessed free will. Did the slave woman exercise this will and significantly control her own child-bearing potential, perhaps through abortion and contraception? Richard Sheridan (1975) has speculated on this possibility and Edward Brathwaite (1971) maintains that it was a valid form of slave resistance. Elizabeth Fox-Genovese (1986) has also pointed to the possibility of both abortion and infanticide as a form of resistance. However, this is difficult to establish for the US slave states where there was a rising birth rate. Such speculations add a novel dimension to the debate on slave fertility, free from external factors over which the slave woman had little or no control. They imply a conscious policy on the part of slaves towards parenthood which planters were powerless to control or even influence.

Caribbean planters frequently accused women of procuring abortions and frustrating their attempts to increase the slave population. Long linked this to promiscuity, arguing that slave women were no better than 'common prostitutes' who frequently took 'specifics' to cause abortion in order that they could resume their immoral activities 'without loss or hindrance to business'. Dr John Quier gave professional support to this view, blaming promiscuity rather than 'ill-usage and excessive labour' as the reason for the 'frequent abortions' on slave plantations. As Dr David Collins noted, it was commonly believed that slave women induced miscarriage through 'violence' or through the use of 'simples of the country . . . possessed of forcible powers'. The Reverend Henry Beame wrote of Jamaican slaves in 1826 (when there was a far higher percentage of creoles, indicating, perhaps, the durability of transmitted African cultural knowledge):

> The procuration of abortion is very prevalent . . . there being herbs and powders known to [slaves], as given by obeah men and women . . . these observations respecting abortion have been collected entirely from Negroes, as the white medical men know little, except from surmise.[15]

Reports from other parts of the Caribbean, Latin America and the Southern United States also accuse slave women of secretly destroying their unborn children, frequently out of malice to spite their masters.

It is necessary to distinguish between procured abortions and spontaneous miscarriage; no such distinction is made in contemporary accounts and the two terms are used indiscriminately.* Many 'abortions' were probably spontaneous but premeditated abortion cannot be ruled out. Slave women would almost certainly have possessed the inherited knowledge from Africa and, as primitive abortion techniques, mechanical or drug-based, can be dangerous, their use by slave women may have contributed to the high incidence of sterility and gynaecological complaints reported by whites. Greater insight into the practice of abortion by slave women can thus be gleaned from a cross-cultural analysis of the practice in African societies. Major abortifacients used by African women include infusions from herbs, leaves of special shrubs, plant roots and bark from certain trees. Common plants used include manioc, yam, papaya, mango, lime and frangipani. Mechanical means are less popular and rely, for instance, on the insertion of sharp sticks or stalks into the vaginal canal.

Among the Mandingo, abortifacients were often used under three months with 'apparent safety' for the mother. The root of the cotton tree was used or a shrub called 'corset leaf' in the form of an infusion. These infusions were also taken if the afterbirth failed to come away naturally during the post-birth period (Harley, 1941). In southern Nigeria, women aborted after drinking certain medicines prescribed by old women; Dahomian women drank the boiled juice of lime with a yellow 'stone' substance in it when two months pregnant (Herskovits, 1938). Abortifacient techniques were thus known and utilised in many areas of Africa which were the tribal homelands of West Indian slaves. Some of the methods used were by no means safe. The Guinea pepper used by the Efik of Old Calabar (southern Nigeria), for instance, caused 'serious constitutional disturbances and organic lesions' (Devereux, 1960). It is a common practice still today in rural areas in Ghana to tie a piece of twig of Jatophra to string. This is then placed in the womb and pulled out by the string to procure a 'spontaneous miscarriage', which also induces haemorrhage (Cutrufelli, 1983).

Praise of motherhood and a real desire for it do not exclude the practice of birth control or abortion where strong reasons exist. Maria Cutrufelli argues that the very structures of traditional African society may drive women to refuse motherhood. Abortion is used when taboos are broken through adultery or in polygynous relationships where there is jealousy between co-wives and women fear separation from husbands as a result of taboos surrounding childbirth. It is particularly common in patrilineal societies where mothers resent the fact that when their children grow up they have no rights over them as they are claimed by the father's family (obvious parallels exist here with the situation under slavery). Other modern anthropologists

---

*Abortion is simply expulsion of the foetus before it is 'viable' in medical terms. This is distinguished from the modern legal definition of *artificially induced* abortion.

have noted that an almost universal reason for abortion was an unsanctioned pregnancy during the lactation period when a taboo on sexual intercourse was in operation. It was also common to abort girls believed to be too young for pregnancy, for, while some controlled sexual experimentation was allowed by many African tribes, young girls were not expected to conceive (Devereux, 1960).

Cutrufelli argues that abortion allows women the only real choice in societies where female reproduction is subject to strict patriarchal control, although there is often a high price to pay for it. Apart from wide birth spacing through long lactation, ritual abstinence and abortion as well as elaborate forms of contraception are more widespread in traditional African societies than is generally recognised. Abortion is the method of birth control most in demand among women in traditional cultures as it is technically simpler than chemical or mechanical contraception. Unlike coitus interruptus (the withdrawal method), it does not require the co-operation of the couple and, finally, it can be carried out at any time during gestation. There is also, however, evidence that certain substances such as pineapple juice and frangipani juice are used as spermicides and certain vegetable products are used to promote amenorrhoea. There is no way of telling how efficacious such abortive and other techniques are but, as Cutrufelli concludes, the variety of procedures is certainly impressive.

Attitudes to, and reasons for, abortion vary, as do methods used by women. However, many common factors emerge such as the use of similar drugs and the important role played by 'medicine men and old women'. Older women were skilled in techniques of midwifery and herbalism. (Cutrufelli notes, for example, that traditional midwives knew of 'efficacious drugs' administered orally or rectally to induce labour and how to massage the abdomen with medicaments.) Such women carried their skills with them to the New World and Sheridan's analysis of slave medicine stresses the importance of these skills in caring for sick slaves (Sheridan, 1985). As in Africa, 'doctor women' were generally old. They were typically midwives and provided postnatal care for mothers and infants. Although some European doctors derided such folk practices (possibly out of professional jealousy), as noted above, black healers and nurses were generally regarded as indispensable to the running of hothouses (plantation hospitals) and the more perceptive Europeans acknowledged the efficacy of many folk remedies derived from Africa.

In this context, the practice of abortion by female slaves is a feasible proposition. On the slave plantation the formulae for herbal concoctions to induce abortion would have been passed on from mother to daughter, as in Africa. Some evidence does exist as to the use of abortifacients. Sheridan cites contemporary evidence that wild cassava and other substances were administered by slave midwives and Dr Dancer recorded the names of a number of plants indigenous to the West Indies used for 'promoting terms' in women. These included Cerasee (an emetic also mentioned by Dr Barham), Barbados Pride, Wild Passion Flower, Water Germander and Wild Tansey (a widely recognised abortifacient Herbert Gutman (1976) maintains was also used by slaves in the Southern USA). Sometimes strong emetics, such as the seed of the sandbox tree, were used to bring on menstruation. John Stedman referred to herbal remedies used in Surinam to induce abortion, including the use of 'green pineapple', and observed that (as in traditional African cultures) young girls were reputedly aborted 'to preserve themselves as long as they were able'. Jealousy in polygamous marriages was another motive for abortion according to Sheridan's evidence, whilst Janet Schaw, a contemporary female chronicler, alleged that women who mated with whites possessed knowledge of 'certain herbs and medicines' used to abort which were harmful to their health.

Although there are problems with speculation about societies in the past on the basis of evidence from modern anthropological studies, the endurance of African cultural forms in the New World black diaspora is highly significant. In the Djuka societies of Surinam – arguably the closest to the type of societies which would have existed in eighteenth-century Africa (allowing for cultural change and adaptation necessitated by a new environment and intermixing of slaves of different tribal origin) – there is evidence of the type of abortion and contraception techniques which may have been used by slave women. These include the use of herbs and 'crude instruments' similar to the pointed sticks used in some African societies (Kahn, 1931). Black women in the modern Caribbean still buy herbal concoctions from old women to procure abortions; Herskovits and Herskovits (1947) noted that in Trinidad salt, green mangoes and lime juice were used to abort successfully.

In societies where contraceptive knowledge is poor, abortion is the only means women have available to control their own reproduction. Absence of hard evidence should not be taken as proof that the practice did not exist. Because of the strong taboos against abortion in most patriarchal societies, knowledge of abortion practices has always been in the shadowy and hidden world of women outside the orbit of mainstream history. In many traditional African societies abortion was arguably more accepted as social practice than in the more centralised states linked to Islam or Christianity. All such factors lend support to the contention that abortion was a positive response to enslavement on the part of slave women.

Throughout history, women, often in defiance of the religious and secular laws of the society in which they live, have resorted to abortion and contraception as a means of terminating or avoiding unwanted pregnancies. Anthropological studies indicate that many pre-literate societies practised some form of abortion, commonly using either crude mechanical methods or simple vegetable drugs. The drugs mostly work by poisoning the system, causing vomiting or diarrhoea which induces miscarriage. Many of these primitive methods are dangerous and can cause permanent sterility or even death. It is in this context of the universality of abortion that its practices in slave society and relevance to the fertility of individual slave women should be gauged.

Low fertility or high mortality? Some reflections on slave infant death

The focus so far has been on the low fertility of slave women but the death of slave infants was also cited as a contributory factor in the low rate of natural increase. Kenneth Kiple asserts that high infant mortality, not low fertility, may have been the prime reason why slave populations failed to increase. Comparative fertility rates for West Africa, he argues, remain high despite extended breast feeding and early sterility of women; female fertility may indeed actually have been high in some cases but this was counteracted by excessively high infant mortality (Kiple, 1984). Infant mortality is here defined as deaths in the 0–5 age range but the main concern of contemporary observers was the unusually high death rate within the first two weeks of infant life.

Jamaican planters reported that slave infants had 'a very precarious tenure' on life and that 'one fourth perish within fourteen days of birth'. In the first nine days of life infants were particularly vulnerable and, according to Higman, contemporary estimates placed the mortality rate within this period at between 25 and 50 per cent of all live births (Higman, 1984). The biggest killers, according to contemporary sources, were peripneumonic fevers caused by damp air and infant tetanus or *tetanus nascentium* – the 'jawfall' or 'lockjaw' regarded by many Europeans as the main barrier to population growth. The Jamaican Committee reporting to the 1789 enquiry into the slave trade stated that many children were born to slaves in the island and if only they could survive the 'locked jaw, smallpox, measles, yaws, and worm disease' a greater proportion of negro children would be reared. Bryan Edwards reported that this disease generally affected infants 'between the fifth and fourteenth days' after birth and he 'supposed' that 'one fourth of all the negro children' perished from this disease, the remedy for and cause of which were 'as yet undiscovered'. The incidence of tetanus may even have been higher than the above estimates. Dr William Sells, for instance, accused managers of estates of 'the common practice' of omitting to list in their 'increase and decrease lists' those who died within the ninth day.

Not insignificantly, perhaps, 'jawfall' appears to have afflicted only black babies. Dr Dancer (who felt that 'in general' a warm climate was 'favourable to infant life') wrote that 'few deaths' occurred among young children in the West Indies except from tetanus, which 'rarely attacks any but [children of] negroes', who were 'carried off in great numbers'. Despite such authoritative statements descriptions of *tetanus nascentium* (*tetanus neonatum* in modern medical terminology) in slave babies were rather cursory. 'The locked jaw and jaw fall,' observed Dancer 'though contradictory in terms, signify, in general, one and the same complaint; *viz*, a fixed spasm of the muscles of the jaw as in tetanus.' On the incidence of the disease in the American South, and of which the slaves 'complained much', Fanny Kemble wrote that it commonly resulted in babies 'refusing the breast', their mouths 'gradually losing the power to open'. Tetanus was contracted through the umbilical cord or stump and symptoms appeared at the end of the first week after birth. These included spasms of the neck and muscles leading to convulsions and later rigidity. Contemporary medical treatises record some incidence of the disease in England and other parts of Europe in the eighteenth and nineteenth century. Infant tetanus still occurs in modern Haiti but has disappeared from most other parts of the Caribbean.

During the period of slavery, mortality rates for infants were high in most parts of the world and slave doctors such as Dr John Quier (1738–1822) asserted that deaths among slave infants 'were no greater than that of any other children born into the same circumstances'. He alleged that slave mothers were largely to blame for the death of their babies because of their 'known want of Cleanliness arising from the obstinate Attachment . . . to their Old Customs'. In addition to bad African childrearing practices planters also blamed infant deaths on 'inadequate maternal attention' and 'negligence' linked to women's promiscuous behaviour.

Planters and slave doctors were agreed that 'bad' treatment of the umbilicus was a primary cause of this disease. Dr Dancer wrote that 'the negro usage' of tying up the cut navel string with burnt rag and never examining it for nine days (a practice derived from Africa and still practised today in Haiti according to Kiple (1984)) 'was attended sometimes with bad consequences'. His theory, he added, was confirmed by the 'superior good effects of laudanum and turpentine' which, when applied to the cut umbilical cord, prevented the infant contracting tetanus. Other interested parties firmly believed in the beneficial effects of the improved and more extensive care of newly born infants. Dr Sells advocated lying-in houses and 'properly instructed' midwives ('a matter deserving most serious attention'). These measures, he declared, would render lockjaw 'almost as rare among negro as among white infants'. Many contemporary observers believed that the remedies advocated by doctors such as Dancer and Sells worked. An English doctor, Caleb Parry, argued that improvement in the treatment of the 'navel-string' (umbilicus) soon checked the mortality rate amongst West Indian slave infants. Generally, however, as the good paternalist 'Monk' Lewis conceded, 'care and kindness' and European medicine failed to check infant mortality. Dancer admitted 'no adequate solution . . . sufficient to prevent the disease' had been found and concluded that

> from the inefficiency of any usual precautions and from the disease occurring only within the ninth day, that how much soever any of the supposed causes may conduce to the bringing on of the disease, it more immediately depends on a certain state and condition peculiar to infants within that period.[16]

Similarly, Dr John Quier who was in charge of between 4000 and 5000 Jamaican slaves for 21 years, proposed that the 'lockjaw' of new-born infants was not, in effect, tetanus. In his opinion, 'the symptom which generally attends approaching Death' had frequently been mistaken 'by people unacquainted with medicine' for this disease.

Certainly the conditions for the development of tetanus existed on slave plantations. Slaves lived close to livestock pens which were also used for making compost where tetanus spores could live. They also laboured in highly manured fields, another fertile environment for tetanus (Sheridan, 1985). However, deaths from tetanus for the slave population as a whole were generally low compared, for instance, with deaths from yaws or the 'bloody flux' (dysentery). It is also hard to explain the marked difference between the incidence of the disease in the Caribbean and Europe. Although techniques of midwifery in the slave quarters were highly deficient by modern standards and held a high risk of infection, they were, in the main, no better and no worse than those in current vogue in eighteenth-century Europe, where the treatment for infant tetanus was similar. (Indeed, the 'burnt rag' with which, according to Dancer, negro women covered the cut umbilicus, may even have afforded some protection against infection.) Moreover, if the tetanus organism was present in the vicinity of the childbed in the slave quarters, surely mothers, as well as infants, would have been at risk. In England during the early nineteenth century this disease was observed in women a fortnight after delivery. However, contemporary observers make no reference to puerperal tetanus in their discourses on childbirth.

Further doubt is cast on the 'tetanus' explanation for the high infant mortality rate if we look at societies where conditions of childbirth exist similar to those on an eighteenth-century slave plantation. A useful glimpse into the kind of conditions slave women would have given birth under is provided by the bush negroes of modern-day Surinam and Guyana (who still live according to a seventeenth-century life-style, unlike communities in modern West Africa). Morton Kahn recorded in the 1930s that amongst the Djuka tribes of Surinam, where precautions taken at childbirth were 'crude', *tetanus neonatum* occasionally occurred due to 'extremely unclean conditions' surrounding childbirth. In general, however, he found that the infant mortality rate was relatively low in the first six months after birth, although child mortality in general was high. Similarly, there was a low rate of infant tetanus in Africa at the time of slavery (Kiple, 1984) although Sheridan attributes this to the absence of large domestic animals which dropped the tetanus spores into manure.

Closer examination of contemporary records shows that they fail to record neonatal tetanus as a major cause of death (although, Higman (1976) notes, this may have been because deaths in the first few days went under-recorded). Sheridan's data indicate that by 1830, the leading cause of infant death in the 0–10 age range was whooping cough and only 4–6 per cent of births were in the first month of life. This decline in tetanus suggests better treatment of the disease and the infants (Sheridan, 1985). However, the contradictory nature of the contemporary evidence and modern demographical and bio-historical controversies suggest that additional factors may have been involved in the mystery of the nine-day syndrome, principally other diseases and the attitudes of the slaves themselves.

In his biological history of the Caribbean, Kenneth Kiple (1984) places considerable emphasis on the link between nutrition and disease. Rates of death from infant tetanus, he argues, were fairly uniform in the nineteenth century, comprising betwen 5 and 10 per cent of infant deaths, but many alleged deaths were not neonatal tetanus. He suggests that slave doctors may have confused neonatal tetanus with tetany, a condition derived from maternal tetany (the deficiency of calcium and other vital minerals during pregnancy). This condition results in hypocalcaemic or hypomagnesaemic convulsions in infants. The symptoms of tetany and neonatal tetanus are thus identical but the former was medically unknown even in the latter half of the nineteenth century. Kiple attributes the high rate of tetany to the neglect of the diet of slave women, which resulted in calcium levels falling with each pregnancy. He thus explains the decline in infant deaths towards the end of slavery to better nutrition. However, there are flaws in this argument. Tetany is linked to vitamin D deficiency and this is less common in climates with ample sunshine. It is also generally not associated with mothers who breast feed. Finally, Kiple's evidence suggests it afflicted only black women although poorer white mothers at the time must also have suffered dietary deficiencies. Speculation about the past on the basis of modern scientific data is problematic, particularly when it ignores the cultural context.

The key to a fuller understanding of the crucial variables of infant mortality on slave plantations lies, perhaps, in the symbolic nature of the first nine days of an infant's life in both African and Afro-Caribbean folk-lore, a factor which contemporary observers were either ignorant of or chose to disregard, although they frequently alluded to this period as a significant feature of tetanus in infants. When 'Monk' Lewis discussed the problems of caring for slave infants with his slave midwife, she fatalistically replied, 'Oh Massa, 'til nine days over, we no hope for them.' Thus many planters believed that if more care were given to infants during this period, far fewer would be lost.

In West Africa a new-born infant is not regarded as part of this world until eight or nine days have passed, during which period it may be ritually neglected. The infant is regarded as no more than a 'wandering ghost', a capricious visitor from the underworld. Amongst the Akan of Ghana, for instance, a child remains within the spirit world until this period is over and it becomes a human being, recognised by its father. The hair of the infant is known as 'ghost hair', the infant's excreta as 'ghost's excreta' and the cooing of infants as 'the language of ghosts' (Rattray, 1927). If a child dies before this time it is considered never to have existed, which may explain the under-reporting of infant deaths. Similar traditions are found amongst the Ga people (Cutrufelli, 1983). The durability of West African practices relating to childbirth has already been observed and it may be argued that the nine-day period when slave midwives reputedly held 'no hope' for infants may have reflected the endurance of African beliefs rather than deliberate neglect and fatalism because of the high risk of tetanus, as Orlando Patterson (1969) suggests. Evidence to support this is found in John Quier's reference to the 'obstinate attachment' of Jamaican women to their 'old customs', in particular

> the injudicious Custom of suckling a new born child for the first week after its birth . . . with Milk of a Woman who often has a child at her Breast a year Old or perhaps Older,[17]

a practice strikingly similar to that found amongst the Akan (Rattray, 1927) and possibly linked to the 'ghost status' of the infant. Edward Brathwaite (1971) clearly links the apparent 'neglect' of slave infants to West African cultural beliefs. Evidence of the strength of such traditions further exists in the fact that, in Jamaica in the 1920s, termination of the nine-day period was marked by a ritual bath and a ceremony to ward off 'evil spirits' (Beckwith, 1929). Herskovits (1947) noted a similar ritual observation of the nine-day period in Trinidad.

As slave women retained a large degree of control over their reproductive potential, they may also have determined the fate of their own children, in accordance with the traditional values and beliefs which they had brought over with them from Africa. For instance, when 'Monk' Lewis tried to introduce the practice of plunging negro infants, immediately they had been born, into a tub of cold water (a measure, he had been assured, which 'infallibly preserved them from tetanus'), the slave mothers 'took a prejudice against it' and were 'so obstinate in their opposition' that he had to abandon the idea.

Within this framework of cultural persistence it cannot be discounted that slave babies may have been deliberately 'encouraged' to die. This possibility does not rule out premeditated infanticide in the true definition of the word. Under normal circumstances, infanticide in West African societies occurs only when abnormal infants are born. But circumstances were not 'normal' on the slave plantation and infanticide may have been more prevalent.

As yet, few scholars have seriously contemplated the possible relationship between the high neonatal mortality rate of slave populations and infanticide, although the latter has been practised, for a variety of reasons, in many diverse societies from 'time immemorial' (Langer, 1974). A number of strong motives for infanticide existed in slave society and slave women would almost certainly have known of suitable methods to use, as they did in the case of abortion and contraception. As Eugene Genovese, writing in the context of the Old South, has remarked:

> [Slave] women who did not want children knew how to abort or arrange to have a child die soon after birth; with infant deaths so common from natural causes, the deed could not be detected.[18]

Infant deaths suspected as infanticide may, of course, have been the result of Sudden Infant Death Syndrome which was linked to slave mothers' labour in the fields rather than to conscious attempts to deprive the system of slave infants (Johnson, 1981). However, given the slaves' inherited knowledge of herbs and techniques of abortion and contraception, infanticide, like abortion, may have been a valid form of resistance. If such practices existed in the American South, where better material conditions prevailed, even stronger arguments for the practice of infanticide apply to the Caribbean.

Infanticide is the natural corollary of abortion. For ethical reasons, it is generally less common than abortion, but, where a 'strong desire' to limit infant numbers prevails, it may be used in conjunction with abortion or contraception, or as a final resort if the latter fail (Aptekar, 1931). In 'letting' their infants die slave women would have painlessly released them from a dismal future. The mystical West African religious beliefs surrounding the first nine days of a child's life may have provided them with the necessary ethical rationale. As Rattray observed of the Ashanti (Akan), during the eight days after birth no one is very certain whether the infant is going to turn out a human child or prove, by dying before this period has elapsed, that it was never anything more than a wandering ghost. If West Indian slaves, like their West African ancestors, did not regard the new-born child as human until nine days had elapsed then they would not be breaking any religious taboos if they ended their infants' lives during this period. Moreover, in West African belief, an infant child, alive or dead, does not have any power for good or evil and is regarded as relatively 'harmless' (Rattray, 1927). (In certain cultures there is a strong resistance to infanticide because of the belief that the dead, of whatever age, take revenge on the living.) If slave mothers regarded their own infants in the same light, they would have had no cause to fear reprisals from the spirit world if they deliberately let certain infants die.

The infant mortality rate from natural causes was undoubtedly high but the unusually high death rate within the first week, given the controversy over the extent of infant tetanus, may signify that women used preparations which effected apparently natural death, acquired from obeah men and women or herbalists reputed for their dangerous knowledge of poisons of which whites were largely ignorant. (In Europe in the early nineteenth century 'artificial tetanus' resulting from strychnine poisoning was not unknown.) Infanticide is a highly emotive word and, in the absence of evidence, the arguments presented here can only remain speculative. However, as the historian Eric Hobsbawm points out, there is a place for informed speculation and creative approaches in history (Gott, 1988). Indeed, in the case of the oppressed, this may be essential in order to develop a fuller empathy for the people and the period. According to Sheridan, there was a decline in infant deaths from tetanus by 1830 and this cannot be explained solely by better conditions, as planters and doctors tended to be disappointed by their efforts to cut infant mortality rates. It may be explained more satisfactorily by the creolisation of the population and greater impact of Christian beliefs which diluted the mystical justification of the nine-day period.

Women slaves had a number of powerful reasons for procuring abortion and releasing newly born infants from misery through 'letting' them die. Too many children can be an excessive burden when mothers have a hard and bitter existence. (Poor women in Victorian England were also accused of infanticide which resulted from the 'misery, hopelessness and utter degradation' in which they lived.) Dr Robert Jackson, who practised in Jamaica, argued that slave mothers were not naturally deficient in parental affection but 'hard usage' rendered then indifferent or made them wish 'that their offspring may fail' rather than be subjected to the plantation regime.[19]

In pre-industrial societies, attitudes to infants and infant death (indeed to child mortality in general) differed sharply from those held by modern western industrial society. Among non-Christian peoples in particular infanticide has always been an accepted procedure for the disposal, not only of the deformed or sickly, but of all such new-borns that might strain the resources of the individual family or larger community (Langer, 1974). In this context the practice of infanticide as a reason for the excessively high mortality rate in the first two weeks of life has plausibility.

An enduring enigma

The controversy over the low fertility rate of slave women (restricted to the Caribbean and Latin America, as slaves in the USA had healthy birth rates) may never be adequately resolved. Deborah Gray White (1985) has argued that, under slavery, motherhood rather than marriage constituted the most important passage in black female life. But in the Southern USA there were arguably more positive policies encouraging motherhood. In the Caribbean birth rates remained low even after more pro-natalist policies were introduced. The birth rate for creole slaves in Jamaica was estimated at 25–27 per thousand in the nineteenth century, compared with 50–55 per thousand in the American South, a rate similar to that of modern West African societies (Klein and Engerman, 1978). If higher rates are related to the peculiarly paternalist nature of slavery in the USA, as Genovese (1974) contends, rather than better material conditions, then the minority of paternalist planters like 'Monk' Lewis may not necessarily have been 'uneconomic' in their desire to conserve slave life and promote fertility. In the long term there may have been gains (Littlefield, 1981). Such policies, however, were generally introduced too late and with insufficient conviction. For most slave owners, squeezed by changing economic conditions, the productive role of the slave woman remained pre-eminent.

The arguments put forward for abortion and infanticide are not conclusive but do emphasise the importance of African cultural retentions and the autonomy of action of slaves themselves. This arguably operated on two levels, the psychological – the impact of slavery on the desire to have children – and the practical – the transmission of folk knowledge about contraception and abortion. A paramount reason for the lack of will to have children, as well as for the existence of abortion, was the institution of slavery itself. As Bryan Edwards declared:

> I see no good reason why it should not be frankly admitted, that slavery in itself, in its mildest form, is unfriendly to population. The human race, to encrease [*sic*]

in numbers, must be placed in favourable circumstances, and unless reason or sentiment in some degree cooperate with corporeal instinct, its offspring is born but to perish.[20]

The abolitionist James Stephen made a similar comment.

After emancipation in the 1840s, Caribbean populations began to reproduce naturally although conditions had barely improved and in some ways may arguably have deteriorated. The birth rate in Jamaica rose to 40 per thousand in the 1840s but infant mortality did not decline definitely until the 1920s (supporting arguments that it was low fertility and not mortality that kept the rate of natural increase low). These developments may have been due to the fact that women abandoned field labour and devoted more time to childrearing. Sheridan's data indicate that by 1891 only 36 per cent of women of working age were employed in sugar production compared with 81 per cent of men and contemporary accounts from the 1850s confirm the disappearance of women from the cane fields (Sheridan, 1985). But these developments also lend support for Edwards's observations. The fact that slaves were deprived of free agency meant that their children were also doomed to perpetual enslavement. There is no doubt that slave women loved and cared for the children they had but no incentive existed for them to have large numbers. Deliberate management of their own fertility may have been a form of hidden, individual protest against the system over which slave masters had even less control than more overt forms of collective resistance.

Slave women in Caribbean slave society were influenced not only by traditional patriarchal structures but by white patriarchal intervention in both their productive and reproductive functions. This deeply affected their attitudes to childbirth and arguably led to conscious control over their own reproductive capacities. In refusing to 'breed' as well as labour, women were voicing a strong protest against the system of slavery. Such intervention was part of a wider pattern of resistance informed by African cultural practices and the personal and institutional relations which developed in slave societies.

Further reading

Aptekar (1931)
Craton (1978)
Thomas Blizzard Culing,
A Treatise on Tetanus (London, 1836).
Cutrufelli (1983)
Greer (1984)
Gutman (1976)
Higman (1984)
Karasch (1987)
Kiple (1984)
Caleb Hillier Parry,
Cases of Tetanus (London, 1814).
Sheridan (1985)

8

'Daughters of Injur'd Africk'

Women, Culture and Community in Slave Society

In West African society there is a remarkable degree of unity of traditional cultural practices. Religion, mysticism, magic and political and family organisation are unified into one complex cultural code. Music, dance, art and oral tradition are the concrete, tangible expressions of this culture, seminal in the cohesion of society and facilitating communication and effective interaction. Amongst slaves in the West Indies, the retention of certain key facets of their traditional culture, in conjunction with the creation of unique cultural forms out of their new environment, was a crucial element in the self-preservation of the slave community.

Although West Indian slaves lived under more extenuating physical circumstances than their kindred in the American South, they were not subjected to as great a degree of paternalism and cultural deprivation. Cultural traditions were retained and jealously preserved. When planters, fearing subversion, tried to ban various cultural manifestations such as drumming, dancing or funeral ceremonies, the slaves became highly secretive. Richard Madden, writing during the 'apprenticeship' period between emancipation and abolition in 1838, noted that the blacks, in reaction to enforced suppression of their cultural activities, sought to keep their community life free from white intrusion. Their huts, he observed, were often concealed 'in the centre of a thick grove of fruit trees', which totally secluded them from observation. Long argued that Ashanti slaves built houses distant from others where they were at liberty to hold their 'dangerous cabals'. Because of their numerical supremacy and relative autonomy of action within their own community, West Indian slaves were thus able to channel their cultural beliefs into various areas of resistance against dehumanisation.

The traditional role of women in West African society equipped women

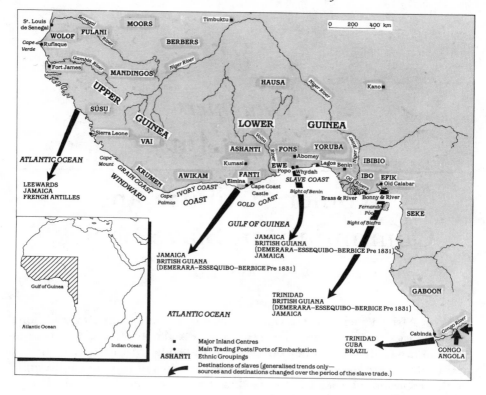

Major Inland Centres
Main Trading Posts/Ports of Embarkation
ASHANTI Ethnic Groupings
Destinations of slaves (generalised trends only—
sources and destinations changed over the period of the slave trade.)

3 *The West African coast 1650–1807: the origins of West Indian slaves*

slaves to play a vital and indispensable part in the cultural activities of the slave community. According to Melville Herskovits, a distinctive characteristic of black societies in the New World was the role women played as the 'principal exponents' and protectors of traditional (African-derived) culture, a factor which 'takes on the greatest significance' for any understanding of the nature of the adjustments that blacks have made to their varying situations. Black women were not only the 'essential bearers of tradition' but also the 'primary agents' in maintaining conventionally accepted modes of behaviour (Herskovits and Herskovits, 1947). This important cultural role of black women in the New World is strongly evident in the activities of women slaves in the Caribbean. Their significant contribution to the preservation of African values within the slave family and wider community has already been discussed at length, but they were no less prominent in other important cultural activities.

As in West Africa, in the cultural life of the slaves religion was a fundamental, unifying bond. Many contemporary writers believed, however, that Africans had no religion as such, for the practice and philosophy of African religion bore little relation to Christianity. ' 'Tis true that [the slaves] have several ceremonies, as Dances, playing etc.', observed Sloane, 'but these . . . are so far from being acts of Adoration of a God, that they are for the most part mixt with a great deal of Bawdry and Lewdness.'[1] Later commentators associated slave religion almost exclusively with obeah and myalism (discussed in Chapter 5), which they regarded as evil and harmful.

Traditional African religion permeates every aspect of an individual's everyday existence and is very much of this world, as opposed to the otherworldliness of Christianity. Its life-affirming traditions contrast strongly with the dour doctrines of original sin and guilt promulgated by Christians. There is a uniformity of supernatural beliefs centred round a supreme being remote from ordinary life and a pantheon of non-human spirits or gods associated with natural forces, ancestor worship and the use of charms and fetishes. Whites worked harder to change slave religious practices than any other area of slave culture yet some of the strongest African survivals, even in modern West Indian culture, are embodied in Afro-Caribbean religions. In Eugene Genovese's opinion, slave religion constituted 'a determined resistance to the pressures of despair and dehumanisation' (Genovese, 1974). Slave religion in its various forms, from myalism to later Afro-Christianity, played an important role in organised slave revolts; but it was also crucial in preserving the individuality of slaves. It provided them with a strong sense of group autonomy and the will and strength to survive.

Black women in the Caribbean played a prominent role in religious ceremonies and resistance stemming from religious practices, and slave religion, even after the introduction of Christianity, had a high African content. In traditional West African religions women often held positions of authority and were endowed with high priestly office. 'One of the singular customs of the people of Grewhe as well as those of Popo', commented John Adams, 'is

153

the admission of females into the order of priesthood',[2] an observation supported by historical and anthropological evidence for West Africa in works by, for instance, Walter Rodney (1970) and Maria Cutrufelli (1983).

West African men and women were not uncommonly accorded equal respect as religious leaders, magicians, healers and seers, and slave women, in keeping with African traditions, came to hold respected positions in the slave community as obeah and myal practitioners, herbalists and 'doctoresses'. Contemporary commentators, however, confused the different aspects of slave religion and magic, especially obeah and myalism, regarded as a politically dangerous tendencies. Women were often persecuted as practitioners of obeah (regarded by whites as evil witchcraft) even if they were merely harmless priestesses or healers.

Age determined to some extent the degree of participation of slave women in the religious life of the community (which included witchcraft *and* healing). 'Old women rule the negro race,' declared the amateur sociologist, Vidor the Vagabond.[3] Vidor lived on modern-day Providencia Island (off the coast of Colombia but part of the English Caribbean in culture) but his observation contains a kernel of truth. In traditional West African society old women held highly respected positions, for example, as leaders of women's secret societies. The latter, together with parallel male societies, played a vital part in regulating community life (Van Allen, 1972). Ashanti lineage leaders were assisted by a senior woman and, in matters of state, a high degree of equality existed (Forde, 1956). When women reached menopause they were regarded as no longer chained to their biological functions and took their place alongside the old men, having a say in the government of the village and taking leading roles in religious ceremonies, and evidence indicates that elderly women were accorded similar respect in slave society.

Old women and old men alike were looked up to for their wisdom and knowledge of folklore and medicines. John Stewart wrote that negroes were acquainted with the use of 'many simples' for the cure of certain disorders and added that the care and management of 'afflicted negroes' were generally confided to 'an elderly negroe woman, who professes a knowledge of this branch of physic'. According to Dallas, the maroons of Jamaica sometimes took simple herbs, 'prescribed to them by their old women'. Undoubtedly, some old 'magic' women *were* obeah practitioners and hence a potential threat because of the power they wielded amongst the slaves. But many female slaves were simply healers or priestesses.

The link between religion and healing was rooted in African beliefs in the supernatural origins of disease. Both 'bad' and 'good' medicine existed. Bad medicine was the province of sorcerers and witches who had control over the 'crises of life and death' or the knowledge of substances capable of producing 'an unusual effect', either good or evil (Harley, 1941). In Jamaica blacks consulted such 'witches' or obeah practitioners

For the Cure of Disorders . . . revenge for Injuries or Insults . . . the Discovery and Punishment of the Thiefs or Adulterers and the Prediction of Future Events.[4]

It was this branch of traditional medicine upon which whites focused as it was connected with poison and threats against whites. 'Good' medicine – the use of herbal remedies, ritual and mystical beliefs to cure illnesses – was frequently dismissed as mere superstition. The attitude of most European doctors is summed up by Sir Hans Sloane who wrote that the slaves' 'ignorance of anatomy, diseases and method' rendered even their knowledge of herbs 'not only useless but sometimes pitiful to those who employ them'. Scientific medicine still derides folk remedies even today. They are equated with 'backwardness' and their socio-psychological effect on individuals has not been acknowledged. In the contemporary context, as Sheridan notes, African-derived medicine may have been as efficacious as European medicine, which was generally of a low quality in the West Indies; no proof of qualifications was required and practitioners were often quacks who had little knowledge of tropical medicine. More importantly, blacks were alienated from white society and mistrusted white doctors, fearing dying alone in the plantation hospital. On a psychic level alone, Afro-Caribbean medicine may have had more success. Black doctors could communicate in native tongues or creole dialect and, even if their herbal remedies did not cure, they were preferable to the purgings and bleedings, opium and mercury of Europeans (Sheridan, 1985).

Recent medical histories of slaves have indicated that they were afflicated by a range of diseases and parasitic infestations. Both Sheridan and Kiple have argued that, in the treatment of diseases endemic to the tropics, African-derived practices were more effective than European medicine. Sheridan maintains that slaves made use of many rational remedies both internally administered and external, such as bone-setting (Sheridan, 1985). Kiple's evidence indicates that black preventative medicine was more advanced than European. The smallpox vaccine, for instance, was administered in some parts of Africa before it was discovered by Europeans (Kiple, 1984). The chief medicaments used by blacks in the West Indies were lime-juice, cardamom, the roots, branches, leaves, bark and gums of trees and about thirty different herbs. Such remedies were examined in depth by one of the few European doctors to learn from the folk wisdom of slaves, Dr James Thompson, who treated slaves in Jamaica in the early nineteenth century.

As Sheridan clearly illustrates, folk medicine developed in the Caribbean with essentially the same features as in Africa. Because women in traditional African society had a vital role in healing, particularly in the practical application of herbal remedies (as opposed to the magical or hypnotic medicine with which men were more familiar) they were prominent also in healing in the slave community. In Sheridan's estimation, women's contribution as healers and nurses outside the plantation hot-house may have exceeded all the health services provided by the white establishment. Indeed the importance of women is underscored by the continued prominence of women healers up to the present day in the Caribbean.

Given the fundamental importance of religion to slave culture and their key contribution to its practice, it is not surprising that female slaves of all ages often exhibited an aversion to Christian dogma and refused baptism. As the abolitionist John Riland observed, women were 'well acquainted with all the customs and mythology of their native country' and they may have rejected Christianity to a greater degree than men. In the later period of slavery Christian conversion represented a form of social advancement and was more popular, therefore, amongst skilled, elite slaves, the majority of whom were men. Furthermore, women had little to gain from the Christian religion; the strict Pauline doctrines of Christianity emphasised female inferiority and subordination in sharp contrast to the sexual egalitarianism of West African religions. Cutrufelli (1983) notes a similar rejection of Christianity by African women under colonial rule.

Christian baptism, in particular, was often viewed by slave women with strong suspicion. At a christening occasion on 'Monk' Lewis's estate, for instance, the women voiced certain serious misgivings. One 'Eboe mother' agreed to have her children christened but staunchly refused to be christened herself. Another woman, although her father and husband had been baptised on a previous occasion, objected to going through the ceremony herself as she was with child 'and did not know what change it might produce upon herself and the infant'.

Creole women slaves were not necessarily more receptive to Christianity. A neighbour of Lewis's used all his influence to persuade his 'foster-sister' to be christened, but in vain, 'for she had imbibed strong African prejudices from her mother' and frankly declared that she found nothing so alluring in the Christian system to her taste as 'the post-obit [death] balls and banquets promised by the religion of Africa'. In Lewis's opinion this was a common attitude among women slaves.

Amongst the *rites de passage* of the slaves, funerals held a pre-eminent position. European and African attitudes to death and the respective funeral ceremonies differed considerably. 'Negroes do not see death as an evil,' wrote William Beckford, 'their principal festivals are at their burials . . . a happy occasion, not melancholy as in Europe.'[5] Europeans could not comprehend this element of celebration in African funerals, in which women were prominent. This is conveyed thus in a contemporary poem:

> Mahab dies! O'er yonder plain
> His bier is borne; the sable train
>   By youthful virgins led;
> Daughters of injur'd Africk, say
> Why raise ye thus th' heroic lay
> Why triumph o'er the dead?[6]

Slave funerals were viewed as riotous affairs by whites and were banned, ostensibly for their pagan and irreverent content but probably on account of the fact that they attracted large numbers of slaves and planters feared their potential for subversion. Nevertheless, the slaves clung tenaciously to their own way of death. Equiano, for instance, maintained that slaves retained 'most of their native customs' such as burying the dead with 'victuals' and 'running with the corpse', as in Africa. Thus, women, who often played a prominent part in funeral ceremonies, may have rejected baptism in order to ensure for themselves a traditional African funeral. Bryan Edwards cited one ancient black woman, Flora Gale, who died at 102 years of age and who:

> always refused to be baptised, assigning for reason her desire to have a grand negro dance at her funeral, according to the custom of Africa; a ceremony never allowed in Jamaica at the burial of such as have been Christened.[7]

Before the abolitionist movement, planters paid little heed to the religious conversion of their slaves, although they suppressed religious manifestations such as obeah. Any attempts at conversion were frequently encountered by resistance. Long talked of 'involuntary proselytes' who eschewed Christianity and clung to African forms of religion. Naturally, Edward Long's impressions were not free from an anti-abolitionist/missionary bias, but the advocates of religion encountered a similar situation. John Riland, who heavily encouraged conversion to Christianity on his father's Jamaican estate in the early nineteenth century, admitted that by no means had all the black population of the estate become Christians, 'nor generally such'. The importance of religion as an area of conflict in the later, disintegrative period of slavery has been discussed in depth in a study by Mary Turner (1982).

The conversion and indoctrination of slaves was intimately linked with controlling slaves, for Christianity stressed submissiveness on earth in return for rewards in the hereafter. As emancipation approached, slaves may have outwardly accepted Christianity but the content of their religion remained essentially African. Thus, the retention of African cultural patterns in this area represented an important aspect of resistance to slavery, an aspect to which women made a significant contribution. In so doing, they not only ensured the cultural continuity of the slave community but also laid secure foundations for future Afro-Caribbean religions.

It is perhaps a significant reflection on the role of black women in slave religion, that women today in the Caribbean far outnumber men as religious devotees of syncretic religions (religions which combine Christian and African beliefs). Francis Henry and Pamela Wilson (1975) found that in the Jamaican revivalist cults, for instance, the ratio of women to men is four to one. Black churches in the modern-day Caribbean retain the egalitarian basis African-derived slave religions were founded upon. In Shango and other cults, including the Spiritual Baptists, in contrast to the orthodox Christian sects, women are prominent as leaders. The Jamaican revivalists, for instance, are led by a 'captain' and a principal mammy and men sometimes take a subordinate leadership role to women. In modern Africa there are more women than men in 'black' churches which have long stimulated a grass-roots resistance to oppression, in colonial *and* post-colonial times.

But the contribution slave women made to cultural resistance and continuity within the slave community was not restricted to their role in slave religion and medicine. In a general cultural context women were arguably more deeply resistant to European influences than men. Proportionately more women than men were field hands and the African element in field-slave culture was strong. Elsa Goveia (1965) has suggested that planters tended to allow blacks to retain their African culture to emphasise the differences between black and white, thus stressing black inferiority. Field slaves, moreover, once their labours were done, were 'out of sight and out of mind' of the planter and could use their leisure as they wished. Women as field workers were thus less prone to assimiliation than skilled male slaves and had a central role in preserving African traditions.

Cultural defiance on the part of women was often expressed through language and song. Language was a vital area of slave identity, and fundamental to black cultural unity. As Frantz Fanon (1968) stressed, 'to speak . . . is to assume a culture.' Language was a first defence against depersonalisation. A major aspect of cultural resistance to a dominant European culture, the creole language of West Indian blacks, with its rich nuances, *doubles entendres* and trenchant satire, was used effectively in the struggle against oppression. The use of verbal abuse as a form of resistance by women field hands has already been noted in Chapter 5. It was also alleged that black female slaves talked 'worse' than males and their language was frequently described in derogatory terms. But the use of such creole was a vital aspect of cultural preservation (still relevant to black identity in Britain today), for it protected the rich linguistic traditions of Africa.

In slave culture, as in West African culture, language and song were almost synonymous. Through song, work could be rendered less burdensome, slave morale could be raised and white masters mimicked, satirised or even subtly threatened; song and music accompanied all the important events in a slave's life. On the slave plantation, women were often the leading singers. William Beckford remarked that in Jamaica singing was 'confined' to the women, the men 'but seldomly . . . excepting upon extraordinary occasions' joining in chorus.[8]

Slave songs were usually African in structure, built on a statement and response pattern. Apart from work and digging songs, they were customarily the province of women. According to Thomas Atwood, in the fields women sang songs 'of their own composing' which were answered 'in the same manner' by men. Slave women sang 'wild choruses of joy' at cropover but also expressed through song the sorrow of enslavement. 'When the mill is at work,' wrote William Beckford, 'there is something affecting in the songs of the women who feed it; and it appears somewhat singular, that all their tunes . . . are of a plaintive cast.'[9]

Entertainment in the slave village was also often provided by the voices of female slaves, sometimes accompanying themselves with primitive instruments. Although slaves had little time for amusement, what they did have they enjoyed to the fullest. 'Plays' were highly popular, combining verbal dexterity, music and dance. Both sexes participated, forming a ring around a male and female dancer who performed to the music of the drums.

8.1 *'A Negroe Dance in the Island of Dominica'. One of the rare illustrations of life in the slave village, showing slaves at leisure. Note the slave houses in the background, and the women's ornate head-ties. The women on the left are fully participating in the music and dance.*

Saturday-night dances were also held, which slaves from neighbouring plantations attended. According to John Stewart, the music on these occasions generally consisted of 'the goombay, or drum, several rattles and the voices of the female slaves'. On more serious occasions 'a melancholy dirge' was sung by a woman accompanied by an all-female chorus.

Many contemporary writers commended the slaves on their great musical ability and some, like John Stewart, believed 'the voices of the female slaves' to be the best part of slave music. African forms of music, like religion, have vigorously survived in the Caribbean in, for instance, Trinidadian 'kaiso' or calypso, which incorporates elements of slave work songs and 'calinda' (Hill, 1972). Such survivals have contributed in no small way to modern Afro-Caribbean culture. Where song is concerned, women in the Caribbean may even have transcended the prescribed limits of female participation in traditional West African society and thus bequeathed a vital legacy to modern Caribbean music. This is especially true with respect to leading solos and chorus responses. In many West African societies, for example among the Ibo and Yoruba, women only join in with choruses of songs. In the Caribbean this situation seems to have been reversed; the prominence of the voices of women in the musical traditions of the slaves may, indeed, have been a unique response to slavery. Not insignificantly, perhaps, choirs in the modern-day Caribbean are still comprised largely of women, who take the leading vocal parts, the men giving choral support only.

In many areas of their everyday life, then, at work and at leisure, women slaves carried on the cultural traditions they had brought with them from Africa. Frequently, the cultural activities in which they participated, especially in the area of religion, were strongly associated with slave insubordination. Even the manner in which female slaves dressed has been connected with a strong resistance to slavery:

> The custom of wearing . . . headkerchiefs originated in Africa and appeared most strongly in those areas of the New World in which African values retained their greatest strength, in some areas, in some cases, in which revolutionary resistance to slavery had been most pronounced and successful.[10]

From the general cultural perspective, slave women were prominent in all areas of resistance against the dominant white culture. Obeah, ritual magic and folk medicine, though frequently despised and derided by whites, were feared and suppressed through laws and punishments. Yet women slaves, undeterred by the often harsh penalties, preserved and defended the African cultural and religious traditions of the slave community. These formed the essential basis of the unique Afro-Caribbean culture which developed on the slave plantations.

Further reading

Beckwith (1929)
Brathwaite (1971)
Curtin (1968)
Genovese (1974)
Goveia (1965)
Harley (1941)
Herskovits (1941)
Parrinder (1935)
Sheridan (1985)
Turner (1982)

Out of Bondage

Black Women
and the Spirit of Freedom

An old Ibo legend retold by Olaudah Equiano tells of how God decided not to allow women to fight wars since they were so fierce that they might have wiped out the world. There is often some truth in legend and in the Caribbean context the fighting spirit of black women was in evidence throughout the period of slavery (and beyond into a 'freedom' still marred by racism and poverty). At all levels of plantation life they were a force to contend with, despite the odds against them. Slave women did not conform to the image created for them by white society and in so doing presented a strong challenge to the slave system and all that it represented.

Out of New World slavery arose what Herbert Aptheker (1943) has termed 'the colossal myth' of the 'sub-humanity' of black people. To justify slavery, the acceptance of this idea had to be demonstrated by all, black and white alike. Thus the essentially human side of the life of the slaves, their family life, their culture and value systems were denigrated. To preserve what was meaningful to them slaves therefore frequently came into conflict with the system. Often this involved breaking the laws of slavery. This was as true for women as it was for men.

Women slaves reacted as strongly to enslavement as male slaves, and, as this study has shown, this reaction often entailed resistance. But living under slavery also involved positive adaptation, a determination to 'make the best of things' despite the depressing circumstances. Indeed, to survive slavery can in itself be regarded as a major achievement of black men and women. In this context, survival itself can be regarded as a supreme feat in the face of the most adverse conditions. Survival-orientated activities were in themselves a form of resistance and a prerequisite of all higher levels of the struggle against slavery.

Terrence des Pres in *The Survivor* (1976) has made a powerful case for the recognition of the heroism of survival in concentration camps. Survivors, he argues, have not been accorded the respect due to them, but have often been accused of capitulation to the system. The 'martyrs' were the heroes. Similarly, earlier studies on slavery stressed that the good slave survivor was totally resigned to his or her condition, and, accordingly, passively accommodated to the system. But, if we examine Des Pres's concept of survival, 'accommodation to the system' takes on new dimensions. Slaves, like concentration camp inmates, shared a 'unity of misery' upon which they based their resistance, both moral and physical. Thus, on both the concentration camp and the plantation, a duality of behaviour existed. This could in some cases be interpreted as an overt acceptance of the system but effectively it masked rejection and covert resistance.

Except on the level of human response to extremity, there can be little meaningful comparison between slavery and concentration camps, but survival as related to human dignity is a theme which has forcibly emerged from this particular piece of research. In order to survive, slaves, both men and women, had to face first of all the basic problems of existence. They had to avoid despair and keep their moral sense of dignity intact. Des Pres defines such dignity as a 'self-conscious, self-determining faculty', something felt to be 'inviolate, autonomous and untouchable' (Des Pres, 1976). Much of the behaviour of the slave woman examined in this work can be interpreted as a struggle to retain dignity as defined in this sense.

Closely connected with the slaves' struggle to survive was the continual affirmation of free will. As Eugene Genovese has remarked:

> the humanity of the slave implied his action and his action implied his will. Hegel was therefore right in arguing that slavery constituted an outrage, for in effect it has always rested on the falsehood that a man could become an extension of another's will. (Genovese, 1974)

Slaves, both men and women, tenaciously preserved the right to exercise free will and this was crucial to their survival.

The greater the human degradation, the more fierce was the desire to survive, to refuse to submit abjectly to the system. Survival with dignity was a highly positive response to slavery. The essence of all resistance on the part of slaves was a fundamental tenacity for life, an appreciation of life itself, for itself. More perceptive planters like 'Monk' Lewis and William Beckford were sensitive to this. 'Monk' Lewis admitted that production on his estate continued to go down although he had done everything to improve the conditions of his slaves. 'Still they are not ungrateful,' he mused, 'they are only selfish; they love me very well, but they love themselves a great deal better.'

This sense of self-worth was reinforced by the inherited culture of the slaves and expressed at all levels of their everyday existence. Women have been the subject of this work, but their story can tell us much about survival, free will and self-worth among slaves in general. Women, in their role as childbearers, had the major responsibility for the survival of the community. How they reacted to slavery can perhaps help us to more fully understand the mechanisms of survival in slave society. Their fight to maintain dignity, especially as mothers and wives, was fundamental to the slave community's co-operative struggle against slavery. Slaves developed a philosophy of survival which enshrined concepts fundamental to humanity. Survival and all that it entailed was the ideal motivating the individual slave, resistance on all levels and positive adaptation was its concrete outcome.

Within this general framework of the spirit and practice of resistance and survival, several broad conclusions about the slave woman's role can be drawn. In the work sphere of her life, the woman slave played a vital part in the economy of the West Indies, both in her formal capacity as field worker and in her informal activities as a marketeer. The fact that the majority of women slaves worked in the fields, where contact with white society in a cultural sense was at a minimum, partially contradicts the view that they assimilated white culture more readily than male slaves. On a superficial level, female domestics, like the male skilled elite, may have adopted white customs more readily than field slaves, but this did not necessarily imply an uncritical acceptance of enslavement.

In the course of her work life, the woman slave suffered the same indignities, miseries and cruelties as her fellow men. Harsh laws and punishments were essential if profits were to be maximised and the aspirations of the slaves suppressed; in brief, they made slavery workable. Paradoxically, the harsher was the repression, the greater was the resistance on the part of the slaves. On the obvious level this involved accepted forms of resistance. On a less obvious plane, it involved the efforts of the slaves to create, preserve and fiercely protect their own values and culture.

In her work life, the sheer force of circumstances rendered the woman slave equal to men and she reacted to slavery with the same intensity and commitment as her menfolk. Far from being more accommodating and submissive than the male slave, evidence presented in this work indicates that the slave woman's contribution to conventional slave resistance was considerable. There is no factual basis to the myth that her unenviable sexual position *vis-à-vis* the white man made her particularly vulnerable to betraying her own people. On the contrary, it placed her in an excellent position to carry on subversive activities. As Edward Kamau Brathwaite stresses, women traitors were probably the exception rather than the rule; the woman slave from the beginning was 'as deeply committed as her brother to the act and art of subversion and liberation' (Brathwaite, 1975). But women suffered a double burden as women and workers and hence were involved in both collective and individual resistance.

In Elizabeth Fox-Genovese's (1986) view, it is important to look at the specific experience of women as women but also their struggle for an 'individual soul or consciousness' against objectification, alienation and dehumanisation. Nowhere was that struggle so complex and multi-dimensional as in the intimate sphere of women's lives where sexual power combined with patriarchal structures to oppress women. Women's productive role affected their reproductive capacities and the formal sphere of plantation labour and punishment intermeshed with the private sphere of slave life. But that private sphere remained largely secret from whites and within it slaves retained a strong degree of autonomy.

Women were vital in the struggle to build, maintain and cohere the slave family and community. This involved not only positive adaptation but also resistance to the erosion of African-based cultural beliefs and practices. The slave community provided a highly effective emotional shield against the harsh realities of enslavement. Organised resistance was important but it could be argued that the strength of the slaves lay in the building of the slave community together with the retention of traditional cultural forms, forged into what Herbert Gutman has termed 'a dynamic, adaptive slave culture' which was part of the 'cumulative slave experience' transmitted down the generations through families. Thus, the creation of the slave community can be interpreted as 'a record of simultaneous accommodation and resistance to slavery' (Genovese, 1974). Dehumanisation was prevented by the slaves' maintaining their own culture, family, community life and religion. The slaves' autonomy and exercise of free will within the slave community was a tangible expression of their constant commitment to freedom.

In order to suppress slaves and define their own power, whites had to denigrate black culture and moral values. In their struggle to resist this suppression, to assert their right to freedom and to preserve their self-esteem, slaves retained an alternative, African-based belief system. Two value systems consequently developed in plantation society, which were 'constituents of a single, sociologically dynamic system', interdependent but in conflict. As the anthropologist Peter Wilson notes:

> Seen from the perspective of history and beginning with the entire value system, the total social system of both slave-owner and slave, was centred on freedom. The one sought desperately to withold it, the other tried desperately to secure it. (Wilson, 1975)

But, because of the superimposition of white norms and the bias of observers, many wildly inaccurate beliefs about black women arose, especially in the area of sexuality. They have laid many red herrings, in the search for the 'invisible' women whose position in slave society, especially as mother and wife, must be interpreted primarily in the context of African-derived codes of behaviour.

The slave family was the crucial catalyst in this continuing struggle against slavery. In West African society a close bond exists between culture, kinship and political organisation and evidence suggests that a similar bond existed in slave communities. In order to resist and survive slavery, men and women had to co-operate and act together. Kinship, as the basic equaliser in slave society, enabled that co-operation but also instilled a feeling of solidarity amongst the slaves, promoting an 'all ah we is one' sentiment, which inspired and co-ordinated resistance.

Women slaves, strengthened by their traditional African culture, were perhaps the backbone of the slave family and community. In the slave community, the responsibility of keeping families together and transmitting African cultural beliefs and practices often devolved upon them. The slave mother, like the African mother, often had a good deal of influence within the slave family, but the men's role as father and community leader in slave society was by no means moribund. Cultural predominance in domestic affairs did not make the black woman a matriarch, or the black family 'matrifocal'. This would have implied an exaggerated degree of power and authority which the black woman rarely had in the wider context of her life.

The black woman in slave society was neither a matriarch, a sexual temptress, a promiscuous harlot nor a negligent mother. She was merely an ordinary woman struggling to counteract the forces in slave society which militated against her traditional role as mother and wife. This was particularly true where childbearing was concerned. Through her will and determination, white manipulation of black life processes was resisted and childbirth remained largely in the slaves' control, as did the socialisation of children. Some of the most significant contributions slave women made to the general cause of slave resistance can, in fact, be found in their private domestic lives. Women's participation in slave community life was extensive, especially in cultural activities.

With increasing creolisation, slaves may have maintained a veneer of acceptance of white culture. On a deeper, more significant basis, however, they jealously retained the culture which they had directly inherited or adapted from the knowledge they or their ancestors had brought with them from Africa. This culture was of deep significance in slave society, not only in terms of conventional resistance, but also in respect of the spiritual well-being of slaves. It bequeathed dignity and self-respect to the individual slave and constituted a powerful barrier against apathy, despair and defeat.

Although the institution of slavery, its laws and philosophy, sought to suppress this cultural vitality, it was invulnerable. 'The amusements of the negroes', remarked William Beckford, 'betray a contentment and independence of mind which I have not beheld in other people.' Of all aspects of traditional African culture which have survived the experience of slavery, religion and kinship patterns have proved the most enduring. They represent an unseverable link between Africa and present-day black societies in the Caribbean. Because of the egalitarian basis of many West African religions and political systems, black women played important roles in slave religion and, ultimately, in the entire cultural life of the slaves. The intimate link between culture and resistance meant that women were deeply involved in the general struggle against slavery. Without the 'consciously rebellious' black woman within the family and the cultural infrastructure of slave society, the theme of resistance and the strong desire to survive could not have become so thoroughly intertwined in the fabric of the slaves' daily existence.

Several important factors emerge from this particular study of the slave woman of general relevance to future research into slave society in the Caribbean. History can be meaningfully interpreted only if the essential humanity of the anonymous masses is acknowledged. Women slaves and the slave community to which they belonged must be retrieved from what the historian E. P. Thompson (1988) has termed 'the enormous condescension of posterity' which has lost sight of the individual. Admittedly, there are problems in speculating about the past of non-literate societies but informed speculation and empathy for the period are valid if they are strengthened, where possible, by firm, historical evidence.

In recent historical works on slave society in the Caribbean, the essential humanity of the slaves, men and women, has begun to emerge. It is hoped that this study of slave women will contribute to a better understanding of slave society in general. More research is indicated into, for instance, the family, women's attitudes to childbearing, and the development of Caribbean society from a black- rather than white-defined perspective. This is a vital and necessary step in the search for a modern West Indian identity and the development of a less ethnocentric history of Britain's past. 'Knowledge about ourselves is derived at least in part, from an understanding by contrast with the past,' wrote Peter Laslett (1971). This is of particular relevance to modern Caribbean society and Afro-Caribbean communities in Britain where women are still 'the heart of the race' (Bryan, Dadzie and Scafe, 1985). In addition to contributing to the cultural richness of the modern Caribbean, women have participated in struggles against colonialism and, more recently, in political and trade union activity linked to an assertion of independence from continuing economic domination.

As black women, like women of all societies, have been particularly neglected or unjustly treated by history, they have been the focal point of this study. The black woman, by force of circumstances, was thrust into the centre of the slave community. She drew her strength and determination, however, from her African heritage and largely interpreted her role in slave society in this context. She was a fundamental and indispensable part of the black historical process which enabled Africans to survive enslavement with dignity and create a vigorous culture and society. Thus, from Africa, throughout the slave experience, in the modern Caribbean and Britain itself, black women had and will have a crucial role to play in their own societies.

Notes

Chapter 1 The 'invisible' black woman in Caribbean history: an introduction

1 Peter J. Wilson, *Crab Antics: The Social Anthropology of English-Speaking Negro Societies of the Caribbean* (New Haven and London, 1973), 193.
2 L. T. Ragatz, *The Fall of the Planter Class in the British Caribbean 1763–1833* (New York, 1928), 27. For similar views, see U. B. Phillips, *American Negro Slavery* (New York, 1927), 341–2; F. W. Pitman, *The Development of the British West Indies 1700–1763* (New Haven, 1917), 62.
3 E. Terry Prothero and Levon H. Melikian, 'Studies in Stereotypes versus Familiarity and the Kernel of Truth Hypothesis', *Journal of Social Psychology*, 41 (1955), 10.
4 Sidney Mintz, 'History and Anthropology: A Brief Reprise' in E. Genovese and S. Engerman, eds, *Slavery in the Western Hemisphere: Quantitive Studies* (New York, 1975), 493.
5 Cited in Herbert G. Gutman, *The Black Family in Slavery and Freedom, 1750–1925* (Oxford, 1976), 329.

Chapter 2 'The eye of the beholder': contemporary European images of black women

1 Anon., 'The Sable Venus – An Ode' (Jamaica, 1765), in Bryan Edwards, *The History, Civil and Commercial, of the British Colonies in the West Indies* (London, 1801), 5 vols, II, 28.
2 James Walvin, *Black and White: The Negro in English Society, 1555 to 1945* (London, 1973), 54; Winthrop D. Jordan, *White over Black: American Attitudes toward the Negro 1550–1812* (Chapel Hill, 1968), 32.
3 Cited in Jordan, op. cit., 35.
4 'William Towerson's First Voyage, 1555' cited in Walvin, op. cit., 22.
5 Edward Long, *The History of Jamaica* (London, 1774), 5 vols, II, 364, 380.
6 John Stedman, *Narrative of a Five Years Expedition against the . . . Negroes of Surinam, 1772–1777* (London, 1796), 2 vols, I, 52–3.
7 John Riland, *Memoirs of a West Indian Planter* (London, 1837), 202.
8 John Adams, *Sketches Taken During Ten Voyages to Africa Between the Years 1786 and 1800* (London, 1822), 8; Long, op. cit., II, 303–4.
9 Philippe Ariès, *Centuries of Childhood: A Social History of Family Life* (New York, 1962), 145.

Chapter 3 Slave society, power and law:
the institutional context of slave women's lives

1 M. J. Craton, *Sinews of Empire: A Short History of British Slavery* (London, 1974), 158.
2 Edward Long, *The History of Jamaica* (London, 1774), 5 vols, II, 278–9; 412–13.
3 Edwards, Bryan, *The History, Civil and Commercial, of the British Colonies in the West Indies* (London, 1801), 5 vols, III, 36.
4 Craton, op. cit., 175.
5 From Henry Whistler's *Journal of a West Indian Expedition*, cited in R. S. Dunn, *Sugar and Slaves: The Rise of the Planter Class in the English West Indies, 1624–1713* (London, 1973), 77.
6 Elsa V. Goveia, *The West Indian Slave Laws of the Eighteenth Century* (Barbados, 1970), 25.
7 *The Memoirs of Père Labat, 1693–1705*, abridged and ed. by John Eaden (London, 1970), 42.
8 'Report of the Lords of Trade into the Slave Trade', *Parliamentary Papers* (Commons) XXVI, 646a (1789), Part III, Jamaica, Appx. Act 103, Clause X.
9 Long, op. cit., II, 490.
10 'Abstract from the Leeward Islands Act 1798' Act No. 36, Clauses XXII – XXV in Edwards, op. cit., V, 183–5; 'Abstract from the Slave Laws of Jamaica, 1826', Nos 32 and 33 in [Bernard Martin Senior], *Jamaica as it was, as it is and as it may be* (London, 1835), 144.
11 *Edinburgh Review*, Art. VII, IV (April 1832), 148.
12 John Stewart, *A View of Jamaica . . .* (Edinburgh, 1832), 246, 262.
13 Long, op. cit., II, 327–8.

Chapter 4 Plantation labour regimes:
the economic role of slave women

1 William Beckford, *Remarks upon the Situation of Negroes in Jamaica* (London, 1788), 13.
2 Bryan Edwards, *The History . . . of the British Colonies in the West Indies* (London, 1801), 5 vols, II, 118.
3 Richard Ligon, *A True and Exact Account of the Island of Barbadoes* (London, 1657), 48.
4 Beckford, op. cit., 44.
5 Ligon, op. cit., 43.
6 William Edmunson, *A Journal of the Life, Travels, Sufferings and Labour of Love of William Edmunson* (London, 1774), 85–6.
7 *Royal Gazette* (Kingston), XVI, 34, 8 August 1794.
8 John Stewart, *A View of Jamaica . . .* (Edinburgh, 1832), 116, 351.
9 Sir Hans Sloane, *A Voyage to the Islands of Madera, Barbados, Nieves, St Christopher and Jamaica* (London, 1707), 2 vols, I, lvii.
10 Edward Long, *The History of Jamaica* (London, 1774), 5 vols, II, 270–1.
11 Thomas Cooper, *Facts Illustrative of the Condition of the Slaves in Jamaica* (London, 1824), 17–18.
12 Ibid., 20.
13 Sloane, op. cit., I, lii.
14 John Jeremie, *Four Essays on Colonial Slavery* (London, 1831), Essay 3, 78.

Chapter 5 The woman slave and slave resistance

1 Sir Hans Sloane, *A Voyage to the Islands of Madera, Barbados, Nieves, St Christopher and Jamaica* (London, 1707), 2 vols, I, xlvii.
2 Extracted from Anon, 'The Ballad of a Repentant Sailor' (Bristol, 1798), quoted in John Riland, *Memoirs of a West Indian Planter* (London, 1837), 68–9.
3 William Snelgrave, *A New Account of Some Parts of Guinea and the Slave Trade* (London, 1734), 173–4.
4 Matthew Gregory 'Monk' Lewis, *Journal of a Residence Among the Negroes of the West Indies* (London, 1845), 71, 175.
5 These plantation records are part of the Atkins Slavery Collection, which is housed in Wilberforce

House, Hull. The main sources consulted here were Baillies Bacolet Plantation Returns (Grenada), 1820–33, and the Punishment Record Books from the Kings' Guiana plantations Friendship, Sarah and Good Success, 1823–33.

5a See J. B. Ward, Review of G. Heuman, *Out of the House of Bondage*, (1986), *Journal of Imperial and Commonwealth History*, XVI (October 1987), 128.

6 Lewis, op. cit., 92.

7 William Beckford, *Remarks upon the Situation of Negroes in Jamaica* (London, 1788), 13.

8 Mrs A. C. Carmichael, *Domestic Manners . . .* (London, 1833), II, 202–8.

9 Anon., *A Genuine Narrative of the Intended Conspiracy of the Negroes of Antigua* (Dublin, 1737; repr. New York, 1972), 20–1.

10 Phillip Thicknesse, *Memoirs and Anecdotes of P. Thicknesse . . .* (Printed for the Author, London 1788–91), 2 vols, I, 121.

11 John Stedman, *Narrative of a Five Years Expedition against the . . . Negroes of Surinam, 1772–1777* (London, 1796), I, 33–4; 'A Rebel Village in French Guiana: A Captive's Description', in Richard Price, ed., *Maroon Societies* (New York, 1973), 317–19.

12 Edward Long, *The History of Jamaica* (London, 1774), 5 vols, II, 445.

13 Stedman, op. cit., II, 304.

14 Law XLV (1792) quoted in Bryan Edwards, *The History . . . of the British Colonies in the West Indies* (London, 1801), 5 vols, II, Appx XI, 177–8.

15 'Report . . . into the Slave Trade', 1789, Jamaica, Ans. No. 22.

16 Cited in V. S. Naipaul, *The Loss of Eldorado* (London, 1973), 292–3.

17 *The Barbados Report on the 1816 Insurrection*, 8, Appx D, 'The Confession of Robert, a slave belonging to the Plantation called "Simmon's" '.

18 [Bernard Martin Senior], *Jamaica as it was, as it is and as it may be* (London, 1835), 180, 204–7, 212–16.

19 John Jeremie, *Four Essays on Colonial Slavery* (London, 1831), Essay 1, 6.

Chapter 6 'The family tree is not cut': the domestic life of the woman slave

1 William Beckford, *A Descriptive Account of the Island of Jamaica* (London, 1790), 2 vols, II, 324.

2 Olaudah Equiano, *Equiano's Travels – his Autobiography . . .*, abridged and ed. by Paul Edwards (London, 1967. First published 1789), 8.

3 John Stedman, *Narrative of a Five Years Expedition against the . . . Negroes of Surinam, 1772–1777* (London, 1796), II, 376.

4 Ibid., II, 255.

5 Richard Ligon, *A True and Exact Account of the Island of Barbados* (London, 1657), 47.

6 From *A Report of the Committee of the Council of Barbados Appointed to Enquire into the Actual Condition of Slaves of this Island* (London, 1824), cited in Higman (1975), 282.

7 Ligon, op. cit., 47.

8 Edward Long, *The History of Jamaica* (London, 1774), 5 vols, II, 414–15.

9 Beckford, *Descriptive Account . . .*, II, 120.

10 William Sells, *Remarks on the Condition of Slaves in the Island of Jamaica* (London, 1823), 28–9.

11 [Bernard Martin Senior], *Jamaica as it was, as it is and as it may be* (London, 1835), 42–3.

12 Bryan Edwards, *The History . . . of the British Colonies in the West Indies* (London, 1801), 5 vols, II, 148.

13 Sir Hans Sloane, *A Voyage to the Islands of Madera, Barbados, Nieves, St Christopher and Jamaica* (London, 1707), 2 vols, I, lvi, lviii.

14 Edwards, op. cit., II, 175–6.

15 Matthew Gregory 'Monk' Lewis, *Journal of a Residence Among the Negroes of the West Indies* (London, 1845), 90.

16 Quoted from Bickell in Brathwaite (1971), 215.

17 Beckford, *Descriptive Account . . .*, II, 326.

18 'Report . . . into the Slave Trade', 1789, Barbados, Ans. No. 15.

19 Lewis, op. cit., 122.

20 Stedman, op. cit., I, 370.

21 Ibid., I, 112.

22 Long, op. cit., II, 331.

Chapter 7 Slave motherhood: childbirth and infant death in a cross-cultural perspective

1 Edward Long, *The History of Jamaica* (London, 1774), 5 vols, II, 431.
2 From Thomas Roughly, *The Jamaica Planters' Guide* (Edinburgh, 1823), cited in *Jamaica Journal*, 1, 32, (22 November 1823), 449.
3 The Rev. Thomas Malthus, *An Essay on the Principles of Population* (London, 1798), cited in Alasdair Clayre, *Nature and Industrialisation* (London, 1979), 199.
4 Thomas Dancer, M. D., *The Medical Assistant or Jamaica Practice of Physic* (Kingston, 1809), 212–13.
5 John Stedman, *Narrative of a Five Years Expedition Against the . . . Negroes of Surinam, 1772–1777* (London, 1796), II, 368.
6 'Report . . . into the Slave Trade' (Commons) XXVI, 646a (1789), Part III, Barbados, Ans. No. 15.
7 Long, op. cit., II, 437, 403–4.
8 *Lady Nugent's Jamaica Journal*, ed. P. Wright (Kingston, 1966), 69.
9 Long, op. cit., II, 436; *The Diary of Dr Jonathon Troup, 1788–1790*, cited in Sheridan (1985), 225.
10 William Beckford, *Remarks upon the Situation of Negroes in Jamaica* (London, 1788), 24–5.
11 David Collins, *Practical Rules for the Management and Medical Treatment of Negro Slaves in the Sugar Colonies* (London, 1803), 35.
12 Cited in George Devereux, *A Study of Abortion in Primitive Societies* (London, 1960), 240, 275.
13 Matthew Gregory 'Monk' Lewis, *Journal of a Residence Among the Negroes of the West Indies* (London, 1845), 41.
14 Long, op. cit., II, 440.
15 The Reverend Henry Beame, Jamaica, 1826, cited in M. J. Craton, J. Walvin and D. Wright, eds, *Abolition and Emancipation: Black Slaves and the British Empire: A Thematic Documentary* (London, 1976), 141.
16 Dancer, op. cit., 257, 278.
17 John Quier, 'A Slave Doctor's Views on Childbirth, Infant Mortality and the General Health of his Charges, 1788', Jamaica, House of Assembly, *Report of the Assembly on the Slave Issues*, enclosed in Lt. Gov. Clarke's No. 92 of 20 November 1788, CO 137/88, Appx C.
18 Genovese (1974), 50.
19 Cited in Sheridan (1985), 228. For comments on Victorian England see Joseph Kay, *The Social Condition and Education of the People* (London, 1850), 2 vols, I, 447.
20 Bryan Edwards, *The History . . . of the British Colonies in the West Indies* (London, 1801), 5 vols, II, 148.

Chapter 8 'Daughters of injur'd Africk': women, culture and community in slave society

1 Sir Hans Sloane, *A Voyage to the Islands of Madera, Barbados, Nieves, St Christopher and Jamaica* (London, 1707), 2 vols, I, lvi.
2 John Adams, *Sketches Taken During Ten Voyages to Africa Between the Years 1786 and 1800* (London, 1822), 12.
3 P. J. Wilson (1975), 121.
4 Quoted in Sheridan (1985), 78.
5 William Beckford, *A Descriptive Account of the Island of Jamaica* (London, 1790), 2 vols, II, 389–90.
6 'Ode on seeing a negro funeral' in Bryan Edwards, *The History . . . of the British Colonies in the West Indies* (London, 1801), 5 vols, II, 88.
7 Ibid., II, 84.
8 Beckford, *A Descriptive Account of . . . Jamaica*, II, 211.
9 Ibid., II, 120–1.
10 M. J. and F. Herskovits (1936), 4–5.

Bibliography

Plantation records, etc.

Atkins Slavery Collection, Wilberforce House, Hull.

The Barbados Report on the 1816 Insurrection.

Quier, John, 'A Slave Doctor's Views on Childbirth, Infant Mortality and the General Health of his Charges, 1788', Jamaica, House of Assembly, *Report of the Assembly on the Slave Issues*, enclosed in Lt. Gov. Clarke's No. 92 of 20 November, 1788, CO 137/88, Appendix C.

Official records

'Report of the Lords of Trade into the Slave Trade; with the minutes of evidence', (British) *Parliamentary Papers* (Commons), vol. XXVI, 646a, 1789.

Newspapers and periodicals

Edinburgh Review
Jamaica Journal
Jamaica Mercury and Kingston Weekly Advertiser
Royal Gazette

Books, articles and memoirs published or written before 1900

Adams, John, *Sketches Taken During Ten Voyages to Africa Between the Years 1786 and 1800* (London, 1822).

Bibliography

Anon., *A Genuine Narrative of the Intended Conspiracy of the Negroes of Antigua* (Dublin, 1737; repr. New York, 1972).

Anon., *A Rebel Village in French Guiana: A Captive's Description* in R. Price, ed., *Maroon Societies* (New York, 1973).

Atwood, Thomas, *The History of Dominica* (London, 1791).

Barham, John Foster, *Considerations on the Abolition of Negro Slavery* (London, 1824).

Beckford, William, *Remarks upon the Situation of Negroes in Jamaica* (London, 1788).

Beckford, William, *A Descriptive Account of the Island of Jamaica* (London, 1790), 2 vols.

Burton, Sir Richard, *A Mission of Gelele, King of Dahomey*, ed. by his wife Isabel Burton. Memorial Edition, 3, 4 (London, 1892), 2 vols.

Carmichael, Mrs A. C., *Domestic Manners; and Social Conditions of the White, Coloured and Negro Populations of the West Indies* (London, 1833), 2 vols.

[Collins, David], *Practical Rules for the Management and Medical Treatment of Negro Slaves in the Sugar Colonies* (London, 1803).

Cooper, Thomas, *Facts Illustrative of the Condition of the Slaves in Jamaica* (London, 1824).

Curling, Thomas Blizzard, *A Treatise on Tetanus* (London, 1836).

Dallas, Robert, C., *The History of the Maroons - From Their Origin to the Establishment of their Chief Tribe in Sierra Leone* (London, 1803), 2 vols.

Dancer, Thomas, *The Medical Assistant or Jamaica Practice of Physic Designed Chiefly for the Use of Families and Plantations* (Kingston, 1809).

Douglass, Frederick, *The Life and Times of Frederick Douglass* (New York, 1883).

Eaden, John, ed., *The Memoirs of Père Labat, 1693-1705* (London, 1970).

Edmunson, William, *A Journal of the Life, Travels, Sufferings and Labour of Love . . . of . . . William Edmunson* (London, 1774).

Edwards, Bryan, *The History, Civil and Commercial, of the British Colonies in the West Indies* (London, 1801), 5 vols.

Equiano, Olaudah, *Equiano's Travels - his Autobiography; The Interesting Narrative of the Life of Olaudah Equiano or Gustavus Vassa, the African*, abridged and ed. by Paul Edwards (London, 1967). First published 1789.

Falconbridge, Alexander, *An Account of the Slave Trade on the Coast of Africa* (London, 1788).

Jeremie, John, *Four Essays on Colonial Slavery* (London, 1831).

Kay, Joseph, *The Social Condition and Education of the People* (London, 1850), 2 vols.

Kemble, Frances Anne, *Journal of a Residence on a Georgian Plantation in 1838 to 1839* (New York, 1863).

Lewis, Matthew Gregory 'Monk', *Journal of a Residence Among the Negroes of the West Indies* (London, 1845).

Ligon, Richard, *A True and Exact Account of the Island of Barbadoes* (London, 1657).

Long, Edward, *The History of Jamaica* (London, 1774), 5 vols.

Macaulay, T. B., 'The Social and Industrial Capacities of Negroes', *Edinburgh Review*, XLV (March 1827), 402.

Madden, Richard R., *A Twelve Month Residence in the West Indies* (London, 1835), 2 vols.

Newton, John, *Thoughts Upon the Slave Trade* etc. (London, 1788).

Newton, John, *The Journal of a Slave Trader . . . 1750-1754. With Newton's Thoughts on the African Slave Trade*. Edited with an introduction by Bernard Martin and Mark Spurrell (London,1962).

Parry, Caleb Hillier, *Cases of Tetanus* (London, 1814).

Ramsay, James, *An Essay on the Treatment and Conversion of African Slaves in the British Sugar Colonies* (London, 1784).

Riland, John, *Memoirs of a West Indian Planter* (London, 1837).

Schaw, Janet, *Journal of a Lady of Quality: Being the Narrative of a Journey from Scotland to the West Indies, North Carolina and Portugal in the Years 1774-1776*, ed. Evangeline Walker Andrews (New Haven, Conn., 1923).

Sells, William, *Remarks on the Condition of Slaves in the Island of Jamaica* (London, 1823).

[Senior, Bernard Martin], *Jamaica as it was, as it is and as it may be. By a Retired Military Officer* (London, 1835).

Sloane, Sir Hans, *A Voyage to the Islands of Madera, Barbados, Nieves, St Christopher and Jamaica* (Printed for the Author, London, 1707), 2 vols.

Snelgrave, William, *A New Account of Some Parts of Guinea and the Slave Trade* (London, 1734).

Southey, Thomas, *Chronological History of the West Indies* (London, 1827), 2 vols.

Stedman, John, *Narrative of a Five Years Expedition against the Revolted Negroes of Surinam, 1772-1777* (London, 1796), 2 vols.

Stephen, James, *The Crisis in the Sugar Colonies* (London, 1802).

Stephen, James, *The Slavery of the British West Indian Colonies Delineated* (London, 1830), 2 vols.

Stewart, John, *A View of Jamaica . . . (with Remarks on the Moral and Physical Condition of Slaves and the Abolition of Slavery in the Colonies)* (Edinburgh, 1832).

Thicknesse, Phillip, *Memoirs and Anecdotes of P. Thicknesse, Late Governor of Land Guard Fort and Unfortunately Father to George Touchet, Baron Audley* (Printed for the Author, London, 1788-91), 2 vols.

Thompson, James, *A Treatise on the Diseases of Negroes, as they Occur in the Island of Jamaica: With Observations on Country Remedies* (Jamaica, 1820).

Tracts upon the Slave Trade (London, 1788).

Williamson, John, M. D., *Medical and Miscellaneous Observations Relative to the West Indian Islands* (Edinburgh, 1817), 2 vols.

Wollstonecraft, Mary [Godwin], *Mary a Fiction and the Wrongs of Woman*, ed. with an introduction by Gary Kelly (London, 1976).

Wollstonecraft, Mary [Godwin], *A Vindication of the Rights of Woman with Strictures on Political and Moral Subjects . . .* (Dublin, 1793).

Wright, P., ed., *Lady Nugent's Jamaica Journal* (Kingston, 1966).

Books and articles published after 1900

Abzug, Robert H. and Maizlish, S. E., eds, *New Perspectives on Race and Slavery in America: Essays in Honour of Kenneth M. Stampp* (New York, 1986).

Achebe, Chinua, *Things Fall Apart* (London, 1958).

Achebe, Chinua, *Arrow of God* (London, 1964).

Anstey, Roger, *The Atlantic Slave Trade and British Abolition, 1760-1810* (London, 1975).

Aptekar, Herbert, *Anjea: Infanticide, Abortion and Contraception in Savage Society* (New York, 1931).

Aptheker, Herbert, *American Negro Slave Revolts* (New York, 1943).

Archer, Léonie, ed., *Slavery and Other Forms of Unfree Labour* (New York, 1988).

Ariès, Philippe, *Centuries of Childhood: A Social History of Family Life* (New York, 1962).

Banton, Michael, *Race Relations* (London, 1967).

Barrett, Leonard E., *The Rastafarians* (Kingston, 1977).

Bauer, A. Raymond and Bauer, Alice H., 'Day to Day Resistance to Slavery', *Journal of Negro History*, XXVII (1942), 388–419.

Bay, Edna G. and Hafkin, Nancy J., *Women in Africa: Studies in Social and Economic Change* (Stanford, 1976).

Beckford, George, *Persistent Poverty: Underdevelopment in Plantation Economies in the Third World* (New York, 1972).

Beckles, Hilary, 'Black Men in White Skins: The Formation of a White Proletariat in West Indian Slave Society', *Journal of Imperial and Commonwealth History*, XV; 1 (Oct. 1986), 13.

Beckles, Hilary, 'The 200 Years War: Slave Resistance in the British West Indies: An Overview of the Historiography', *Jamaican Historical Review* (1982), 1–10.

Beckwith, Martha, *Black Roadways: A Study of Jamaican Folk Life* (New York, 1929).

Blake, Judith, *Family Structure in Jamaica: The Social Context of Reproduction* (Glencoe, 1968).

Blassinghame, John W., *The Slave Community: Plantation Life in the Ante-bellum South* (New York, 1972; repr. 1975).

Brathwaite, Edward Kamau, *The Development of Creole Society in Jamaica, 1770–1820* (Oxford, 1971).

Brathwaite, Edward Kamau, 'Submerged Mothers', *Jamaica Journal*, 9; 2 & 3 (Feb. 1975), 48.

Brathwaite, Edward Kamau, 'Caliban, Ariel and Unprospero in the Conflict of Creolization: A Study of Slave Revolt in Jamaica in 1831–32', *Annals of the New York Academy of Sciences*, 292 (June 1977), 41.

Brereton, Bridget, *A History of Modern Trinidad 1783–1962* (London, 1982).

Bridenbaugh, Carl and Roberta, *No Peace Beyond the Line: The English in the Caribbean, 1624–1690* (New York, 1972).

Bryan, Beverley, Dadzie, Stella and Scafe, Suzanne, *The Heart of the Race: Black Women's Lives in Britain* (London, 1985).

Buer, M. C., *Health, Wealth and Population in the Early Days of the Industrial Revolution* (New York, 1968).

Bush, Barbara, ' "White Ladies", Coloured "Favourites" and Black "Wenches": Some Considerations on Sex, Race and Class Factors in Social Relations in White Creole Society in the British Caribbean', *Slavery and Abolition*, 2; 3 (Dec. 1981), 245.

Campbell, John, 'Work, Pregnancy and Infant Mortality among Southern Slaves', *Journal of Interdisciplinary History*, 14; 4 (Spring 1984), 793–812.

Cash, Wilbur J., *The Mind of the South* (New York, 1941; repr. 1961).

Chioma Steady, Filomena, ed., *The Black Woman Cross Culturally* (Cambridge, Mass., 1981).

Clarke, Edith, *My Mother Who Fathered Me* (London, 1957).

Clark Hine, Darlene, and Wittenstein, Kate, 'Female Slave Resistance: The Economics of Sex' in Chioma Steady, ed. (1981), 289–300.

Coombes, Orde, *'Is Massa Day Dead?' Black Moods in the Caribbean* (New York, 1974).

Craig, Susan, ed., *Contemporary Caribbean: A Sociological Reader* (Trinidad, 1981–2).

Craton, Michael, Changing Patterns of Slave Families in the British West Indies', *Journal of Interdisciplinary History*, 10 (1979), 1–35.

Craton, Michael, 'Hobbesian or Panglossian? The Two Extremes of Slave

Conditions in the British Caribbean, 1783–1834', *William and Mary Quarterly*, 3rd ser., XXXV; 2 (Apr. 1978), 324.

Craton, Michael, 'Jamaican Slave Mortality: Fresh Light from Worthy Park, Longville and Tharp Estates', *Journal of Caribbean History*, 111; 1 (Jan. 1971), 1.

Craton, Michael J., *Sinews of Empire: A Short History of British Slavery* (London, 1974).

Craton, Michael J., *Searching for the Invisible Man: Slaves and Plantation Life in Jamaica* (Cambridge, Mass., 1978).

Craton, Michael J., *Testing the Chains: Resistance to Slavery in the British West Indies* (Ithaca, New York, 1982).

Craton, Michael and Walvin, James, *A Jamaican Plantation: The History of Worthy Park 1670–1970* (Toronto, 1970).

Curtin, Philip, *Africa Remembered: Narratives by West Africans from the Era of the Slave Trade* (London, 1967).

Curtin, Philip, *Two Jamaicas: The Role of Ideas in a Tropical Colony, 1830–1865* (New York, 1968).

Curtin, Philip, *The Atlantic Slave Trade: A Census* (New York, 1969).

Cutrufelli, Maria Rosa, *Women of Africa: Roots of Oppression* (London, 1983: trans. from the Italian).

Dabydeen, David, *Hogarth's Blacks: Images of Blacks in Eighteenth Century English Art* (Kingston Upon Thames, 1985).

Davies, Angela, 'Reflections on the Black Woman's Role in the Community of Slaves', *Massachussets Review*, 13 (Winter 1972), 181–3.

Davies, Angela, *Women, Race and Class* (New York, 1981; reprint, London, 1982).

Davis, David Brion, *Slavery and Human Progress* (New York, 1984).

DeLara, Oruna, 'Resistance to Slavery: From Africa to Black America', *Annals of the New York Academy of Sciences*, 292 (June 1977), 464.

Depestre, Réné, *Les Fondements socio-culturels de notre identité* (Paris, 1969).

Des Pres, Terrence, *The Survivor: An Anatomy of Life in the Death Camps* (New York, 1976).

Devereux, George, *A Study of Abortion in Primitive Societies* (London, 1960).

Dunn, Richard S, *Sugar and Slaves: The Rise of the Planter Class in the English West Indies, 1624–1713* (London, 1973).

Dunn, Richard S., 'A Tale of Two Plantations: Slave Life at Mesopotamia in Jamaica and Mount Airy in Virginia, 1799–1828', *William and Mary Quarterly*, 3rd ser., XXIV; 1 (Jan. 1977), 32.

Dunstan, G. R., 'A Note on an Early Ingredient of Racial Prejudice in Western Europe', *Race*, VI, 4 (April 1965), 338.

Elkins, Stanley, *Slavery: A Problem in American Institutional and Intellectual Life* (Chicago, 1959).

Emmer, P. and Van den Boogaart, E., 'Plantation Slavery in Surinam in the Last Decade Before Emancipation: The Case of Catherine Sofia', *Annals of the New York Academy of Sciences*, 292 (June 1977), 205.

Engerman, S. and Fogel, R., *Time on the Cross* (London, 1974).

Engerman, S. and Genovese, E., *Race and Slavery in the Western Hemisphere: Quantitative Studies* (New York, 1975).

Esike, S. O., 'The Aba Riots of 1929', *African Historian*, 1; 3 (Fall 1965), 308.

Fanon, Frantz, *Black Skin, White Masks* (London, 1968).

Firor Scott, Ann, *The Southern Lady from Pedestal to Politics, 1830–1930* (Chicago, 1970).

Fogel, Robert W., 'Cliometrics and Culture: Some Recent Developments in the Historiography of Slavery', *Journal of Social History*, 11; 1 (Fall 1977), 34.

Forde, Daryl, 'Kinship and Marriage Among the Matrilineal Ashanti' in A. Radcliffe-Brown and D. Forde, eds (1956).

Foucault, Michel, *Discipline and Punish: The Birth of the Prison* (London, 1977; first published, Paris, 1975). Translated from the French.

Foucault, Michel, *The History of Sexuality* (London, 1978-9; first published, Paris, 1976), vol. 1, *An Introduction*.

Fox-Genovese, Elizabeth, 'Strategies and Forms of Resistance: Focus on Slave Women in the US', in Okihiro, ed. (1986), 143-66.

Frazier, Franklin E., *The Negro Family in the United States* (Chicago, 1948).

Freehling, W. W., 'Denmark Vesey's Peculiar Reality' in Abzug and Maizlish, eds (1986).

Frucht, Richard, 'Emancipation in St. Kitts, 1834', *Science and Society*, 1; 2 (Summer 1975), 201.

Galenson, David W., *Traders, Planters and Slaves: Market Behaviour in Early English America* (London, 1986).

Gaspar, Barry David, *Bondsmen and Rebels: A Study of Master-Slave Relations in Antigua with Implications for Colonial British America* (New York, 1985).

Gaspar, Barry David, *Slave Resistance and Social Control in Antigua, 1632-1764* (New York, 1986).

Gaspar, David Barry, 'The Antigua Slave Conspiracy of 1736: A Case Study of the Origins of Collective Resistance', *William and Mary Quarterly*, 3rd ser., 35; 2 (April 1978), 308.

Gautier, Arlette, 'Les Esclaves femmes aux Antilles françaises, 1635-1848', *Reflexions Historiques*, 10; 3 (Fall 1983), 409-35.

Geggus, Patrick D., *Slavery, War and Revolution* (London, 1982).

Genovese, Eugene D., *Roll, Jordan, Roll: The World the Slaves Made* (New York, 1974).

Genovese, Eugene D., *From Rebellion to Revolution: Afro-American Slave Revolts in the Making of the Modern World* (New York, 1979).

Goode, William J., 'Illegitimacy in the Caribbean Social Structure', *American Sociological Review*, XXV; 1 (Feb. 1960), 1, 21.

Gott, Richard, 'The History Man', *Guardian*, 26 Feb 1988.

Goveia, Elsa V., *Slave Society in the British Leeward Islands at the End of the Eighteenth Century* (Barbados, 1965).

Goveia, Elsa V., *The West Indian Slave Laws of the Eighteenth Century* (Barbados, 1970).

Gray White, Deborah, *Ar'n't I a Woman? Female Slaves in the Plantation South* (New York, 1985).

Green, William A., 'Caribbean Historiography, 1600-1900: The Recent Tide', *Journal of Interdisciplinary History*, VII; 3 (Winter 1977), 509.

Greene, Graham, *Journey Without Maps* (London, 1936).

Greer, Germaine, *Sex and Destiny: The Politics of Human Fertility* (London, 1984).

Gutman, Herbert G., 'Persistent Myths About the Afro-American Family', *Journal of Interdisciplinary History*, VI; 2 (Autumn 1975), 181.

Gutman, Herbert G., *The Black Family in Slavery and Freedom, 1750-1925* (Oxford, 1976).

Hall, Douglas, *Free Jamaica, 1838-1865: An Economic History* (New Haven, 1959).

Hall, Douglas, 'Slaves and Slavery in the British West Indies', *Social and Economic Studies*, 11 (1962), 305-18

Hall, Gwendoline M., *Social Control in Slave Plantation Societies: A Comparison of St Domingue and Cuba* (London, 1971).

Handler, Jerome and Lange, F. W., *Plantation Slavery in Barbados: An Archeological and Historical Investigation* (Cambridge, Mass., 1978).

Handler, Jerome S., 'Joseph Rachell and Rachael Pringle Polgreen: Petty Entrepreneurs' in David G. Sweet and Gary B. Nash, eds, *Struggle and Survival in Colonial America* (New York, 1981).

Handler, J. S. and Corrucini, Robert S., 'Weaning among West Indians Slaves: Historical and Bio-anthropological Evidence from Barbados; *William and Mary Quarterly*, XLIII, 1 (Jan. 1986), 111–18.

Harley, G. W., *Native African Medicine* (Cambridge, Mass., 1941).

Henriques, Fernando, *Family and Colour in Jamaica* (London, 1953).

Henriques, Fernando, *Prostitution and Society: A Survey* (London, 1962–8), 3 vols.

Henry, Frances and Wilson, Pamela, 'The Status of Women in Caribbean Societies: An Overview of their Social, Economic and Sexual Roles', *Social and Economic Studies*, 24; 2 (June 1975), 165.

Herskovits, Melville J., *Dahomey, An Ancient West African Kindgom* (New York, 1938), 2 vols.

Herskovits, Melville J., *The Myth of the Negro Past* (Boston, 1941; repr. 1967).

Herskovits, M. J. and Herskovits, F., *Rebel Destiny Among the Bush Negroes of Dutch Guiana* (New York and London, 1934).

Herskovits, M. J. and Herskovits, F., *Surinam Folk Lore* (New York, 1936).

Herskovits, M. J., 'A Note on Woman Marriage in Dahomey', *Africa*, 1; 10 (1937), 335.

Herskovits, M. J. and Herskovits, F., *Trinidad Village* (New York, 1947).

Heuman, Gad, *Between Black and White: Race, Politics and the Free Coloureds in Jamaica, 1792–1865* (London, 1981).

Heuman, Gad, ed., *Out of the House of Bondage: Runaways, Resistance and Maronage in Africa and the New World* (London, 1986).

Higman, Barry W., 'The Slave Family and Household in the British West Indies, 1800–1834', *Journal of Interdisciplinary History*, VI; 2 (Autumn 1975), 261.

Higman, Barry W., *Slave Population and Economy in Jamaica, 1807 to 1834* (London, 1976).

Higman, Barry W., *Slave Populations of the British Caribbean, 1807–1834* (London, 1984).

Hill, Errol, 'Calypso', *New Community*, 1; 4 (Summer 1972), 308.

Hoffer, Carol P., 'Mende and Sherbro Women in High Office', *Canadian Journal of African Studies*, VI, 2 (April 1972), 165.

Johnson, Michael P., 'Smothered Infants: Were Slave Mothers at Fault?', *Journal of Southern History*, 47 (1981), 510–15.

Jones, Jacqueline, *Labour of Love, Labour of Sorrow: Black Women, Work and Family from Slavery to the Present* (New York, 1985).

Jordan, Winthrop D. *White over Black: American Attitudes toward the Negro, 1550–1812* (Chapel Hill, 1968).

Kahn, Morton, C., *Djuka: The Bush Negroes of Surinam* (New York, 1931).

Karasch, Mary, *Slave Life in Rio de Janeiro 1808–1850* (Princeton, 1987).

Keith, Nelson and Keith, Novella, 'The Evolution of Social Classes in Jamaica, 1655–1838', *Plantation Societies*, 1; 1 (Feb. 1979), 81–107.

King, Mae C., 'The Politics of Sexual Stereotypes', *Black Scholar*, 4; 6 & 7 (March–April 1973), 12.

Kiple, Kenneth F., *The Caribbean Slave: A Biological History* (New York, 1984).

Kiple, Kenneth F. and Kiple, Virginia H., 'Slave Child Mortality: Some

Nutritional Answers to a Perennial Puzzle', *Journal of Social History*, 10; 3 (Summer 1976), 284.

Klein, Herbert, S. and Engerman, Stanley L., 'Fertility Differentials between Slaves in the United States and the West Indies; A Note on Lactation Practices and their Possible Implications', *William and Mary Quarterly*, 3rd ser., 35; 2 (April 1978), 356.

Köbben, A. J. F., 'Unity and Disunity: Cottica Djuka Society as a Kinship System' in R. Price, ed., 1973.

Kopytoff, Barbara K., 'Jamaican Maroon Political Organisation: The Effect of the Treaties', *Social and Economic Studies*, 25; 2 (June 1976), 87.

Ladurie, E. Le Roy, *The Territory of the Historian* (London, 1979). Translated from the French.

Langer, William, 'Further Notes on the History of Infanticide', *History of Childhood Quarterly*, 2; 1 (Summer 1974), 129.

Laslett, Peter, *The World We Have Lost* (London, 1971).

Laslett, Peter and Wall, Richard, eds, *Household and Family in Past Time* (London, 1972).

Leith Ross, Sylvia, *African Women: A Study of the Ibo of Nigeria* (London, 1939; repr. 1965).

Little, Kenneth, *The Mende of Sierra Leone* (London, 1967).

Littlefield, Daniel, 'Plantations, Paternalism and Profitability: Factors Affecting African Demography in the Old British Empire', *Journal of Southern History*, 4; 7 (1981), 171–89.

Lowenthal D. and Clarke, C. G., 'Slave Breeding in Barbuda: The Past of a Negro Myth' in Rubin and Tuden, eds (1977).

McNulty, Sir A. S., ed., *The British Medical Dictionary* (London, 1961).

Malinowski, Bronislaw, 'Parenthood: The Basis of the Social Structure' in V. F. Calverton and Samuel D. Schmalhausen, eds, *The New Generation: The Intimate Problems of Modern Parents and Children* (London, 1930), 29.

Malinowski, Bronislaw, *Sex and Repression in Savage Society* (London, 1972).

Manning, Patrick and Griffiths, W. H. S., 'Divining the Unprovable: Simulating the Demography of the African Slave Trade', *Journal of Interdisciplinary History*, XIX; 2 (Autumn 1988), 177–201.

Mathurin, Lucille, 'The Arrivals of Black Women', *Jamaica Journal*, 9; 2 & 3 (Feb. 1975), 2.

Mathurin Mair, Lucille, *The Rebel Woman in the British West Indies During Slavery* (Kingston, 1975).

Medick, Hans, 'The Proto-Industrial Family Economy: The Structural Function of Household and Family During the Transition from Peasant Society to Industrial Capitalism', *Social History* 3; 3 (Oct. 1976), 291.

Mintz, Sidney, 'History and Anthropology: A Brief Reprise' in E. Genovese and S. Engerman, eds, *Slavery in the Western Hemisphere: Quantitive Studies* (New York, 1975), 493.

Mintz, Sidney, 'Caribbean Marketplaces and Caribbean History', *Radical History Review*, 27 (1983), 110-20.

Mintz, Sidney and Hall, Douglass, 'The Origins of the Jamaican Internal Marketing System' in S. Mintz, ed., *Papers in Caribbean Anthropology* (New Haven, 1970), 3.

Moynihan, Daniel P., *The Negro Family: The Case for National Action* (Washington, 1965).

Naipaul, Vidia S., *The Loss of Eldorado* (London, 1973).

Nnamdi, Asikiwe, 'Murdering Women in Nigeria', *Crisis*, 37 (May 1930), 164.

Nwapa, Flora, *Efuru* (London, 1966).

Okihiro, Gary, ed., *In Resistance: Studies in African, Caribbean and Afro-Caribbean History* (Amherst, 1986).

Parrinder, G., *West African Religion* (London, 1935).

Parry, John H., 'Plantation and Provision Ground: An Historical Sketch of the Introduction of Food Crops in Jamaica', *Revista de Historia de America* (Mexico), 39 (June 1955), 1–20.

Patterson, Orlando, *The Sociology of Slavery* (New York, 1969).

Patterson, Orlando, 'Slavery and Slave Revolts: A Socio-Historical Analysis of the First Maroon War, 1665–1740' in R. Price, ed. (1973), 246.

Patterson, Orlando, *Slavery and Social Death: A Comparative Study* (Harvard, 1982).

Paulme, Denise, ed., *Women in Tropical Africa* (Berkeley, 1963).

Phillips, Ulrich B., 'A Jamaican Slave Plantation', *American Historical Review*, XIX; 2 (April 1914), 543.

Phillips, Ulrich B., *American Negro Slavery* (New York, 1927).

Pitman, F. W., *The Development of the British West Indies 1700–1763* (New Haven, 1917).

Price, Richard, ed., *Maroon Societies* (New York, 1973).

Proctor, Samuel, 'Persistance, Continuity and Change in the Jamaican Working-Class Family', *Journal of Family History*, 7 (1982), 135–61.

Prothero, E. Terry and Melikian, Levon H., 'Studies in Stereotypes versus Familiarity and the Kernel of Truth Hypothesis', *Journal of Social Psychology*, 41 (1955), 3.

Radcliffe-Brown, A. and Forde, D., eds., *African Systems of Kinship and Marriage* (London, 1956).

Ragatz, L. T., *The Fall of the Planter Class in the British Caribbean 1763–1833* (New York, 1928).

Rathbone, Richard, 'Some Thoughts on Resistance to Enslavement' in G. Heuman, ed. (1986).

Rattray, R. S., *Ashanti Proverbs (The Primitive Ethics of a Savage People)* (Oxford, 1916; repr. 1969).

Rattray, R. S., ed., *Religion and Art in Ashanti* (Oxford, 1927).

Rawick, George, P., *The American Slave: A Composite Autobiography* (Westport, Conn., 1972–3), 8 vols.

Robertson, Claire C. and Klein, Martin A., *Women and Slavery in Africa* (London, 1983).

Rodman, Hyman, *Lower Class Families: The Culture of Poverty in Negro Trinidad* (London, 1971).

Rodney, Walter, 'Upper Guinea and the Significance of the Origins of Africans Enslaved in the New World', *Journal of Negro History*, LIV; 4 (Oct. 1969), 327.

Rodney, Walter, *A History of the Upper Guinea Coast, 1545–1800* (Oxford, 1970).

Rogers, J. A., *Sex and Race: Negro-Caucasian Mixing in All Ages and All Lands* (New York, 1944), vol. 2.

Rosenberg, Edgar, *From Shylock to Svengali: Jewish Stereotypes in English Fiction* (London, 1961).

Rover, Constance, *Love, Morals and the Feminists* (London, 1970).

Rubin, V. and Tuden, A., eds, *Comparative Perspectives on Slavery in the New World Plantation Societies* (New York, 1977).

Sabeen, David Warren, 'The History of the Family in Africa and Europe: Some Comparative Perspectives', *Journal of African History*, 24 (1983), 163–71.

Savitt, Todd L., *Medicine and Slavery: The Diseases and Health Care of Blacks in Ante-bellum Virginia* (New York, 1978).

Schuler, Monica, 'Ethnic Slave Rebellions in the Caribbean and the Guianas', *Journal of Social History*, 3 (1970), 374.

Scott, R. J. and Andrews, G. R., 'Slave Emancipation', *Journal of Social History*, 20 (1987), 824–45.

Sheridan, Richard, *Sugar and Slavery: An Economic History of the British West Indies 1623–1775* (Barbados, 1974).

Sheridan, Richard, 'Mortality and the Medical Treatment of Slaves in the British West Indies' in S. Engerman and E. Genovese, eds, *Race and Slavery in the Western Hemisphere: Quantitative Studies* (New York, 1975), 285.

Sheridan, Richard, *Doctors and Slaves: A Medical and Demographic History of Slavery in the British West Indies, 1680–1834* (London, 1985).

Shorter, Edward, *The Making of the Modern Family* (New York, 1975).

Sides, Sudie Duncan, 'Slave Weddings and Religion', *History Today*, 24 (Feb. 1974).

Smith, M. G., 'Social Structure in the British Caribbean about 1820', *Social and Economic Studies*, 1 (1953), 55.

Smith, M. G., *The Plural Society in the British West Indies* (Berkeley, 1965).

Smith, R. T., *The Negro Family in British Guiana* (London, 1956).

Smith, R. T., 'Culture and Social Structure in the Caribbean: Some Recent Work on Family and Kinship Studies', *Comparative Studies in Society and History*, VI, 1, (Jan. 1964), 24.

Solien, Nancie L., 'Household and Family in the Caribbean: Some Definitions and Concepts' in M. H. Horowitz, ed., *Peoples and Cultures of the Caribbean* (New York, 1971), 403.

Spruill, Julia, *Women's Life and Work in the Southern Colonies* (New York, 1938).

Stampp, Kenneth M., *The Peculiar Institution: Slavery in the Ante-Bellum South* (New York, 1956).

Tajfel, Henri, 'Stereotypes', *Race*, V; 1 (Oct. 1963), 1.

Terborg-Penn, Rosalyn, 'Black Women in Resistance: A Cross Cultural Perspective' in G. Okihiro, ed. (1986), 188–210.

Thompson, E. P., cited in Richard Gott, 'The History Man', *The Guardian* (26 Feb. 1988).

Turner, Mary, *Slaves and Missionaries: The Disintegration of Jamaican Slave Society 1787–1834* (London, 1982).

Van Allen, Judith, 'Sitting on a Man: Colonialism and the Lost Political Institutions of Igbo Women in High Office', *Canadian Journal of African Studies*, VI; 2 (April 1972), 165.

Walvin, James, *Black and White: The Negro in English Society, 1555 to 1945* (London, 1973).

Wilson, Peter J., *Crab Antics: The Social Anthropology of English-Speaking Negro Societies of the Caribbean* (New Haven and London, 1973).

Wilson, Peter J., *Oscar: An Enquiry into the Nature of Sanity* (New York, 1975).

Documentary collections

Augier, F. K. and Gordon, S. C., eds, *Sources of West Indian History* (London, 1962).

Craton, M. J., Walvin, J. and Wright, D., *Slavery, Abolition and Emancipation: Black*

Slaves and the British Empire: A Thematic Documentary (London, 1976).

Williams, Eric, ed., *Documents of West Indian History, 1495–1655* (Port of Spain, 1963).

Unpublished theses and articles

Brereton, Bridget, 'Brute Beast or Man Angel: Attitudes to the Blacks in Trinidad 1802–1888' (Unpublished Paper, Dept of History, University of the West Indies, Trinidad, 1974).

Duffield, Ian, 'From Slave Colonies to Penal Colonies: The West Indian Convict Colonies Transportess to Australia' (Paper given at the Colloque International sur la Traité des Noirs, University of Nantes, July 1985).

Gautier, Arlette, 'Les Soeurs de solitude: histoire des esclaves femmes aux Antilles françaises, 1635–1848' (Doctoral Thesis, University of Paris, 1982).

Marks, Linda, 'Sugar Planters in Jamaica, 1766–1800: Raising Cain or Planting Seeds?' (Unpublished Paper, Johns Hopkins University, April 1973).

Mathurin Mair, Lucille, 'A Historical Study of Women in Jamaica from 1655 to 1844' (PhD, University of the West Indies, Mona, Jamaica, 1974).

Reddock, Rhoda E., 'Women and Slavery in the Caribbean: A Feminist Perspective' (Unpublished Paper, Institute of Social Studies, The Hague, Netherlands, 1983).

Riviere, William, 'Active and Passive Resistance to Slavery' (Lectures in Caribbean History, University Library, University of the West Indies, Trinidad, 1972).

Index

Numbers in italics refer to maps and illustrations